NEW AND COLLECTED POEMS

ALSO BY IAN McDONALD

Fiction
The Hummingbird Tree (1969)

Poetry
Selected Poems (1983)
Mercy Ward (1988)
Essequibo (1992)
Jaffo the Calypsonian (1994)
Between Silence and Silence (2003)
Selected Poems (2008)
The Comfort of All Things (2012)
River Dancer (2016)

Drama
Tramping Man (1969)

Non-Fiction
A Cloud of Witnesses (2012)
A Love of Poetry (2013)

IAN MCDONALD

NEW AND COLLECTED POEMS

1957-2017

P E E P A L   T R E E

First published in Great Britain in 2018
Peepal Tree Press Ltd
17 King's Avenue
Leeds LS6 1QS
UK

ISBN 13: 9781845234034

Mercy Ward and *Essequibo* were first published by Peterloo Press;
The Comfort of All Things was published by
the Moray House Trust, though many of the poems in "The
Garden" are previously unpublished;
River Dancer was first published by Hansib Publications,
though the poems appear here in
a revised and resequenced form.
All other poems were or are first published in book form
by Peepal Tree Press.

Supported using public funding by
ARTS COUNCIL
ENGLAND

CONTENTS

JAFFO THE CALYPSONIAN

MERCY WARD

ESSEQUIBO

BETWEEN SILENCE AND SILENCE

III

NEW POEMS

1: Annals

4: Speculations

5: Questionings

6: Maturities

TO MY WIFE MARY ANGELA McDONALD

WITH LOVE AND THANKS

JAFFO THE CALYPSONIAN

For
Mary, Jamie and Darren

TEMPLE BULLOCK

Strong bullock tugs a corn-laden cart up the dirt hill,
saliva drips down the slippery black of cut lips,
falls into the dust at the end of long elastic threads of cowspit,
bright glue in threads like spider silks hung from trees some
mornings.
Clumsy testicles sway, hitting big legs as he treads on.
The driver beats him methodically without any anger
and the bullock moves not one beaten muscle;
the flies are not disturbed from his mouth.
On the hill stands an Indian temple with white clay walls;
on the walls are painted blue herons and peacock fans,
strange men in colour-beaded high hats,
on their faces different grimaces of pure emotion,
cruelty and delicate love.
High white dome of the temple stands strong on the sky,
good white stone reflecting stars like a pool of water.
Pots of corn stand under the walls.
Drums beat in the bright courtyard.
The soft peculiar wail searching for sadness
of the religious chant of old Indians
sweetens the gold air on the hill.
Today is celebrated, you see, the prophet Hossein,
lover of men and all oxen.

RUMSHOP GIRL

Walked the burnt red roads, looping the green hills
like red ropes around nine green tons of cane.
Thirsty hours on the road under the honey sun.
Came up to a rumshop on the bright-stoned way,
ordered hard yellow cheese, thick slices of earth brown bread,
four tall beers dewed with cool keeping.
Life was good. Kicked my boots off under the counter.

It was a joy when the big girl came
with dancing step, full of sweet eyes,
black face full of dark shining, breast stuffing her blouse.
It was marvellous how she leaned them on the counter
like fat young pullets, how her thighs bounced.
She clapped down the plate with a sideways look
and poured the cold beers for me with a lazy smile;
while I gulped the beer, cold as creeks,
she stood arms akimbo, making her dark sweet-eyes.
Good to be hungry and eat that cheese, that soft bread.
Good to be thirsty and drink the cold-dewed beer in a gulp.
Good to be a man and see the girl, arms akimbo, make her eyes
        sweet for me.
The sun floods the red road outside;
smell of warmed flowers, song of corn-birds, dream in the air.
What joy to live! Far, far away is death.
Suddenly the girl laughs, I laugh also, we do not speak.

BRIGHT COCKEREL

I find a fowl will eat flesh as well as grain and blades of grass.
Here is a bright cockerel picking the bones of a frog
        under the lemon tree.
The bird is finely plumaged, at his tail a cascade of
        white and purple
and at his back a ruff of small red and golden feathers.
Now, bright cockerel, proud bright fowl, red-combed lion,
how could you pick with your white splendid beak
this poor small frog green and delicate as a lily leaf?
How employ the sharp curved sword of your armed and
        golden head
upon little green frogissimo meek and jewel-bright?
Why peck, bright cockerel, the life out of this little
        mud lover?
Why sully the rich bracelets of your feathers

with blood from out this fish-pawed lesser emerald breed
unless the stink of frog bones smelling in the sun
appeals to you, great bright cockerel of death.

MAIS OF JAMAICA

His own life died but he has not truly died.
There, man! Look, look at him, the writing man,
muscles of Jamaica's hills carved in his face,
his skin coloured above the blood in brown drought sun,
his hands strong like a carpenter's, his eyes strong,
his work strong, his theme the terrific future of the poor,
commonplace and powerful as the sea's green weight.
Do not forget him in your ordinary days.
See his paintings there gaunt as starved oxen –
he put his hand to them in no search for praise.
His own life died but he has not truly died.
Man, you have seen a great tree put to the flame
how it roars up red above the land
and nothing will stop the red and fiery tree
until the red flames eat the tree-heart out,
and then it dies, the good fire dies,
but no dying can put the glory out.
So! Touch his life, your heart burns like a fire-tree.

DECORATED FOR A KISS

I come to her house for love with a basket of red petals.
Man-friend tell me what a fool to go to the girl.
Come, man, come fish shark, strong white shark,
at midnight, come fish, golden snapper along the warm black rocks.
But I decide my mind and come to her for love.
Her dress is patterned with blue dragonflies.
She has put a red bead in each ear.

Green lizards run in her eyes.
Her body has the scent of sun-dried khus-khus grass –
the sweet fibres she has put between the linen since midday.
She has washed her mouth with milk,
she has rubbed her lips with bay leaves,
made her limbs clean with water from a green calabash.
now she offers me a few plums and palm-wine from a gourd
of scarlet leather.

YOUNG HARPOONER

At low tide the jetty stands with socks of moss on its
caterpillar feet.
He lies on his belly on the warm and slippery planks of wood,
fishes for eels and peacock fish with cork and hook and shrimp-bait.
Ah! the smell of salt and tar in the wood and the feel of the green
waves pulling the cord.
Suddenly! gliding bat fish, black stingray, passes at
three yards distance,
a small one only but enough to set the boy's heart mad with courage
for the open sea,
for standing like the one-legged seaman in his boot
shining harpoon in young hand,
with landless eyes on the waves coming like giant redfish
as the sun flames at the horizon.
His soul fills with the silence and the fierceness of the sea.

LONELY NEAR EDUCATED WATER

Here evening spends its hundred hours –
drinking red water from white-jellied coconuts,
sharpening itself on blue rock,
buying from the merchant with golden cloths,
climbing green Japon hill,

jubilant in the red heavens
like a paradise of fair-boys
visiting the moon for bundles of silver sticks,
chasing the wild black pigs in the black bush.
Wrecks of gold and scarlet barques float
in the immense India of the sky.
I am seated in the nut grass by this green pond
quiet amidst the Israelic chirring of brown grasshoppers.
I have been so for one hot, still evening hour
at watch on the goldfish burning in the water,
slender unquenchable ingots in this gentle green element.
Round the pond is a mosaic of ordinary bright stones.
Patterns of flowers and lions create themselves in the mosaic.
A lizard green as grass slips away in the amber light.
I am lonely near educated water.
I have nothing better to do than suck quite dry
a yellow hairy mango seed old as yesterday,
long after it has lost its last, lost flavours.

OLD MOON RISING

It is late at night.
As we talk gently,
sitting by one another,
life is as beautiful as the night.
The old moon is rising
across the black slope of heaven
like a fire started among the trees.
There are the stars
shining like bees of gold.
Your beauty threatens my heart
like sweets of ambergris on a white beach.
The night air breathes outside;
the frogs ring in the canefields
near and far away.

The hibiscus close their red hearts;
the sea retreats, making silver noises.
The days without you go like dull-winged birds.
Let us sit like this all night,
my love, under the moon.

PORT OF SPAIN HARBOUR

It was years for me that the exciting gates were closed
    by the steady policemen there,
so now I visit with adventure the quayside in the tarry harbour.
Each step buffets the eyes, colour is god.
Blueness of the sky pierces me, sunfire burns me,
each piece of dust on the asphalt walk is a grain of spice.
I see the ibis-bird in pigeons and feel a tremendous palace
    in the brown customs shed.

Ay! The whole green anchorage is crowded with boats,
for today, sweet day, is cargoes day.
A rusty tramp loads out flour and pines,
cakes from Cuba, sweet potatoes from the islands;
a white launch takes tongues of hummingbirds and scarlet lilies
    to its master ship.
Then an old history of romance is bright again against my eyes,
for now I see swung in nets on board this ship
ten sacks of muscovado and four cages of orange monkeys.

THE LEGEND OF MANGAMUCH AND LA COUR HARPE

Our epics begin to form.
I know the great stickfight is one: the stone pictures have been
    carved of it.
It was near Rio Claro, between the champions of the batoniers,
the giant Mangamuch, hard bitter La Cour Harpe, the two fighters.

* * *

The Negres jardens with their jointed tambour bamboos, goat-skinned,
many-coloured,
beat the news of a major bataille bois days and days ahead,
honoured to be proclaimers.
Men came from seventy villages barefoot or in donkey carts
and the women carrying melons and coconuts to sell
in the hot afternoon.
And even three sunburnt Englishmen in white drill and brown
cork hats came!

* * *

When the last goat-skin drum faded in silence
all was very quiet around the fighting pit and the sun very hot
there on the charred ground.
Small boys in the surrounding plum and calabash trees watched
with flaming eyes;
these men in khaki shorts and belts of dogs' teeth were the strongest
champions of their blood.

* * *

The wary beginning, the skilful work of the stick-stick, sweet to the eyes
of the old men.
Then the heavier direct blows with their weight of knotty black
muscles.
They fought all morning with hard watchful eyes
and all afternoon the hard poui sung wapp, wapp, a tinge of
iron in the wood.
They rested for one hour when night was coming like a great
black pig.
All the colours of the day came back to burn and praise them
in the sky.
Then the women bathed their flesh with cool water and gave them
to drink and corn cakes to eat.

Then followers set up the flambeaux on iron drums in the circle
And they fought again by orange flames in the rich, furious pit.
The silence of a thousand silent men around the hard singing
wapp, wapp, of the poui sticks.
Three stars flashed with silver tails above in the black night,
good sign of God's interest.

* * *

Mangamuch had five broken fingers and all his fingernails were
torn off.
La Cour Harpe had deep injuries in his belly and his face burnt
with the sweat in the poui cuts.
But both had their eyes still to judge and hit and parry well,
So they fought, calm-eyed. Man thought they would fight forever
And, indeed, as men will tell you, they fought for longer than forever.
Then Mangamuch with the giant's strength in the hot second
afternoon
Swung his red poui for the thousandth time and La Cour Harpe
had only bitter weakness.
The blow, swung from great shining arms, burst six of all his
white ribs.
A shout more of general glory than of single pride for either man
Sprung around the fighters. Two small boys fell off a calabash tree
in excitement!
Pouches of jumby beads and pennies were cast in the scarred pit.
They sang of it after,
With the sweet-harsh songs, songs of the stickmen for Mangamuch
and La Cour Harpe.
O! The strong kalindas shouted by the red-sleeved jacket-men,
'Je t'aime, Mangamuch, je t'aime, triste Harpe, je vous aime,
grans noirs hommes.'
From the moon of a hummingbird wing to the moon of a rich
plum
The legend springs in the song, finds roots as tough as the nut grass.

WALKING ON LILY LEAVES

The brown boys have a game they play: it is a rare philosophical
game.
In the streams under the old trees when they slow to sluggish
ponds,
Where stick-bodied dragonflies with red paper wings are adroit
in skips on the surface.
Water lilies grow from the stones and their green leaves float
on the water.
Fully grown the leaves are almost tough enough to stand in
but not quite.
So each boy will jump softly from the bank full of ferns to one leaf,
a second
Before it sinks, jump to another leaf as deftly as tallymen and the
game ends at the end of water lilies.
The floating leaves are of course crushed into the sluggish water
and the lily flowers go too.
I played that game. I hear still the laughter on the lady-slippered bank.
Death in the long river of lilies invades my heart, grown old,
grown iron.

JAFFO THE CALYPSONIAN

Jaffo was a great Calypsonian, fire ate up his soul to sing
and play calypso iron music.
And when he was small he made many-coloured ping-pong
drums and searched them for the island music,
Drums of beaten oil-barrel iron daubed in triangles, with stolen
paint from a harbour warehouse.
Now he seized the sorrow and the bawdy farce in metal-harsh
beat and his own thick voice.
He was not famous in the tents; he went there once and not a
stone clapped and he was afraid of respectable eyes,
The white-suited or gay-shirted lines of business men or tourists

muffled his deep urge.
But he went back to the Indian tailor's shop and sung well and to
the Chinese and sweepstake shop and sung well,
Unsponsored calypsos, and in the scrap lots near the Dry River lit
by one pitch-oil lamp or two
He would pound his ping-pong and sing his hoarse voice out for
ragged still-eyed men.
But in the rumshop he was best, drinking the heavy sweet
molasses rum he was better than any calypso man,
In front of the rows of dark red bottles, in the cane-scented rooms
his clogged throat rang and rang with staccato chant.
Drunk then, he was best, easier in pain from the cancer in his
throat, but holding the memory of it.
On the rough floors of rum-shops, strewn with bottle-tops and
silver-headed corks and broken green bottle-glass
He was released from pain into remembered pain, his thick voice
rose and grated in brassy fear and fierce yoke.
His voice beat with bitterness and fun, as if he told of old things,
hurt ancestral pride and great slave-humour –
He would get a rum if he sung well so perhaps there was that
of it too
He was always the best, though, he was the best: the ragged men
said so, and the old men.
One month before he died his voice thickened to a hard
final silence;
The look of unsung calypsos stared in his eyes, a terrible thing
to watch in the rat-trap rum shops.
When he could not stand with pain he was taken in the
public ward of the Colonial Hospital.
Rafeeq, the Indian man who in Marine Square watches the birds
all day for his God, was there also.
Later he told about Jaffo in a long mad chant to the rum-shop men;
they laughed at the story.
Until the end Jaffo stole spoons from the harried nurses to beat
rhythm on his iron bedposts.

A WHITE MAN CONSIDERS THE SITUATION

Perhaps it is time to retreat from these well-loved shores.
The swell heaves on the beach, angry clouds pile:
The surf is ominous, storms are coming.
I see I am a tourist in my own land:
My brutal tenancy is over, they all say,
The centuries have faded like a dream...

* * *

Every day it is harder for the timid to make plans,
People do not say good morning with the former politeness.
The pavements feel safe only when old men pass.
The grip of power slides away, slides.
Something is missing in days still filled with pleasure;
There is emptiness, dreaming in the air.
Where ruling ends, the ruler cannot stay:
A diminished mastery is the keenest woe.

* * *

The best measure is the use of time.
My father's father planted once
A green tree in this quiet garden:
It was to yield ancestral wood
To grace my grandson's christening chair.
The best measure is the use of time.
I decorate now my dark-skinned love
With hibiscus for her shining hair
The petals fade, the sun burns out
Red hibiscus in her shining hair.

* * *

I lie sleepless in the embroidered sheets,
A sprig of khus-khus scents the room.
The night is dark with cloud, and lonely.
The black sentries are whispering, restless.
My father heard a hurricane of nightingales
Once upon a time, once upon a time.
Now the owl hoots, signalling danger coming,
The moon is half alight, throwing coldness.

* * *

There is no way back, no forward way;
My heart grows clenched from inner grief.
Almost certainly I will have to go from here.
The laagers of the world build higher, black and white.
And no one is to blame except my brother, me.
No one is to blame except my brother.

COLOUR POEM

I make colour-poems of an easy choosing,
Trying to forget, forgive.
I praise the artist, I praise the sun,
I praise black, I praise white,
Colour-poems, easy, soothing.

* * *

Colour of cool green in a river shade,
Drift of Samaan flower
Colour of pink on a black road,
Iron sugar mills etched against the sun,
Flags of bright trees flying in the exuberant wind,
In the rice fields white oxen, red machines,
Gold glare of sea-light on arcs of sand.

Cameos of brightness I collect:
Cane emerald in the ripening sun,
A small church filled with white dresses,
By lantern-light a cartman chopping coconuts,
Red bougainvillea on a sunlit wall,
Cloud-shadows moving on a wild hill.

* * *

Ah, brother man, I know it well!
A mild heart falsifies this art.
The greatest love is never soothing,
The greater truth is bitterness.
Pearl are the tears your mothers wept,
Black are the whips,
Grey is the ash,
Burned villages are ash,
Red, red are the travels of your brothers long ago.

THE FARMER

That mild man, a farmer, lived fifty years
Loving the land, tended it with phosphates, sickled its grain,
Ate his own white bread after humble prayers,
Once a month in relaxation hunted foxes barking in the wood.

* * *

He had no pretensions as regards the posthumous bowing of
the world
But often he thought of ghost's ennoblement,
Supposed his real flag only at present furled
Tight around life's mast, set to rip out in a heavenly breeze.

* * *

This thought, a joyful sustenance through his mild days,
Abandoned him one night. He saw his years like jasper stones
Worn to nothing by nothing, his hope of pageantry mere
        self-praise,
A vanity among his other little hopes and aims.

PINEAPPLE WOMAN

Selling pineapple is she art
Sad old woman pushing cart

Near Dutch Stabroek every day
You can find she minding tray

Full of sunripe 'Quibo pine
'Come an' buy me God-ripen pine!'

When the sun is hot and gold
Old woman get she pineapple sold

Rich lady come with Palmolive skin
Then the bargaining fun begin

Rich woman probably good at heart
But she got to bargain to play the part

So while silver shilling busting she purse
She letting fly with less pence than curse

And old woman with she age and pine
Have to cut the price down fine

So she squatting down beside she tray
Twelve hard hours by the end of she day

Pineapple ripe smelling sweet of sun
Turning she belly by the time day done

Dollar fifty profit from the fat gold pine
If a day make so much she doing fine

And go down Stabroek in Maytime rain
Look for that old pine woman again

She old grey dress busting away
Rotting and fade in the rains of May

But she under the branch of a samaan tree
Still working out she destiny

Selling pines from 'Quibo fat and gold
Until the heart inside she chest get cold

Forty years by Stabroek rain and shine
Sad old woman selling pine

And when she dead by a 'Quibo charcoal pit
Nobody bother or care one shit

She was buying pine to sell in the morning
But she never reach to sell that morning

Stabroek look the same old way
In suns of March or rains of May.

MYSTIC AT THE NIGHTCLUB MIRAMAR

He sits by the rum-sweet bar: an Indian mystic.
His eyes are lightless, his cheekbones stretch the dry skin,
His white moustaches are stained yellow up at the roots

From eating curry-cakes or smoking bamboo leaf tobacco.
Every Wednesday he comes to sit, watching the dancers,
Watching with white still eyes the men drinking rum,
The sweaty dance band, trombonist in a red sweater,
Golden Madeline the whore and Jackman full of calypso.
He has a bag of shells and when he goes he leaves one
on the bar.
Then on Thursday morning he walks five miles from his village
To Caroni river where he spits into the brown water
And walks back: penance for a whole world's crazed direction.

THE STICK FIGHTERS

Lives form around facts and the greatest lives around the greatest facts –
So the old men speak of the bataille bois; their greatest fact.
Where are La Cour Harpe and Gros Adams, Tiepin, and Chinee
Patrick, the great stickfighters,
Laptong, Blood, and Muscovi, the old heroes of Cobeau Town?
They wielded the yard-long poui sticks, polished, balanced in a
fine way,
Centred with charms, snake-teeth or bones from the Belmont
graveyard.
The fine ritual is lost of the precise harsh art of it.
They say Placide could with his quick wrist beat away any stone
flung at his body.
Oh fine art! Fierce game for only the calm-eyed!
On Carnival day, Jour Ouvert: the colour of it, the jacket-men
in scarlet sleeves
And their big-hipped women carrying rum and roasted breadfruit
and cassava cakes.
The fighter's challenge then: 'Zingay Talala mettex la main asu moi!'
And the tough-skinned batoniers urged by the stick-cry 'Quaray!
Quaray!' Proud men.
And after: the stick songs, sweet kalindas, beat on bamboo drums
stretched with many-coloured goatskin,

Song throbbing in the red throats of the fight-contented.
Ha! Great days then, hard boys, hard blows, say old men.
Of the blood pits of Sangre Grande can be told endless
strong tales
But in the green hills now only the whine of hill-women cutting
grasses.

THE FOUR KNIVES OF FREEMAN THE CANECUTTER

The four knives of Freeman, the cane-cutter, are famous
in his village.
Man call him Knife-man and praise the marvellous handles and
cold, sharp blades.
One knife is bone-handled and that red-veined bone was the
stamping foot of a black mare once,
Pared and shaped and polished with chisel and rough steel file.
That knife he has cut a man with who hurt his wife near the
water-rock one night.
The handle of his second famous knife is of hard lime wood
seasoned yellow with vinegar.
Like a fat stick of old ivory it is and round it fastened three thin bands
of green leather.
It handles easily, the exquisite balance of it lies deep in his fingers.
This is his throwing knife: with it he can split a dog's wagging tail
twenty feet away.
His third knife is rose-coloured and has small dragons carved in
that blood-stone handle.
Men admire the golden pebbles of wood laid in the dragons'
eye-sockets with infinite, infinite artistry
And they admire the curved blade of it, thin as a leaf and glazed
with silver.
This is the most precious of his famous knives. A collector offered for it
one hundred dollars
But Freeman, the cane-cutter, will not sell: he keeps it at his belt
Beautiful to see in its white-skinned sheath of fringed leather.

And sometimes villagers watch him peel fruit with it or carve
boy's whistles and crucifixes for the Church.
But his fourth knife is different: there gathers in it from a long
remembered history a separate value.
From generation to generation the faith of men has entered into
the long blade and the shell handle.
It is used for only one work; it can have no other; it is a
consecrated knife.
The knife hangs above his bed at night like a holy cross,
holy indeed to him.
For when the slaves were freed an old man took it from the saddle-
sheath of his overseer and ran to the saving hills:
In his mind the story of its special use began. Dying, he gave it to
a son
And from this son the famous knife has come through
generations to Freeman, still the cane-cutter.
What European craftsman toiled to make the knife, its blade rich
and edged to cut-bone sharpness
Its palm-worn handle a treasury of sea colours? Now a symbol
for a black man,
An ancient gesture grown large to hold the meaning of man's
humility and a slave's defiance
For Freeman uses his fourth famous knife only in the fields, uses it to cut
the emerald ancestral cane.

SONG IN SAN FERNANDO

There was silver girl sang in the streets
Sang in the old streets old and silver songs
The tamarind leaves fell like green wings as she sang
And the mountain men came to the black cobbled streets.

* * *

Her hair was drenched with white scent
her face was pale as white candles in a church
Ah, her mouth was like a small fish gulping snow
All her clothes were silver English shillings.

* * *

The mountain men big and black as rocks
They came from hunting birds green in the leaves
And gathered near the silver girl in seriousness
And heard song-sadness old as the policy of God.

* * *

It was the song of death they loved, they remembered:
Who has touched the red berries of my breast and raped my daughters,
Put down my sons, sent donkeys into the shrines?
Despair engraved of the darkness after time has ended.

* * *

It was the song of hunting they loved, they remembered:
The swords swung through pear boughs in preparation,
Used on wild hogs in the gold-bellied cassia forests,
On bright adversaries in man's imperilled future.

* * *

It was the song of lust they loved, they remembered:
The women whom they met in golden creeks
Breasts to move the fingers over like rough brown silk
And warm bellies on the beds of dark-leaved corn.

* * *

It was the song of youth they loved, they remembered:
Entrancement long as one star-dappled night

Ending quick beneath old suns and suffering
Blood burning old in sweet castles of the flesh.

* * *

There was a silver girl sang in the streets
Sang in the old streets old and silver songs
All sadness were her old songs under every moon
Time bittered them always with the end of worlds.

INDIAN LOVE STATEMENT

Tassim loves her like an idiot, makes himself a saga boy,
Puts green cedar leaves to scent his clothes, sweetens his hair
    with bay rum.
He makes sweet eyes at her all day and praises her green eyes.
He does nothing practical, his only gift is sentiment.
I, on the other hand, am determined to make less brittle love
    to her.
Though I am, as I will be, overall gentle, I bring her not a little
    pride and confidence.
Also I bring her faults: she knows the smell of my sweaty armpits
    if I work hard.
I do not hide it: cane-field sweat is good water.
Nor do I hide some roughness in my manners, being unused
    to Tassim and his like.
Yet I bring her also gifts and assurances of love, a basket of oranges
A parasol of rough blue cotton stemmed and ribbed with bamboo,
Beads, candied shaddocks, rings, everything I bring her
    in shrewd love.

THE SEINE PULLERS

On the sand under the loose-leaved tree I watch the seine-pullers:
for me a romance.
There is no romance for the toilsmen as for them it is a plain
work for eating.
They pull the seine in long powerful tugs, pull the seine,
In long perpetual tugs they pull the seine and pull the seine,
Twenty men on the salt ropes to their knees in strong water
In trousers of sailcloth and handkerchief hats and necklaces
of seabone.
Their women ready with baskets for the fish sit at the back
of the beach with their children.
Sharks and cutlass fish which are bright and sharp begin to beat
in the closing urn of water,
The tugs quicken and the corks on the black net toss closer
in the broken green waves.
The men get the smooth clubs ready; the small boys smile
brilliantly with excitement
They, like myself, watch for the terrible shining fish, expect
the sea to unsheathe wonderful swords –
The men and women hope for a profitable catch bringing many
silver pence.
I in the end see a flail from the grave sea beat silver rainbows up
and in its leap with colours
The mackerel shines in the morning air a long time after its
protest at the shallowness.
There is a murmur then for that fish means thirty shillings
in the market.

STATEMENT TO GOD

Things of the world, things of my flesh, facets of all sensual being:
Diamonds in the water-grass, clear stars above
Mount Saint Benedict,

Wood shone by the great sea, the beauty in birds,
Induce me towards God, or at least make me love what they seem
to mean.
This morning I saw a red locust on the fruit of a carob tree,
Its flare of scarlet made me love the maker of such scarlet art.
But I want no sweet signs or tremendous signs of the
unsensed original:
Only to find a bare love come by a plain way,
And take such love to be eternal habit, ornamentless, mild,
Direct as a peasant's drinking cup of clay,
A woman's hand that daily feeds a child.

SON ASLEEP, AGED SIX MONTHS

Before our own sleep of passion, dreams, and clocks
Warm wife and my proud self watch by his sovereign bed.
Over the child our smiling eyes like emperor's shine:
In his warm life our hopes spring tall as spears.
Pray God he finds a destiny well-designed.

* * *

Against the terrific future how can he sleep so soft?
He is golden-armed, he is not tall or strong
So gently born, so sweetly grown, so calm
He rests soft beyond birth only half a year.
Deathless he must be, no pains will visit him.
He breathes quiet as white leaves of moonlight.
His fist clenches like a young rose in his sleep.
My son's face is serious for peace and good intent.
His small heart is burning like a star.

* * *

This is not so, he is not safe forever.
Death rages in man's bones all the days he lives,
My son's not singular, death rages in him too.
Long time to come, long years past this proud present watching
He will find agonies enough, he will be hurt.
The flesh is kingly but kings' dethronement comes.

* * *

Yet let him sleep so soft as this
Give him some sweet preliminary of life.
Do not warn him too soon of cruelties and sleepless lusts,
The bribery of habits, red wounds, the iron nation's wars.
In this raw age of jealous total moods
When men soon march to order behind dogmatic whims
We watch and deeply love and we determine this:
Take childhood's time and make a dream of it.

GEORGETOWN CHILDREN

Under the soursop silver-leaf tree
The High School children play skip-and-free

Sun burning down like a fire ball
Watch the children before school call

Laugh in their gay time, laughter rich
Jump the jack, bring marble pitch

Black child, yellow child, brown child, white
They all the same if you looking right

Pass by any schoolyard in Georgetown at all
And watch the children before school call

Under the soursop silver-leaf tree
The High School children play skip-and-free.

The biggest thing in life could be
Watching the children play skip-and-free.

HISPANIOLA

Hispaniola is an old white aristocrat
The demon of his life, a black cat

Which he killed as a schoolboy long ago
With a golden arrow from a rosewood bow.

Now it combs his beard with its silver claws
It pads on his heart with printless paws

It scratches his belly with undrawn scar
This cat-ghost relentless, black avatar.

An amethyst glows in vain, in vain
From the iron top of his daggered cane

He cuts and stabs at elusive it
But the cat's a cat that never'll be hit.

History-long Hispaniola asked the Why
With dust in his throat, red-flecked his eye:

The scaffolding of his mind eased down
And soon he lived only in feline town

Where a black cat stood at each street turning
And each street lamp was a cat's eye burning.

Hispaniola old waned to final age
His teeth still ivories of crystal rage

But last night over his ebony incense bowl
Black fur closed on Hispaniola's soul.

And tomorrow night they'll find in his heart I know
A cat's claw shot from a rosewood bow.

RAILWAYMEN

The railway shines like swords through Tunapuna.
Now, stand by the morning market near the bright tracks –
The early sky full of red fruit:
For sale, slain agoutis with golden eyes –
And watch the black trains trample the bright swords:
Storm-arsed, stallion powerful, black iron fire-guts:
Railwaymen are heroes, man!

* * *

Railwaymen discover the way of life, like poets.
They feed the train's fire and roaring life with jewels of coal,
They throw it in with heavy hot iron shovels
And the new flames warm and redden their hard cheeks,
Especially hard cheeks, railwayman's cheeks, tough like black leather.
And the poet might seem a softer man but he shovels too
And flames flush out the black jewels from his iron shovel
Make his stern cheeks lined as old black leather folded for one life,
Clean hard the slag-black jewels into pure diamond.

WALKING TO SUGAR LOAF, ANTIGUA

Walk out down the road made of sun and broken shells
Past killi-killi hawks building nests in the old muscavado mill,
Bringing in their beaks dry twigs, seaweed, and white sea-
    island cotton.
The screech of peacocks comes from the golf-course for tourists.
Walk to wilder earth where agony-trees grow tough and
    stunted
And the thorn-armed cossi bush sifts down its golden ash of
    flower,
And stand at the top of the hill, brown sugar loaf, the best
    tower.

PELTING BEES

By July the bees have built in the samaans:
There are honey-hives in the notches of those burly trees there.
Today is Sunday, I go out and pelt them with white stones;
And duck quick under the river-bank, my feet in the cold water
    on the white stones.
How they get up in golden arms then and make a noise
    like breezes!
I hide and watch and again throw white stones with the strength
    of my arm!
Nectar-sweet streams from the rich red honeycombs,
The golden bees blaze with fury in the sun.
I laugh and laugh, pelting white stones from the safety of
    Easter River.

YUSMAN ALI, CHARCOAL SELLER

Some men have lives of sweet and seamless gold,
No dent of dark or harshness mars those men,
Not Yusman Ali though, not that old charcoal man
Whose heart I think has learned to break a hundred times a day:
He rides his cart of embered wood in long agony.

* * *

He grew rice and golden apples years ago.
He made an ordinary living by the long mud shore,
Laughed and drank like any other man and planned his four
 sons' glory.
His young eyes watched the white herons rise like flags
And the sun brightening on the morning water in his fields.
His life fell and broke like a brown jug on a stone.
In middle age his four sons drowned in one boat up a pleasant
 river.
The wife's heart cracked and Yusman Ali was alone, alone, alone.
Madness howled in his head. His green fields died.

* * *

He burns the wild wood in his barren yard alone,
Sells the charcoal on the villaged coast and feasts on stars.
Thinness makes a thousand bones around his scorched heart.
His moon-scarred skin is sick with boils and warts,
His grey beard stinks with goat-shit, sweat and coal.
Fire and heated dust have rawed his eyes to redness:
The eyes hit like iron bullets in my guts.
No kindness in him: the long whip smashes on the donkey like
 an iron.
The black and brittle coal has clogged his chest with dirt,
The black fragrance of the coal is killing him.

* * *

He is useful still. I shake with pain to see him pass.
He has not lost his hating yet, there's that sweet thing to say,
He farts at the beauty of the rain-dipped moon.
The smooth men in their livery of success
He curses in his killing heart
And yearns for thorns to tear their ease.
His spit blazes in the sun. An emperor's bracelet shines.

POEM ON A BLACK STONE

I walked in a bright river – cool, silver walking.
In the shallows I saw a black stone shining:
Black as the sapodilla seed shining in its flesh,
Charred in the fire of old moons,
Buried in green mountains, covered by worlds of earth,
Tumbled in huge downfalls of cold and sharpened ice,
Washed clean, smooth, in churns of golden ore.
So it was fashioned precisely for my fingers,
Balanced and shone, fruit of the turning suns.

* * *

It is suited for the young girl who is my lover,
Black scarab from the silver river for her breast,
Brown girl, so young, no pain yet come to her.
Gently she sleeps now, but I am sleepless in her arms.
The sheets sweat beneath my heavy body.
She holds the black stone near her unknowing heart.
Her fingers touch it in her quiet sleep;
She has greatly treasured this simple gift from me.
Despair withers my old and blazing heart.
I get up on one elbow to watch her carefully.

She is so young, her beauty is not marked,
Youth breathes with grace in every line of her,
She has thrown her dark limbs like a child,
Suddenly I dread cold death's coming:
Dry bone blowing in the wind,
Pulp of eye unseeing, not anymore flesh curving on the bone,
Death is terrible, terrible, terrible.

* * *

Morning will come.
I will take the black stone from my love.
I will smile at her and explain nothing.
I will carry the black stone up the mountain path,
Walk through the green ferns dewed by night,
The early sun rising, warming the roots of the trees.
I will throw the black stone in the cold and silver river,
Secret it will lie a thousand centuries more.

ON AN EVENING TURNED TO RAIN

Visiting the seaman's ward a hot afternoon
I discovered the old man dying, dying fast,
The rattle in him, the black crow flying near.
The walls dewed grey, the hard beds crowded close,
The smell of deaths, the old routine of cure,
Of alcohol, rough sheets cleaned a thousand times, urine
splashed like holy water.

* * *

No one saw the dying of the old man –
All, all encased in dreams of life –
Until a nurse came with some tenderness
(I well remember her, she hard and tall as a post)

And took his hand, with some tenderness I say,
Hand frail as ash waiting for wind to blow.
And she held his hand until the black crow settled firm.
I wandered near, death's mystery a lure,
And heard the low words almost break his teeth:
'I live a good life, and now I dead!'
To write it straight as bone is not to say it well.
Slimed by black belly juices the tongue fell out of him:
The nurse stood up and cleaned his vomit up.
I knew him well, a strong man in his day.
The black crow cawed, rattling a joyful wing
And so the old man died, leaving his words to me.

* * *

There is a bureaucracy for moving people on: they buried him
quick
That evening, turned to rain.
Your funeral cart, my reader, will be more glorious than his:
Think now of your heaped flowers, not for him!
No man shall go naked to his cavern-rest:
A grey robe sheeted him, rough as cattle tongue,
A lead medallion twined his neck for long identity.
(So, old counterfeit Pharoah! They left you that last treasure!)
When the world overturns, they say, God will know his bones.
He had a pauper's grave, black hole glistening in the earth.
Narrow moats with lilies red and sweet as flesh,
And palms wave above in melancholy green.
In rainy times the trenches swamp the burial places of the poor;
The rich man's bones keep dry on higher ground.
He had his retinue like any other man:
The grave-diggers, brawny-young and laughing,
And the lantern-carrier, uncle of a thousand deaths,
And myself, watchman at a distance, not near enough for love or
work.
An old moon coming up, a cold wind blowing,

The rain drifting in, bringing the smell of the sea.
No one claimed him, no sons came.

* * *

His words pursued me as I followed him.
'I live a good life, and now I dead!'
I puzzle at the old man's meaning.
He was so certain when he spoke,
He had an idea in his mind I'm sure,
He had to say his chosen words out clear,
They almost broke his teeth to say.
Silence was not good enough for him:
The breath inside him screeched like a sharpened bone.
Was it defiance that he spoke?
Proud of living well in full enjoyment,
Women fucked and fondled, wine drunk down,
Every pleasure tasted in *his* young and middling life,
And now he thought of that and spat a curse at death?
Could that be it? Or was it black agony of loss?
Of loss and bitter disillusion, his words an agony:
'I live a good life, and now I dead!'
So much of sacrifice offered up, no justice in return,
Was that the thought that struggled to be said:
Each man who dies, he dies in desperation,
Like a stray cat strangling in a ditch?
Or was it fierce eternal faith,
An echo of the saint's calm prayer:
'Let nothing disturb thee
Let nothing affright thee
All passeth away.
God alone will stay.'?

* * *

The ashes of the old man's words I taste:
I think of Gandhi in his hungering quest,
Of Hitler in his iron hate,
Of emperors polishing bright swords of war,
Of poets practising their songs of love,
Beggarman, I think of you.
The dark evening turns to heavier rain.
My thoughts' confusion troubles me.
All, all are pity's children
All will go out like flame.
The water cleans the old man in his grave forever.

STATE OF THE NATION

Affairs in the young Republic do not go well.
Problems weigh like stones on every man.
In everyone's heart there is growing doubt.
The most placid have begun to grumble:
The playing children notice the unusual scowls.
In the rumshops there is moody silence, with bursts of anger,
And the churches are filled with arid sermons.
The nation seems to trudge a weary road:
On all sides ardour is withdrawn.

* * *

It is not that progress is not made.
No, the burnished buildings grow,
Machinery hums in the new factories,
Bush is cleared and new crops are extended.
Men are urged to be prouder and are probably so;
Beards sprout fearlessly, non-colonial clothes sell in all
 the shops.
Great advances are made in education and medical care.
Our foreign embassies every day report fresh diplomatic

initiatives.
New dances are discovered for the new culture.

* * *

The people are a flame, not easily put out,
Unless you raze wide swathes around their rights.
What has happened? Why are knives pulled in the street?
There is not much time, that is generally recognised.

DRUNK

There is a young man, always drunk,
Nobody has respect for him in this town,
He has let down his respectable parents.
I say he is young, but now he is not so young:
Grey threads of hair sparkle in his beard.

* * *

Ever since, he was badly behaved, this man,
From young days he was always getting drunk:
He would go to the cricket and shout with joy,
He would direct bustling traffic in the middle of Water Street,
Hot noondays would find him feeding birds in the Gardens.
He would go to parties in mad clothes, in ridiculous hats,
Spill drinks, swing pretty girls squealing in the air,
He could never be at all serious in any work.
He entered the Civil Service, the first day he was drunk:
He engaged his superiors in poetic argument.
He would draw bright cartoons on the important files
And say in a loud voice: 'This is cock, man, this is truly cock!'
He did not last long, lacking the necessary application.

* * *

He was idle mostly, rum-soaked in beer pavilions.
Once he went on the savannahs, burning, swept by wind,
He came back with his beard and a little gold,
His pockets full of jaguar blood,
Green locusts tangled in his hair,
Stars of coldness on his tongue.
He spent the gold feting up his friends, and a few prostitutes,
Strangely mixed, but the fete was good, full of joy,
Everybody in town talked about him, laughed scornfully.

* * *

He is getting older now, his vigour more subdued:
People hurry past this drunk man, showing sour faces.
He came to my house Sunday, frailer than I remember,
He asked for bread to eat, and a cup of cool water.
All he wanted – bread, a cup of water, and a little talk:
Talk of his roaring times, the heroes at the cricket matches,
The clashing games of dominoes, the brawling bars of Tiger Bay,
The roistering, the love affairs, the carnivals of rum.
But once, before he ended, he told a different tale:
His eye looked serious in my eye, burning to convince,
From boyhood days he loved wild birds:
In books he wrote their colours down,
Their ways of flight, their gleaming wings,
He had them all in memory,
Every bird in this wide land,
He told me how he followed them,
Not drunken then in his wild chase:
Not drunken then in that devotion.

* * *

My drunken visitor has gone,
His begging bowl is full with bread.
I sit in silence in my home,

Sober in this quiet town,
The peace of Sunday settles down,
He walks away, his back hunched up
The grey hairs sparkle in his beard,
The sunset on him burns and glows.
I see him through the mist of years:
He goes to chase the gold-winged hawks,
His eyes ablaze for hummingbirds.

The spurwings circle around his head,
The corn-birds land upon his arm,
And drunken in their sun-filled games,
The river-swallows dance for him.

THE THREAT TO THE CITY

The town is mighty: steel battlements towering in the air,
Intricate traffic roaring, crowds peering in the glass avenues,
Everywhere important things proceeding in smooth order.
Men full of power share the rich, well-built town.
Strong animals roam in the recreation parks, green, calm;
In the gardens, filled with sun, birds are flying:
These are good places to visit, everything under control.

* * *

I am part of it, life is full of grace.
If you follow my sleek car with a tracing lamp
It makes an elegant pattern through the roads:
Clean-lined office, country club, opulent apartment block,
Distinguished diplomatic party, theatre premiere with the new elite,
Bars hung with wine bottles, the best bookstores in town;
The points, connecting, make a map of ease.

* * *

And so the darkening evening calls me to the cocktail hour.
Briefly I stop to get a pack of aspirin on the way,
The shop is dark, the counter-man is sullen,
The room I see is hung with posters vowing death:
The pattern dislocates; the map no longer tells the way.
Four men look up from a bare table,
They have beers, and knives, and books – reading. Books!
Their eyes are hard when they look up at me,
Then they turn back to drink beers and read the open books.

* * *

The beetle with a cinder in its belly
Can burn the town, any soaring city,
Fire spreading where it goes, it hides,
Flame dripping from its stick-toes every inch,
Red sparks flicking as the beetle crawls,
Slowly crawls from the dry sewers, burning, burning.

ON AN OLD WOMAN, HALF GONE MAD

I remark the old woman in the poor-house room
The sun brightens the corner where she stands alone,
Alone, as if she was buried in the evening air,
Sun surrounding her like the thick gold earth.
She pats immaculate hair, ready for her evening talk.
She has half gone mad, her wits awry.
But in her madness she is not rough,
She does not curse or throw her bible down
As others have been known to do,
Or mess her weekly linen with black excrement.
She is gentle and sometimes smiles,
Her only madness a conversation with the trees.

* * *

She murmurs to the palm trees in the poor-house garden.
Intently she whispers to them each day,
And they believe she thinks they answer her,
The green branches moving in the wind,
The wind which blows down silver Brickdam from the sea.
She talks to no one else at all, they say,
Since no one comes to visit her this year.
She takes her food with care and cleanliness,
She prepares her bed with neatness in the mornings:
She needs no nurse for care, no priest for comfort,
Sufficient are the green trees in the wind.

* * *

She dresses carefully each day at evening,
She makes her hair up, and pins it with a comb.
She dresses in a black dress of ordinary style,
Faded but respectable, for Church fairs long ago,
An old brooch shining at her mad old throat.
She goes each evening to have her quiet talk;
It is the custom of her heart.
She talks plain sense, she describes her day,
The green trees in the wind reply.
She speaks with comfort if there is storm,
And when the sunshine blesses she has joy.

* * *

Her talk is commonplace and plain,
She holds fast to the mood of sense,
I heard her speak of bread today:
She said her mother baked brown loaves,
And there was one loaf always for the hawks,
Blood-mixed for their brilliant eyes.
She followed this with talk of sons,
Two sons she had, but they had died,

And she had sorrowed for them many days:
As plain as that, no emphasis of love or hurt,
And she went on to talk of other things,
And thanked the trees for being friends.

* * *

All pity taints the pitier.
In my huge pride I hug the thought:
Her agony she cannot bear:
And feel for her tormented scorn
That she has burned beyond despair.
But she is quiet all her way,
The green trees murmur in the wind,
And no one knows the human heart.

COLLEGE

(I)
HISTORY LESSON

'Ghost' we called him:
He walked in quiet shoes.
He was so ram-rod straight
Seemed always to be holding back:
Part of his reserve, his distance
From us that preserved respect.
The love came with the teaching.
We read books they set for us,
His look was one of slight disdain.
'Be sceptical of hallowed texts:
Before you learn, convince yourselves.'
He made the dust of history glow.
He read us the Periclean speech:
The Greeks were marvellously few

But down the darkened centuries
They gave light to all the world.
Our scattered nation too was small
Yet to be noble was not beyond our reach.
He traced the steps of Hannibal.
Of all men in history most magnificent,
Driving the great, grey, betowered beasts
Through avalanches of blinding ice and snow.
'I don't know how to make this live.
Imagine thrusting through the Northern Range
When forests stood without a path:
That might be as mad a task,
But how will you feel the bitter cold?'

* * *

The dexterous beauty of his blackboard writing
Fascinated us: it was a mystery:
The care to practise such strict art.
Why spend love on this
To be expunged before an hour was out?
We, his scholars, asked him this one day.
Of all his lessons I remember best –
The silence of the 'Ghost', we knew so well,
And then the deliberate, unfading words:
'There are creatures that live half a day.
Princes of the world, do you not think
They also strive to perfect their lives?'

(II)
ACHILLES

Born amid purple-fruited cocoa trees
In Caura Valley – old plantation family:
What soaring hopes a father had of him

You can easily guess, I think;
Achilles he was named at birth.
Forty years a teacher when he taught us first,
Dauntless, Dauntissimus, or just Old Daunt,
Taught us Latin when we reached the Sixth.
Moon-round, pallid face, moustache patch
Stuck, unclipped, untidy on his upper lip:
He looked like Himmler in the Picture Post.
Inelegantly dressed in white: white baggy pants
Held up by an unchanging, old, black belt,
White crumpled jacket, stained with breakfast egg.
Discipline! He missed it by a mile:
Shoes invariably undone: 'Sir, sir, your laces!'
And down he bent with apologetic smile.

* * *

He loved to roll around his tongue the sonorous metre
Of Virgil's mighty tale of adventure and survival.
The generations had not changed his joy in it one jot,
With brightened eye he beat tirelessly the great verse out:
A firmament flickering continually with heroic fire,
Singing thud of sword, the blood, the battle mire,
Dido in a flaming sea of endless passion
Amid strange, armed men with silver-circled eyes,
Half-Gods that gold-clawed tigers suckled,
Ancestral ashes desecrated and avenged.
To us he gave all as miracle and gift
To keep with us always as his great favour
Long as life to wonder and to savour.

* * *

Old Daunt, we scorned him behind his back.
'Can he be human to have loved one old book so long?')
We scoffed because we knew, bright boys,
Our flashing minds flew way beyond his ken:

We had, contempt and genius, what he would always lack,
And took success for granted when success came along.
To us his dowdiness deserved no real attention,
His ancient mannerisms made us all rejoice
With secret laughter, to see him conduct the Siren's song
And make such pretence to have the lion voice.

* * *

Forty years have gone since then.
Why is it that I still dream
of Dauntless on his Sixth Form pedestal
Shoes, unlaced, moustache, egg-stains, all
And see the golden armies clash?
Beyond pale visage and the baggy pants
Watch the Achillean anger flash
And hear, what never until late awoke,
The undying thunder of the words he spoke.

(III)
HODGE

Imagine! Such an ordinary Englishman,
John Hodge, thousand year oldish name:
Good earth tilled for Saxon centuries
Under open skies and slow rain.
Plaster patches on his ill-shaved throat,
He taught Literature for the Scholarship.
One day without any reason: Hopkins!
Hopkins wasn't on the syllabus.
'I caught this morning morning's minion, king-
dom of daylight's dauphin, dapple-dawn-drawn falcon...'
The words flashed and sung and silvered
The grey sky of school-imprisoned boys
Waiting for picnic and the weekend girls.

* * *

That Sunday on the beach at Blanchisseuse,
Watching the high waves leap and shine,
The gleaming, marvellous words came back
And back and back again and back
Suddenly took flame and flight.
The double-dawning of the Jesuit priest
Could not get out of my head at all.
Words sang as birds sing striding in the air
And the high waves arched and shone.
My eyes dazzled in the white noon blaze
Off the sea of heaven and the heavenly sea.

* * *

Monday the dusty room was new.
The old Englishman with the spectacles,
The stolid agricultural name we knew,
Had changed the angle of how the world is seen.
Talk once was meant for only living,
To get through ordinary days,
Perform the basic chores of time:
Plain statements telling truth and lies –
Not conversations with the Gods
Explaining how one views Their work.
Ill-shaven, homely Englishman,
John Hodge, I praise you down the years.
The complex value of the word was born,
Roots began to branch and sing:
At Blanchisseuse waves curled and shone
And language took ecstatic wing.

(IV)
THE CROCODILE

Hair cut brutally short, a gauleiter's
Look, eye patched with velvet black.
The one blue eye, beautiful but cold,
Searched and found and fixed you
An irritating fly held and pinned,
Specimen ready for display.
'This boy', quiet, curled gash of lips
Snarled. 'This boy', the whole class frozen:
I found the blue eye worse than licks,
Scorn is the great cruelty of schools.
'This boy', menace rising in his throat,
He jingled small change in his pocket
Ominously, the esses hissed:
'Who thinks the simplest word to use
Describing groups of men at arms...'
The pause lasted until youth was done...
'Is expeditionary force! Good grieving God,
One word, boy, one word I said
And you give me an essay pages long!'
Unsure laughter, cold eye swept the class,
Fear knotted in the stomach's pit
Worse than a bully's fist, the mind tormented
Stuck. Still the cold eye grimly
Waits for answer that will never come.
'Army' haunted me for weeks unending.

* * *

Is that the way to teach? Fear
And cold, unsparing threat?
It seemed not then, and all the books say no,
But forty years have gone, vivid
In my mind he stalks his victims still.

I learned, I learned, by grieving God, I learned:
Books became my friends by force
And what he said was best in books
Became my ally in a survival course.
He hated adjectives, pretentious words,
Colour, anything that makes language gleam
Or had the least romantic touch.
'Clean your sentences, the muck and dirt
Is worse than on your filthy hands!'
Clean! I think only of a sentence clean.

* * *

Forty years have passed. I meet again
This formidable man, this 'terrorist' of boys.
The iron hair now silky white, neatly brushed,
The pirate patch still there, ice-cold eye grown dim.
The years have clearly drawn his teeth:
Confident, I tower over him
And cannot quite imagine it.
He extends a shaky hand, not rising from his chair.
'You've done well,' he says. 'I could have told.'
The softness in the voice I do not recall
Deepens the sadness of how the years unfold.
'To teach a boy, you must know very well
Who will be strong enough to crucify.
I liked the way you fought me back:
Plain sentences I could never make more plain!'

A certain crookedness in the lips, old crocodile,
Makes the years roll back, I glimpse the snarl
Of certainty that what he taught was right.
Lacking clarity, nothing could atone:
All the flesh of language he removed
Leaving bone, no decoration allowed,
You wished to polish, well, you polished bone.

MERCY WARD

To my wife, Mary,
and in memory of
my grandmother, Hilda McDonald

LIFE/DEATH

Sudden,
quick as light:
skin shine,
then
bone white.

JUST JOHNNY ON HIS CHART

Johnny on his chart,
simply Johnny,
helplessly small.
his large head slips sideways,
a stick arm hangs listless out the cot
like a last gesture for help.
Eyes look at you:
blue-black in the corners,
flickering, searching, ending.
Don't look at the eyes.
I feel like shouting out
Hold him quick!
He slips on the world like grease.
Soon fall off.

NURSE GUYADEEN AND THE PREACHER

Best nurse in here was Sati Guyadeen,
bright, loving, strict, humorous and clean.
Dealt briskly with every single chore
yet strove beyond "Accept, endure."
Sati Guyadeen, fresh morning breeze,
stepping in on edge of dance,
you made a difference in this place.

Who claims even half-perfection?
Hope and bravery in every glance
you nudged life in the right direction.

Big feud broke out once in here;
it livened up the Ward a while.
They brought in Herman Forrester
a pavement-preacher all his life.
He had his pitch in Water Street;
up and down the pave all day,
"Save your soul: Repent, repent!
The world it end tonight at eight.
Repent, repent! It not too late!"
Every Friday eleven o'clock
he took his stand by Royal Bank:
"Money is the root of all evil,
it eat out your soul like biscuit-weevil!"
And Wednesday by J. P. Santos store
he lectured on Mosaic law.

In here he didn't stop for breath,
all day you heard his preacher-mouth:
"Repent your sins before you die!"
If you were God's children, then all right:
he pointed straight up in the sky.
But when he said where sinners go
he pointed dramatically low,
implying that those he saw around
would taste hellfire underground.
In all the Ward distress began;
they frighten of this preacher man.
Who with, say, a month to go
likes to be condemned below?

Nurse Guyadeen, brisk and firm,
decide herself to handle him.

"People can't have peace in here?
Hush up, or water pour on you!"
(She would have poured a drop or two).
The big feud start up straight away.
Preacher-man forget to preach,
he have a new thing now to do:
bad-talking Guyadeen black and blue.
"Parrot-monkey, La Penitence rat,
Guyadeen more ugly than that!"
He spends his hours thinking hard
and looking happy when he could shout,
"Someone smell like pit-latrine;
it go have to be Nurse Guyadeen!"
And Guyadeen giving as good as got,
lip match lip, hot for hot.
And when she think he gets too fas'
she jam an enema up his arse.
The quarrel kept the whole Ward bright:
who win today was the talk tonight.
For a good ten days they had it out
row for row, shout for shout,
but I noticed how she took her cue:
he began to weaken, she weakened too.
The last few days it didn't count,
his mind wandered North and South.
Sweet Jesus walked in Stabroek Market
and honey rained on Zion's Mount.
"Good riddance!" claimed Nurse Guyadeen
when she came to hear he died at noon;
set straight about her many tasks,
brought clean sheets, plumped up the pillows.
The empty bed was filled by six,
the new chart written up and fixed.
She made sure the night-lamps all were lit
and then she cried a little bit.

BELLE OF THE BALL

"Why is she in rags?"
Silk dress, but in shreds now
flowered, faded, aged, and filthy.
It was made for bigger breasts
and plumper hips and sweeter thighs –
eighty pounds at least are missing.
A heap of bones in this strange silk.
"She wanted to wear it;
she is dying, why not let her?"
What dance does she remember,
what dancing days,
when that nice dress once made her
Belle of the Ball?

WALKING IN THE STARS

Last words are not remarkable as a rule.
They drift away, have nothing much to say,
murmurs hardly loud enough to catch the ear:
"Please for some water", "I so cold in here".
Not more nor less than this or that.
Dying is a puzzled, incoherent act.
But this one! He described his desert days,
rose-coloured forts and old battalion pals.
"Servant of the Crown", one of the old school,
he served the King in postwar Palestine.

One still, clear night in Galilee
the stars dripped silver in a midnight sea.
He and his platoon went wading out
far from shore so that they could shout
loud among the stars and be heard by God.
He ends before he ends the story;

a sentence cut in half is his last word.
His exultant voice clamours to be heard:
"I, walking in the stars, in great glory..."

AXED MAN

"Bad-bad case of sugar:
they had to cut him down."
The old man sits upright, rigid,
spine straight against heaped pillows.
He grips the bedclothes on both sides,
big-torsoed, bull-necked, muscled man,
wears faded-red, short pyjama pants
just folding over both new bandaged stumps.
No toes, no feet, no shins, no legs,
no knees to kneel on any longer
to pray to God for mercy, rest.
Yesterday they "cut him down" again,
but still an obscure stink prevails.

Matron knows his story: strong once,
a timber man, big as the trees he killed.
He lived in forests and towered over men,
a rollicking and famous working man:
ten times won at Mashramani time
who could chop a great tree down the fastest.
He logged purpleheart and teak and silverballi;
trees falling give a sense of exultation.
Look at his stumps now!
The axe in the end
missed horribly.

FIRE IN THE WARD

Young, new nurse, serious in her job:
white uniform, white as roses,
brushed lustrous hair, brown skin shining.
She seems a banked immortal fire,
warm beauty, such glow of life.

She passed between the beds
full of vigour, dance, and glory.
As she passes, they sink lower down,
they seem ashamed, avoid her eyes.
She blazes; they shrink far away.
You think they should die quicker,
get out of the way of health and beauty.
What is the use of living any more?
Hips will never sway like that again.
She is burning this place down.
They will all be lost.

Motherly old dump, old Matron,
with your greyness, limp and sighs,
better you walk this ward.

GRANNY ISAACS VERSUS DEATH

Granny Isaacs, from the time she came,
fought death like a tiger.
She looked ready to go from day one:
frail as a stick in the sun,
tissue paper for her skin,
old, toothless mouth caved in,
hair lank and loose and ivory.
So thin, bones showed;
the next thing would be skeleton.

But she battled for life
and would not give in.
She hurried to take her food,
sat up when and where she could,
was eager to keep presentable,
and tried conversing quite a bit.
She would not just go.

And, most of all,
she made it clear,
she placed her faith
in God's arrangements,
and that beyond
this fierce encounter
other ceremonies are planned.

It could be said
death came out top.
Who can be sure?
She made me think
now she has gone
we'll have to wait
a little more
to see who won.

TIME PIECE

There is no clock in here:
the tick-tock of what time is left
tells too sad a doom.
And it disturbed the restless night
to hear the loud knock-knocking;
it was like drip-drop, drip-drop,
blood falling to the floor
and no one ever coming.
So they took it out.

It wouldn't matter now;
they could bring back a clock.
These days
clocks are different:
soft, no noise.
They do not beat
like hearts
that stop.

THE LAST CLASSROOM OF HUBERTUS JONES

Hubertus Jones was teacher to the bone:
fifty years in schools in Golden Grove.
His wit unvarying as the texts he taught:
mark him down five in scale ten to naught.
Term after term infinitely unwound
plain and strict and dull and sound.
Taught unchanging what he could teach,
the generations soared beyond his reach.
Cord-thin, very neat, and spare
his routines recurring, his rules austere,
he made no money, so he ended here.

People lonely, sick, and old
have strange dreams in Mercy Ward;
when they "go off" no fuss is made,
they are soothed or chided, then tucked back in.
So Schoolmaster Jones pursued his career,
taught a full class and set them homework.
Once a week he had Matron fired
for failing to do what he required
and confirmed in writing to Central Board
all that was wrong in Mercy Ward.

What eases the heart should never be grudged;

when anyone departed his last classroom
Hubertus Jones called for paper and pen,
and it was seriously brought for him to compose
a concise and lucid term's review
of conduct, aptitude, and future ambitions
for possible use by the powers that be.
He carefully handed them in on completion
and Matron would promise to deliver them safe.
Meticulous in all he ever did
he kept file copies for easy referral.

When Hubertus Jones departed in turn
I had a look at his filed returns.
Everyone was given precisely his due
but I noticed something shining through:
in the very worst cases of condemnation
he always added a last recommendation:
"Whatever his misdemeanours here on earth
he should be given a chance to prove his worth".

Scrappy little man, Hubertus Jones;
God spare us all, and rest his bones.

NOT HERE

Somewhere
a bird sings.
Sound of ping-pong balls
batted to and fro,
kitchen-clatterings,
a shooing of dogs.
Wind-murmurs
in green trees.
Laughter-spiced talk
somewhere.
Not here.

SCREAMING GIRL

It is no use to pretend otherwise:
this is not a pleasant, airy place.
They try their best with pots of flowers,
prints of sunny seas and bright savannahs,
but it would be foolish to expect good cheer.
In fact, it very much surprises one,
with so much pain and sickness all about,
how quiet it is always: a few low sounds, creaking of a bed.

Alarming and mysterious, then, suddenly to hear
a girl screaming as if her life gave out,
screaming and screaming as they hold her arms;
it must be worse than pain that visits her!
She screams, it is hard to pity or excuse it;
the thought of death is worse than death itself
and she is young, you think: so much to lose.
It is not quite so simple, as you soon discover.
For hygiene's sake, and discipline, and work routine
they can't allow this girl's hair shining to her thighs,
and she disturbs the whole room with her agony.
They snip it off in lustrous curls piling on the floor
and the girl screams, more and more and more.

There is, I must suppose, a deeper wound to bear
than any mortal injury that doctors diagnose,
but what it is in this girl's case
I find, amid the screaming, I do not know or care.

ROYAL VISIT

Once Mercy Ward was heaped with flowers.
A serious princess from the British Isles
asked what more duty she could do

to fill a Sunday morning she had spare.
They really spruced the place up then:
cleaners scrubbed the floor with non-carbolic soap,
swept roach wings, mouse shit, all away,
air freshener used to help the winds of May.
Mercy Ward was clean as heaven.

And everywhere it blazed with flowers.
The Parks Commission sent their gardeners.
Truckloads of greenery and flowers came:
great, lovely clumps of flaming bougainvillea,
roses in profusion and Barbados Pride,
blue plumbago and sweet jump-up-and-kiss,
vases lent and filled with fragrant plants,
exotic orchids pale in beds of fern,
blood-red hibiscus and flowers of the sun.
(Would all their funerals fetch half so much?).

Only old Mangru, not known for being difficult,
spoiled the great occasion somewhat.
When she stopped and asked him very nicely how he was
he sucked his few teeth quite hard and long.
For all the sour stares from Matron at the back
he simply would not smile or say a single word.
Even worse than that, old-stager Mangru,
when she was three beds further on,
amidst the healthy dignitaries, all those lovely blooms,
gave forth the loudest fart you ever, ever heard.

DISCHARGED

They cannot keep you in this place
if you are sure you do not want to stay.
You can discharge yourself at any time:
you have that option, it is your privilege.

Naturally they try to persuade you differently.
Mostly it is possible to ease the patient back
but sometimes a little vigour must be used –
the tough attendants use a slap or two
to make a man see sense, and only for his sake.

But one night, dismal with a rainy moon,
the young man in row 6, bed 22,
solitary, silent, making no fuss at all,
broke a hidden drinking glass
and under the covering sheets pulled right up
cut both his wrists, deeply, surely,
one by one, carefully, firmly,
and discharged himself.
They came running in the morning
but not even the tough ones
could coax him back.

THE LAST GOOD SHOUT

To people clinging on to life
it takes not much to satisfy;
it's also not fully understood
in what extremity life still seems good.
Things are measured differently:
simple gifts are jamboree.
Please God, stretch the hours out,
might perhaps be one last good shout!

Diwali festival one year
a big rice farmer sent piles of fruit:
ripe mango, pine, and golden apple.
Who too sick to eat enjoy to look:
"We just feel good we get it free".
The same day by coincidence

rampaging children visited.
Throwing, catching, red balloons
they soon escape their mother's care.
"Man, don't concern, let them make noise".
Race round laughing, bumping into beds,
playing catcher and bounce-balloon.
A good thing matron isn't here:
a playground buzz hangs wildly in the air.
Pray God this day not end too soon!

FUSS-POT

The old woman never stopped complaining;
it seemed her sign of life, her signature.
The food was bad or salt or made her sick,
water had the bitter taste of aloes in her mouth,
bed was hard or full of lumps or flea-infested,
the light was bad, mosquitoes stung her toes,
the place was hot or cold, whichever was most trouble,
and she never got the right amount of good attention.
And whenever the children visited, she let them have her tongue.

She deserved the suck-teeth she all the time received.
Strange, then, at the end, when agony came on,
she was calm and quiet as the day is long.
Lay back and never made a single petty call
and seemed to try and find a deepening peace within.
And when the children came you noted, with surprise,
how close they clung to her with many signs of love.

Who can delve into all the years gone by?
All one can tell is in behaviour now.
She takes on strength and certainty and love,
she summons seriousness in place of spite.
Death for her is drama worth her while,
too big, it seems, to make a fuss about.

THE MASTER

The old man carries on so:
he has no bravery.
But we don't know
how hard he tried to
keep the cries inside,
then let go.

Pain won't go
with screaming;
pain feeds on screams.
Praying's no good;
please go,
please let it go!
Drugs work a while,
lock the pain away.
It's still there,
waiting.
Show kindness, love;
abashed, pain backs away.
Not for long;
it comes back again,
the hard master
that sings no song.
Pain teases;
it'll let go
for a whole hour.
That's worse;
it keeps its power.

One thing though:
have patience,
it will go.
Old man
wait, wait.
At last
it will go.

CANDLELIGHT

No beauty
is here.
It is stark.
But one night
light failed
over half the town;
the old generator
took its time to start.
In that instant
candle-flies in season,
brightening and fading,
were hundreds in the room
as if girls
had flung them
at a wedding.

That once,
such beauty
in this sad place,
the glimmering
of candle-flies.

NIGHT FEAR

"Fast-Finish" Kowlessar, famous cyclist,
and, later, rum-shop raconteur,
ended up here when his good wife died,
stricken and trembling like water in a wind.
Sons found good reasons not to keep him,
but sent of course the fruit and cigarettes he needed,
for which he thanked them when they visited –
which was twice a month unless otherwise engaged.

The darkness he hated the most I've ever seen,
as if the sun went out for him alone.
He cried with fear and loneliness at night,
this brave man who once won famous races.
He could not bear the coming on of night.
The rose of evening, and his fear would start,
and never until morning would it depart.

Night's the worst time, that's sure,
people die much more.
More people do not die,
death is just much more.

One nurse kept him company for a while at night
listening to stories of his young days and his sons
wide-opening her eyes; she had the art
to show her fascination for all he said.
I think she kept the dark from closing round his heart.
But she was reprimanded, as she was bound to be,
for neglecting other chores for "Fast-Finish" Kowlessar.
The night she suddenly was not there,
for those who saw it, it was hard to bear.

There's one good thing about what we really hate:
the end of it is sweet beyond compare.
They could have told him, or he should have known,
the longest night of all contains no fear.

CHASING FLIES

The day is over in the Ward.
The dark time gathers in my room.
In and out of cloudy caverns
a silver, chill moon falls and floats.
Rain spots the window where I sit.

Too much to do today:
the blur and fade of routine work.
The mind that holds a universe
will keep a single memory fresh.

In noon-time's sultry heat
a beaten old man falls asleep,
snoring toothless mouth agape,
yawning in a ravaged face.
Not much there to talk about.
With tender art that will not last
a young nurse coming up to him
bends down so carefully concerned,
gently shoos some flies away,
secures the boon of sleep for him
and steps away with quiet grace.

The silver moon streams where I sit;
three years at least have passed away
and still I sometimes think of it.

TEST MATCH

When cricket is playing
this place has a special mood.
Naturally, in the town there's little else.
For miles and miles and miles around
attention centres on the Test Match ground:
stands besieged from early morning;
transistored cyclists weave one-handed,
risking crashes every wicket down.
Heroic men are just down there
and the greatest heroes are our own.
Latest score is all that counts;
there is a feel of fairground in the air

that catches on in Mercy Ward.
The excitement rises in the days before,
the desperate centring on self departs.
The subject concentrated on is changed,
the endless question unexpressed:
how much time have I got left?
Now other questions supervene:
the boys in trouble or the boys on top?
Their minds, diverted and released,
fly out to where the cricket plays.
For a little while at least
those broken on the wheel of life
feel at their throats a different knife.

STEALING BUXTON SPICE

What has made the veterans so upset?
Even the garrulous are silent and faraway.
Old Farnum shakes his head and mumbles something odd.
Shading the Ward veranda, in the yard outside,
three tall old mango trees are full of fruit;
rosy Buxton Spice are hanging sweet and low.
Wasps buzz and sip where bats have sucked the holes.
A lovely smell of ripeness fills the noontime Ward.
"Touch them by the stem, they fall down in you' hand".
Boys pelt down the fruit, or climb up the trees and steal.
They do it laughing now, so did they long ago,
as Farnum, who won't go out again, and six other old men know.

MONSTER

Black eyes
without tears.
Terrible seeing a child

that will not cry.
A monster's eyes,
the giant worm of hunger,
swells her belly.
It lies curled there,
it has wound itself upwards
and stares out the sockets
of her emptied eyes.

THE DWARF DOGS OF MONTSERRAT

Jumpy on twin leashes
panting pink tongues
gold-speckled eyes
scarlet-collared
silver-tagged like gifts
miniature and manicured:
a fine lady brings them,
luxury-lap things.
She is sleek too.

What are they doing?
Dogs are not allowed.
This fine lady is allowed,
and of course her pets.
How in this place?
You scc that old woman
crumpled in a corner bed,
ulcers on her cheek?
The fine lady sleek as silk
comes from Montserrat –
a mansion by the sea
terraced with sea-grapes.
She's purchased beauty.
Two different lives ago
this old auntie minded her.

Favours are bestowed now,
new clothes and drugs.
Old woman nods and nods and nods.
The little dogs jump and yap,
pink tongues lick her oozing cheek.
The fine lady cries.
Old auntie smiles and nods,
she puts up a hand again.
Shoo, shoo, dry the tears
she dried a thousand times,
time gone like forty years.

ART EXHIBITS

A most joyous thing in the Ward
was once when an old lady was admitted.
She brought pictures coloured by small children
and stuck them up on the wall above her bed:
bright cartoons of green dogs and red cats
and blazing suns in cloudless skies
and perfect blue seas with white birds flying.

The last one she pinned up glowed superbly:
Grandma, no doubt, in necklaces and purple gown
sitting in a golden chair, smiling all around.
When she went the pictures stayed a few days
then began to fall off and were swept away.
I remember feeling sad; no one ever came for them.

WHITE GRIP

At first you couldn't see her beauty;
this young girl was too-too thin,
bones were too near the skin.

Where could the blood find room to move?
No soft bosom, just nipples on a chest.
Look hard again, you see it soon:
no beauty ever matched hers in this room.

Oh, it is sad, sad to tell her story;
she did not expect to be here for long.
A man who went away has now come back;
they are matched; she will go with him.
The day she cannot wait for comes along;
she sits for hours combing out her hair.

He walks in and you know: nothing for her there.
He sits, her eyes fasten on his face;
his lips make up a smile, he scorns this place.
Eyes slip and slide from early on.
Five minutes, he turns to check a noise,
ten, the first look at his golden Seiko watch.
Meanwhile she hungers, devours all of him.
His well-fed frame is squirming all about;
he's embarrassed, how quick he can get out?
Half an hour; it's his time to go, not hers.
Her lustrous eyes cannot, cannot believe it.
It's a simple thing: he made it, she has not.
He quite roughly puts aside her hand;
she grasps his arm most desperately.
No good asking how it ended
with any hope that all went well.
He went away; she died one day.

Some things once glimpsed remain mind-set:
moon blaze on an Essequibo shore;
hawks riding high above this waiting place;
how once a boy looked at Orion's Belt;
an old man crying in the Silver Chapel.
Her white grip on his arm I can't forget,
Anyway not yet, not yet.

DARK ANGEL

A bird flew in,
quite big, taloned,
perhaps it was a hawk.
It grew desperate:
flew against shut windows,
battered against rafters,
began to leave droppings.

Much excitement,
great fluttering of wings.
Somebody screamed out:
"Out, out, get it out!"
Full of fear and hate.
The dark angel.

STONE FISH

Abel Washington is eighty-four.
He's the oldest one in here;
life has finished with him completely.
His mouth dribbles open all day long,
eyes have clouded the colour of the sea.
The only time he lifts his head a little:
when ice-cream comes for him to suck.
Hard to find his story when I checked:
he has disappeared before his death.
Booker wharfinger for fifty years
in the old days when sugar sailed in sacks.
No family left at all, all dead or gone away.
Lives condensed like this is history.

Two things alone stick out for me.
He made a famous river swim

across the Essequibo mouth and back;
and he was known as “Stone Fish” in the town.
It’s a mystery; no one now knows why.
I try to ask him, but he makes no reply,
then take his hand and sit by him
and talk about his Essequibo swim.
A sudden thing, his hand no longer slack,
his eyes come level, his head unsags
for a second, for the briefest shiver.
What happened? What came back?
Is nothing lost? Did he feel the river?

GETTING WELL

You can always tell the time for sure
when patients who are getting well
will soon get up and leave the others here:
they do not have that one-way-only-stare.
They seem to see the flowers in the jar.
They do not make a boast of getting well.
“The kindness of the ward”, it’s called.

But outside you can see amazing scenes.
One time a man ran in the glorious sun
and climbed a green tree standing in the yard.
To the very top he climbed, rocking in the wind,
and turned his face up to the burst of sun,
frolicked on a swaying branch, and scrambled down.
“I’m not mad”! he cried,
and swung his mother round and round.

AMERINDIAN

I suppose you'd say with truth
no one here looks all that "right",
but they settle themselves down.
He was all wrong from start to finish;
he squatted in his bed half the time
paddling a strange bateau.

All his life he knew forests,
forests and the great rivers.
Why bring him in town to die?
His soul is damned that way.
Tribal overarching heaven
replaced by rag of sky.

He should have been with brothers,
he should have died with jaguars and stars
and a wind rising in the trees,
a last wood-fire comforting
the coming on of cold.

Dream for him a savage vision:
a multitude of years will pass
when buildings in this upstart town
again are lost in sea-drowned grass.
The forest will stay;
nothing he loved gone down.

WARD WEATHER

The right day to die on:
a grey sky leaking rain,
colour washed out of everything.
Whole week it's like this,

Trees groaning in the sea-wind,
mornings sad after black nights.
Can't blame people dying today!

Last week it was different:
hummingbird sort of weather,
sun flaming in the sky,
rose-smell, hot grass, and ripening pomegranates,
at night stars crackling like sparks from a fire.
In here people died then too!

Draw no conclusions from the outside weather.
Rain or bright shining sun
Ward weather is Ward weather.
I recall the sorrow of all graves
and what the old men say:
What a day to die on
is any day!

A ROW ABOUT THE MOON

Regular as religion, every month,
there is a row about the moon.

When the full moon comes to flower
it floods the earth with silver colour.
A basin of white water spills and froths
and slops over all the town.
A bright pallor spreads in dark corridors.

Some in Mercy Ward complain.
They hate and fear the great white ghost
that makes them think of jumbie-birds.
They want the tall blinds pulled across;
keep out the coffin-colour, these ones say;

keep out the leper-shine,
this fungus-staining of our skin.

Some want the moon let in.
They like the pallid beauty everywhere,
the waxen light of lilies that it throws.
Throw the windows wide and let her in,
the grey fox of the night, our pet;
we may not see again, so sleek, so silvery.
Let her in!

CAGED

The stroke stuns him into just a stare:
mouth screams without a scream being there.
Neck muscles tighten, throat-apple thrums.
Plucks with fingers at his lips and tongue
to rip out songs or words or anything;
he strains and sweats to say a single word.
Paradise would be to let out half a cry.
Nothing comes; his eyes rage.
Think of birds that can no longer fly;
his skull is like a bolted cage,
no opening anywhere.
The slightest motion, a shivering in the cheek,
like wings in flutter before flight.
No further movement comes.
Inside there alone, alone, alone, alone,
wings nailed right through to bone.

SWEET PEPPER SUNDAY

Hook-nosed Amoroso,
eyes blazing,

spade beard bristling white,
demanded the right
to better food.
Slop and sausages
were not his fare,
so he said,
and made it clear
he wanted action.
A buzz arose:
rebellion in the air!
He wasn't just ignored,
he had a victory.
On Sunday, the Ward
served, on special china,
red sweet peppers
stuffed with garlic crab.
Worth remarking,
this Conqueror of Drab.
Not often did you see
such cookery.
Somebody skylarking!
But Amoroso,
eyes blazing,
in the humming Ward
lifted up his fist
in triumph
to the Lord!

RECIPE FOR THE BITTER CUP

Water poured
in bitterwood cup
cleans the liver,
freshens the gut.
Here's the recipe

old nurses say
keeps belly sickness
far away.
Put inside
jumbie-bead,
drop of blood,
pinewood dust,
and, if you feel,
a little bit
of coconut peel.
Pass fire near
three times three.
Cool the water
and let it be.
And, remember,
when you drinking,
don't stop
until you drain
the bitter cup.
When you start
you can't stop
until you drain
the last gall-drop.

MILKBOY

Dazed with sleep, I rise in morning dark.
The call has come: attend a man who's dying –
old Ramkissoon, who no one visited.
His time has come at last to go.
It isn't a big thing, truthfully.
We watched his loneliness so long a time
it's a relief, at least to me.
No one can speak for him, I know.
He wanted nothing as I sat nearby,

except once he asked for water in his cup
(in all the years he said not one hundred words),
wet his lips and looked to see my eyes,
drifted into whispering that was hard to follow.

"Get up, chile, get up, get up!
Time to loose the white cow by the tree.
Bush in flower where bee burn my skin.
Mam so pretty when she vex with me,
Mammy die before my Pappy,
tears came so bitterly.
Hard Pap try to comfort me,
hard he try to comfort me.
He gone too, who going mind this baby?
Why he gone so far away?
Why Mammy you gone so far away?
Hear both you calling: chile, get up, get up!
Don't frighten, Mammy, don't frighten, Pap,
I will mind the white cow in the morning.
Ah, ah, pot so shaky with the spurts of milk."

He sighed and silenced and soon he died.
I rose and went out to hear the morning start.

BENJIE DISROBES

Benjie was getting down;
everyone knew it; he too.
When suddenly one day
he began to take off all his clothes,
everyone thought it must be
simply his senility.
Not so. Seventy years
in the bosom of the Church
he'd lived and now he knew
exactly what he had to do.

So far as he was concerned
his time had come.
"Naked into the world
cometh man
and naked
he goeth out".
He did not feel any more
the need to make a point
which had been made
a long time gone before.

THE LAMENT OF "BIG BULL" COUSINS

Tell me the truth!
This could be me?
God loose me in the world
to love women
and women to love me back.
How this could be me!
So maugre and wrinkly-looking,
so mash-up in misery?

Something inside eating me up
sitting crawly like a slug-king
taking what it want and when,
shrinking up everything.
It like most what most fresh,
sucking the brain, drawing down the flesh.
It shrivel up the good, thick loins,
it hollow out my jouncy cheeks,
mek big-barrel chest like a little biscuit.
It fattening up fat inside:
everything else getting trembly and thin.
Years and years it eat and eat;
now it nearly finish and done
like it want to eat up everything.

It starting East, it going West,
soon it going leave alone by itself
and only the heart in the breast,
then that eat too and all done!

Skin shine once like silk, man,
smooth like pure molasses flow,
not a mark on this black man.
Muscle in my belly-pit
hard as stone, not a fat-ounce.
Knock it, your hand bounce.
Who could mock me,
match my mastery?
Now look at me good!
This could be me?
Eye never see glass until sixty,
could sight the old chimney up the coast
from so far like a close-up post.
While people straining, I laughing and reading.
Clear-clear eye, storm-sea grey,
now everything gone and fade away.
Eye full of pink string and boo-boo;
who could play joke so? Who?

Who is it abuse me so?
How who it is could ben' so low?
You could tell why it is,
why He it is allow this wickedness,
bitter-bitter after so much sweetness?
I fresh and spright and young,
next day donkey-drop-dung!
Why life can't fix up a different way?
Why night have to follow bright day?
It could have been organise so
you getting greater as you go.
First is sour, then is spice,
the direction is to Paradise.

So why it couldn't be all we fate
to end up young and bright and straight
from old and scrawny and wither and grey?
It could damn well be fix up that way!

A big, brawly man I was,
big everywhere I tell you,
big down there too –
ask any women I know.
Now look how I scrawly!
How this could be so?
There wasn't a woman in town
didn't know my renown.
Every night
they testing my might.
I tekking my pick;
when one done, I ready fo' next.
Night have no woman, I vex!
How these days done so quick?

But one woman this heart beat fo' still –
I think she dead now forty years.
Sweet, sweet as morning wind,
oh Lord, Lord, she drink like wine!
Eye get heavy with hold-back tears.
Watch me now, so dry-up and old;
she lucky bad she never get old.
Out of so much she was my One.
How quick-and-go that sweet time done.

You could tell me what sense it make
to build something good only fo' break?
I don't understand this big mystery:
a priest-man say it is God decree!
Before I done I going have my say,
cuss I going cuss, not pray I pray:

I going cuss this God before I die
and He ent have no reason to ask me why.

REQUEST FOR SOFTER SPOONS

You could get some thicker socks?
Toes turn cold like ice today.

Rice pap, bran, and water-soup;
"A shot of red rum, sweetie doo-doo!"

Cobwebs festoon the dead-dark roof;
clean and colour it sky-blue.

Door creaking somewhere far away
"like a funeral parlour hearse."

Raise the bed-head one foot more.
Why, Heaven not near enough for you?

Old man murmuring dirty songs
disturbed the Ward for one whole week.

Look, she lip paint up so red!
Who she think she is at all?
Matron, what going on in here?
It could be Hotel Belvedere!

Woman only got tears like rain.
Don't let she in here again!
Why all you can't hire bus,
take we all to a matinee?

Balgobin gone too far this time,
he open the window and take a pee.
What sort of conduct that could be!

So many flies they have in here
we could be carcass-meat one time!

Nurse skirt too, too thin,
or she petticoat didn't put on.
She stand against the sun;
look how brazen panty wearing!

Sweetheart, you know, just thinking this:
never again I going to get kiss
until I dead and lay out flat,
me cold and marble burying.

Gums hurting every time I eat;
you can't get softer spoons in here?

Mammy used to tell me so,
lonely is a stone pillow.
I miss everything at home so bad;
why you just can't carry me back?
What medicine when the heart choke up?

Chink-chink frogs too loud at night.
Board got barefoot splinter wood.

Old this old place old, old, old,
they should done and pull it down!
The blasted day, it last too long!
Why are all the plates here round?

Procedure exists to hear each case.
Having to die is a grievance too.
No point registering that complaint,
though naturally there are some that do.

A LEOPARD IN THE SKY

In October
on pure, moonless nights
there is a leopard in the sky.

Above the black outline of trees
amidst the thousand glittering stars
I trace the daring of its leap.

Night after night
at sea in the terrible boat
he saw the leopard burning in the stars.

Bound from Calcutta
to the sweet green plantations,
Gopaul Singh, grown old, remembers only this.

He died here yesterday.
Forever he has made me see
a leopard burn and leap among October stars.

BETTY KUMAR

In the canteen yesterday at four
amid the noisy washing up of cups
a simple ceremony a few attended.
The notice set it all out plainly:
"A presentation will be made today
to Betty Kumar well known to all.
Fifty years she served this place:
she goes with Mercy Ward's best wishes".
The new Administrator, young and businesslike,
cracks some jokes and chats to everyone.
No doctors came: none can spare the time.

Matron's there, who knew her as apprentice-nurse.
Cook Stevens from the kitchen came,
the shine of pot-heat on her face,
and Thomas who guards the outside gate:
old retainers of this ancient place.
A photographer came to take a shot of her.

Tough and stringy Betty Kumar
I look on her in wonder.
Sweet young woman when she started here,
"She had googly eye but silken skin".
And Matron says her back was arrow-straight;
spine-bone curves now into a humpish shape.
Fifty years she emptied slop-pails in the Ward,
morning, midday, nine o-clock at night,
cleaned out the urine, spit, and vomit,
swilling disinfectant, scraped out shit;
running water sluiced them clean, clean, clean.
The plump young Admin speaks his words of praise
to scattered clapping amid the noisy cups.
"Washroom attendant" is the name he calls.
She hesitates to take his wrapped gold gift,
she does not seem to know what she must do.

Is this a proper way to pass the time on earth?
What Madonna smiles to see this juggling act?
The mind cannot assess a fate like this,
put value on a lifetime emptying slops.
Fifty years of mornings, noons, and nights
made brutal habit of Betty Kumar's days;
what can there be that's noble in all this?
I wish I knew much more about her life,
not only how much shit she moved about.
Did she enjoy the act of love? Did she have children?
What was her home like? What laughter? Dreams?

She puts up her hand in great distress,
the tears come in her googly eyes.
Clutching what she's got, she stumbles slowly back
and then seems loath to leave and go.
She stays as if she fears some doom;
what has she got but tin pails in a stone and scoured room?
Matron takes her by the stringy arms
and leads her to the back door out.
The apprentice-nurses play and nudge and giggle:
their eyes don't turn a moment as the old ones pass.

THORN BUSH

One day a corn bird, flash of gold,
got caught in the thorn bush outside.
Something happened: a bird should know bushes.
An old lady saw it from the Ward.
It worried her, she made a great upset.
Brisk nurse Guyadeen went down herself,
got out the bird and threw it free.
It soared above the mango trees.
The old lady grew pleased, quieted down.
Not such a big event, you'd say.
For some reason I recall that day:
the corn bird fluttering in the thorn.
I was forty and the world seemed old.

GOD'S WORK

Mister Edwards, more my good friend
than gardener and handyman at home,
served me well for half my life.
Prince, they called him, born about that colonial time:
I called him Mister Edwards until the hour he died.

Strong black face, handsome old man,
ashy cap of curled short hair,
never sick a day until a day he sick.
"Wind by the heart", he said,
but the heart was sound, too sound;
it took months of agony to kill him,
ripping his guts away slowly
until that strong, good man was nothing.

"God's work", he would say
when the rain pelted down
and floods rushed in the rivers
and storms lashed the treetops.
And "God's work" now he said
when the pain wracked him,
spasms crumpling up his face,
sweat dripping in the effort to hold back
the gut-contracting cry not quite escaping.
"Prince Edwards, he too strong for cry".
But his last day in my arms he cried.
"God's work!"
God should play more.

CALYPSO

Here is not for emergency,
but sometimes there is overflow
and they have to bring them in:
like this pretty girl in pretty party dress
and tall, young, handsome smashed-up man.
You can tell it's month-end Friday night:
money in his pocket, a girl to court,
after rum and dancing, show-off time:
80 down the avenue by the old train-line.
Life good, the wind sweet.
They're ugly now, butcher's meat.

Try of course, hustle about,
but they're dying, nothing to do.
They're completely out of place too;
they make the Ward restless,
barging in, no patience, such a mess.
Dying has rhythms, fast and slow:
the Ward is waltzing, they calypso.

THE CANCER

Strange case.
Rich, debonair, and completely with it,
young Whittaker, the lawyer.
He got cancer and would die.
They made no bones about it,
opened him and shut him up again,
told him he had three months, no more.
He took it well – you never know who will;
straightened all his business with his wife,
set up a Trust for John Whittaker, his son,
drank the best malt whisky while he could,
played the hero part to absolute perfection.
The sun will boil the earth in any case.

Then he seemed to go a little mad:
he checked himself in here, in Mercy Ward.
Understand, this is for the poorest of the poor,
and Whittaker was on his way to being very rich.
He came in alone, not even with his wife,
signed the forms, and settled in his bed.
Visitors who came were most embarrassed.
No plea could budge him; his end came here.
I never found the reason out for sure
(whoever finds a reason that is sure?).
Turning up the records when he died

I found another Whittaker, named John,
died in Mercy seven years before.

I puzzled at it, not for long –
why dig for agonies that are gone?
It lies too near the desperate human heart
to tell for sure how sons and fathers part.

THE FIX

You have to get out sometimes,
take a few days to far away.
The Ward-tension gets too much:
the suffering and lonely pain,
the bursts of unreasonable joy,
the waiting on, the waiting on in vain.
A man whispering, "No hope, none, none!"
Always on the point of wondering
how lives will end, not how they go on.

The drug of beauty taken pure –
beloved Essequibo where my soul will go
if hereafter good things happen.
The ballahoo slides in the slow river,
rose-black water smooth as glass.
Tonight a clear moon lights the land;
the paddle drips silver.
Gold fires in the Mazaruni far away;
silence and the barking cough of ocelots.
Travel all night and rest at dawn,
dew glistening on the green banks,
birds calling before the red comes in the sky
and speeding kingfishers kiss the water.
A bell from somewhere lost in trees,
and then a clearing: one man setting nets

and women squeezing white cassava roots.
Waving, we slip through the rose-black water;
they are full of smiles and so are we.
The sun floods over the thick vigorous forest,
air hums and shines with dragonflies and rocket-bees;
between piling clouds and blue sky blazes,
poui petals, like gold leaves, drift on the river.

These dream-days pass and pall.
My mind drifts back to Mercy Ward:
the ending-up of people in great sadness.
I wake to feel a yearning restlessness;
the itch starts up which needs rough rubbing.
Disturbing things a man must fully face,
a swarm of demons he can't do without.
The gut-attraction of those at risk,
wounds and danger and utter fear:
love grows for it when you are safely near.
There's intensity in living through
a dying that's not your own.
There's always power in the air,
shine of courage flicking off and on.
The hard habits and the daily dealing
with mortal crises in the Ward
gives life a pitch and rigorous meaning,
from which, I think, there is no weaning.
Why do you think that wars go on?
No mild or sacred wand can catch
the lightning from the sky or match
the fascination of the sword.
After beauty's gentle fix, I need
the sharper fix of Mercy Ward.

MOTHER TANGO

There is always some cruelty in nicknames.
They called her Mother Tango in the street,
not because she, being young and strong,
became some legend on the dancing floor.
She got her name, and no one knows another,
since she was very small and fell
and never was the same again:
a hip disjointed and a stunted-leg
made of her walk a comic twist and dip.

It must be bitter to be laughed at all your life.
There never was a sign of bitterness in her,
nor is there now that anyone can see.
She smiled at all and never was affronted.
She lived a frugal life, she served her Church.
In place of those she never had, or could,
she mothered orphans fifty years and more.

Her life ends here; she will never go back out.
In part-thanks for her love and work she's done
a young Jesuit comes to visit her.
He holds her hand and gives Communion bread.
The young priest looks disturbed: he's sad.
Perhaps he hears the jeers of "Mother Tango!" still.
He should not be sad; when all is said and done,
she can sideways drag herself to Heaven
faster than you or I can ever walk or run.

BIRD SONG

Sky, colour of agouti, drips rain,
a strong wind blows in the gulls from the sea.
Young boy in a blue jacket, head hunched,
bicycles in carrying a pan of milk.

Every morning he comes without fail.
The pan clanks against the bike's side:
it's for his grandmother in Mercy Ward.
The sound wakens me like bird-song.

LAST BREATH: STILL LIFE WITH FAN

Silence from the sea;
the still night
holds its breath.
In the lamplight
her living face
carved by shadows
looks not very different
from what is soon to be
her decomposing face.
She has left uneaten
rose-fleshed pomegranates,
bread, and chickpea brew.
Pearls of pale sweet
bead her high brow.
It is a stifling hour;
the few deep breaths she takes
seem precious things to do.

On the brown, iron bedside table
she's dropped an old fan delicate as fern.
Ivory stems pinned with silver pins,
torn yellow silk opening in between
shows red plums on a tree with birds.
Lace gone black tatters on the spray of bone.
Sweetheart's gift now nearly all used up,
it lies abandoned, heirloom at its end.
Framed beyond all further composition
she'll never pick it up again it seems.

Glossy grape-skin once, now so raisin-withered,
blue-veined, liver-freckled hand
plucks weakly at the congealed sheet.
A nurse, in passing, senses what is wanted:
an ancient grace is reasserted.
How honourable are simple, well-learned ways!
A practised gesture with a lovely thing
at once transforms the gesturer.
What gathered round this death's defeated,
what is brutal falls away;
momentarily all's not lost.
Life's pattern knits up anew,
what's to come has been before,
what has gone may reappear,
All's not settled, all's unsure.
The picture can be drawn again.
If only briefly, she fans the breathless air.

LOVE AFFAIR

At four precisely every afternoon,
she starts preparing for the visitor.
She smooths the sheets and tidies up all round:
her house to keep has narrowed down to this.
She dresses carefully and puts sweet talcum on,
grey hair she combs as much as can be combed,
and settles in her chair, folds her hands and waits.
Her day, her life, concentrated in this hour:
her eyes intently turn towards the opened door.

At five precisely every afternoon
he comes in through the door at visiting hour.
His suit is shiny-old but pressed and clean.
He takes off an old beret on entering the Ward,
he leans quite heavily upon a worn-wood cane.

Without fail he shyly gives a wave towards her bed,
then slowly stumps towards her and she looks content.

Quietly they sit together near the tidy bed:
they hardly speak a word the whole hour he is here.
She bends a little closer, he gives a halfway smile.
She rocks a while and he relaxes.
But there is something in the closeness of the chairs:
strangers would be further, even friends not half so near.
They doubly occupy a single space in time:
that space is empty if he for one's not there.

At five to six he rises from his usual place.
She looks at him, he gives her half a nod,
and bends stiffly down and touches her old cheek,
and takes her hand in his and she takes his.
No words exchanged, and that is all there is.
At exactly six o'clock, when visiting hour ends,
he goes towards the door and does not turn at all.
Her sadness deeper than our customary sorrow,
she turns away and yearns towards tomorrow.

THE PLACE THEY HAVE TO GO

When someone checks into Mercy Ward
one of the particulars you have to get
is what provision has been made
for a burial costing nothing, net.
They look restless and turn away.
Even if you have a few days only
you don't want to think of the black hearse
pulled by the half-blind City horses,
or about Merriman's fourth-best limousine
rattling unattended through the streets.
And you don't want to know

about that part of the graveyard
where no flowers grow, just tussocky grass
and nettles and black-ant nests.

You often have to visit where they go:
a bare field where goats are grazed,
rust-coloured grasshoppers whirring as you step.
Across the way the splendid tombs arise,
white and shaded by huge impressive trees;
marble blossoms deck them down the years,
and ornaments and wreaths in perfect alabaster.
But here, of course, no monuments arise:
graves dug in line straight into earth.
When freshly dug slapdash dirt-mounds show
with wooden crosses stuck awry on top,
rain crumbles them shapeless in a month or so.
This field of grass and goat-weed
holds a bare and hopeless dignity.

The Supervisor's office is a simple place:
a chair, a desk, a concrete vault
where archives of all burials are kept.
The leather-covered volumes stretch centuries back.
This sets things in perspective right away –
the record is equal in these careful books,
inscribes for all an austere common fate.
No space for high, or space for low,
the line of written detail does not change;
all are put down here the same,
bare, unblemished soul-mates, row on row.
In the field you do not get to see
the part of burial that does not show
obscurity or utmost fame:
The scene below is much the same.

HAWK-WING OR STONE

Walk around outside the Ward
there's so much bustle about nothing.
The streets busy with what?
Some sort of treadmill:
people passing and re-passing.
The having to eat and to plan eating.
The purchasing and delivering.
Where's the edge on anything?

Back here, deep in each one,
life or death's the thing:
even that's minor in the end.
No more lies.
Nothing, everything?
Clean down to bone.
Will I rise
or fall
like hawk-wing
or stone?

RUNTEE

"Runtee" Tang-Choon, yellow as a Lima bean,
was brought in like a bundle by the police.
"Little grasshopper, he light as leaf", they said.
They found him in the cold morning crumpled up,
old clothes tied with string, small torn black boots,
by Alonzo's rum shop in Anira Street.
He could have been dumped out of a rubbish bin.
The nurses roughly rubbed his skin, roughly wrapped him up
to make him last a little while at least;
Matron brought him dumpling soup he would not take.
Black eyes dying, he never said a word.

He had a sort of pride not easy to describe:
a fearlessness when fear has ceased to count.

Scuttling little four-foot huckster man
(calf-muscles hard as iron even at the end),
sold roasted peanuts around the town for years,
moved so fast from crowded street to street
the children called him "Mile-a-Minute" man.
His whole life spent in carrying nuts and walking;
savage sun or pelting rain was all the same,
he never seemed to stop for long enough to sell.
The worst among the urchins robbed him once a week,
set him a-sprawl and laughed as he got up:
"Mile-a-Minute on the road again!"
He'd look away, hoist his sack, hustle on his way.
He seemed to have no friends or anyone at all,
and nobody ever knew what hole he had to go.

Chinamen don't end up here; they mind their own.
None ever came for "Runtee" Tang-Choon though.
Five days here he lasted, never said a word.
Black eyes like shining beads, hardly winking,
trapped animal, except he never trembled once.
Small as a child, his chest sunk in,
he frightened me more than anyone I know.
Something about him far beyond forlorn;
this little man should never have been born!

I cannot think that: no man's life is waste.
No one stopped in kindness or gave him half a thought.
A life and death so lonely teaches best:
"All that lives needs help from all the rest".

BLUE POTARO HILLS

Old Oudit Ram seemed, to those who knew,
to have taken up permanent residence
in the coveted corner bed on the Western side.
He had even accumulated a few belongings,
a litter of small items to grace his stay,
a sort of shrine to give a sort of meaning
to his life: a holy Hindu picture, a tattered book,
a bag of stones (I don't know why), a faded Panam bag.
He seemed to have settled in for good – or bad,
and he behaved himself and said his prayers and ate.

Without any warning, at evening time one day,
he surprised the Ward by getting up and walking out.
He showed every sign of knowing what he did,
collecting up his picture, book, and rocks,
and also his small bag, and making for the door.
He got quite far, almost to the stairs outside,
before the shouts brought order back again,
and he was hustled back to stay in bed
where he belonged, the nurses told him scoldingly,
but not where he was trying hard to go,
as he explained: home, home, one time more,
home, far away and far to go,
home where he remembered in the evening mist
Blue Potaro hills of young days long ago.

ESSEQUIBO

"To my Father and Mother
For so much bestowed
On their 60th Wedding Anniversary"

AMERINDIAN

I think of woodskins,
I think of quick arrows. I think
of things Indian. And still
I think of their bright, still
summers when these hills
and meadows on these hills
shone in the morning
suns before this morning.

RIVER MEMORIES

River along whose shores
the shadow of memories
and long-lost delights
hang like morning mist.

No moon but one bright star
shines in the black river.
Go carefully: there are rocks,
but the captain laughs confidently.

Jetty posts rotting in the water:
boats once loaded muscavado,
coffee, coconuts, and purpleheart.
A few birds settle on the black posts.

Blueness of the sky blazes,
a white-sailed boat comes near.
It is fast in the gleaming river:
lettered on its side the name: 'Wind-Song'.

A girl in scarlet blouse
beats clothes and sings.
Her voice comes over the water.
Sliding past, we turn and wave.

The sun burns on the cold river.
Put a hand in the water wrist-deep,
the rose-black water is cold and sweet.
Savour the two sensations.

Cloud-castles pile up far away,
a storm sweeps up the river.
Curtain of silver rain fast approaches.
The first drops gleam in the sun.

Hush and shiver of wind,
chuckle of water at the bow,
silence of green forests all around:
senseless to say a word.

Stop in the shade of bamboos:
the creak of wood, rustle of leaves,
white orchids in the tree hollows
and mauve butterflies flying.

The river fills with blaze of orange:
suddenly wild pigs are seen swimming.
Black and shimmering in the burning river,
caught in a net of golden shadows.

River-beach with dogs barking,
white chapel in a small clearing.
A boat bobs up to the steps,
a man all in black gets out.

Green parrots fly in the blaze of blue.
Far away the river stretches
into deep mists and mountains
wrapped in shadows.

TRAPPED AGOUTIS

('It is good that the animal rushes about in desperation. The level of lactic acid, which builds up in the muscle tissues during exertion, tenderizes the flesh.')

Hardly silver light of morning;
shouts of pleasure, sound of pain.
The lithe-running village boys whistle and cry:
they have caught and held a bright-eyed agouti.
They dig a strong stake in the open ground
and bind the small, resisting, pet-shop thing
so that by the neck it spins and spins and spins,
dashing for freedom to the safe, green trees
until the stake-rope pulls it sharply up.
Again and yet again it makes its freedom bid.
It does not give up, it seeks the trees without despair.

The village life returns to peace.
Deliberate hurt is not the aim.
Nor is it thoughtless cruelty –
as children pull bright wings off flies.
They know the purpose in their blood:
old huntsmen tell the sons of sons.
Past noon the rope has worn its throat
but not so deep that it can die.
The arc defining freedom's end
is beaten bare and marked with blood.
The children walk about and play,
the women nurse the evening fires.

If Gods are good, why is there pain to bear?
What ignorance! To think that Gods are fools!
Of course they cannot interfere:
before time began they made the rules.
Forgive the Gods that fashion fear!
Forgive the Gods that crucify!
It depends on what our souls are for:
agoutis at the torture stake
cannot know that they endure
such agony for a simple sake.
It is not love, it is not hate,
but prelude to a higher fate.

When the village feast is done
go out and watch the icy moon.
However long our story runs
man will not have his mercy soon.

IT IS GOOD TO LOOK OUT ON GREAT RIVERS

Late afternoon, gold starting in the clouds,
wind-ripples on the shining river,
five rods down the bank fishermen come home,
tether the boats, scoop water out with pans.
Children speed down to cling around their legs,
are lifted up and shouting to the sky.
All about gleam fish threaded on long lines:
good workday and they swing the children high.
Food is preparing: sweet pots sing and sizzle,
fat yams bake black on split-wood fires.

In a clearing of white sand under grass,
near enough to smell the cooking pots,
by evening custom a rocking chair is put,
dark mahogany carved with heron-shapes,

stouter made than any house for miles.
Old lady, tiny as a doll, sits there
dressed in black, white ruffles at the neck,
sits and rocks and looks out on the river.
The hours pass, she rocks and dozes.
Sky and water stain with gold and rose.
For years like this she's watched the river
every day before the dark rose leaves the sky.

She's not left the river all her life:
her birthplace and her death-place will be a walk apart.
To grow to love what anyway you've got
is one way to find an earthly satisfaction.
You get accustomed to what you've always had.
After a while you do not want to choose
even if what's offered millions say they want.
She sits at evening in her dark chair carved with herons
and watches what she's grown to love so well.
Small gold flowers sift down at certain seasons,
fish break the surface in bubbling silver streaks,
birds flash down and up, mirroring themselves.
A song drifts across the water from some burly men:
she shades her eyes to see a little better.

What happens now has happened long ago:
the drama of the river entertains her.
Farmers paddle to Parika on the coast
with piles of mottled pumpkins big as boulders,
mangoes rosy-gold, and green plantain stems.
Schooners bound for Skull Point's landing stage
with orchids, tractor parts, and drums of oil
pass and hoot: old lady gives a wave.
Gold dredgers move slowly up towards green creeks.
Drunken axemen out of Willem's timber yard
sing and holler across the silver water.
Strong steam-tugs pulling greenheart rafts

push slowly, heavily, against the flooding tide.
Soiled and battered little boats drift down
loading blue gravel quarried out of Monkey Jump,
charcoal burnt in Makouria pits, sacks of cashew nuts.
Corrials carrying gold men and young police,
surveyors going to Northern forest posts,
shopkeepers bound for Bartica and beyond
– a tin of cornbeef worth a fleck of gold –
glide across the sun-path on the river.
Sunday families in white put up black umbrellas
returning from the small church past Kyk-Over-Al.
Three women dressed in red pass rum around
and shout with laughter in their motorboat.
Old lady claps her hands, she's seen it all before.

Men head up-river on a thousand quests.
Deadpan Amerindian scouts slip past in ballahoos
to guide determined men in teams of three or four
in long batteaus brim-filled with food and fuel.
They aim towards the dark interior creeks
to seek what treasure's now the latest fashion,
still full of yearning to find the Gold-Dusted One:
precious letterwood to make a cello sing;
rough diamonds found in secret green-deep pools
in pear-drop perfection will gleam in metropole;
fish with red-fringed tails caught under waterfalls
end a-gape entanked in New York drawing-rooms;
a thousand grasshoppers, russet, gold, and green
fetched from tops of balata for science far away;
ancient Amerindian herbs to daub on modern sores
and bat's blood to test for some new corruption's cure.
The cargoes on great rivers change and do not change.

The trafficking is only centuries old;
old eyes near death see something more than that.
The river dreams beside the huge and golden forest.

It grows dark, still she sits and watches.
What dreams possess her? How the years pass
and she grows old? How should she prepare?
Out of the timeless forest, darkness nears.
Fireflies fill the air, birds come home;
if children wept, the tears are brushed away.
Cold brings a low mist on night water:
with gentleness they take her in to sleep.
The soul grows strong on beauty
like a child's bone fed on milk:
it is good to look out on great rivers.

HALF-MAN IN A STORM

Upstream sweeps the storm past Stampa Point,
unbanks the river and makes it like a sea.
Fat clouds, swollen black, billow up like hills:
the storm rumbles in its thick beard far away.
We sit in sun and view the black horizons:
rain-curtains in the distance fall like silver lace.
Big wind begins to shake the gold-leaved trees about,
the bright sun gleams on storm-outriding rain.
Soon it is darker, the river grows uncalm,
a strong wind rises and makes a nearing roar,
it blows froth off the tops of rising waves:
a dust of flour-white on heaving grey confusion.

The storm strikes, howls, darkens everything:
now it's nearer night than golden day.
The river looks rough and huge and live,
great grey bear-coat ruffling the wrong way.
The wind is strong ocean-wind,
the waves crash on black rocks like the sea.
Towering treetops like green sails unfurl,
torn and tattering on long, bending forest masts.

The house groans like an old boat in a storm.
We stand soaked on this veranda-deck.

The rain pours down, we can't see more than yards.
Suddenly far out a red batteau appears:
it seems in trouble, the sails are taken down,
it drifts and wallows in the wild sea-river,
wind-torn driftwood at the mercy of high water.
It looks as if the waves are pouring in to it:
we run down to the weekend cabin cruiser,
big and powerful and more than safe enough,
unanchor her and go to save the day.
Even this big boat is heaved and smashed.
The rain streams down: the hungry sound of wind.
We steer towards the red boat in the waves.

The batteau nears, crimson in the grey:
the waves are tossing it, water's getting in.
Firm set on the steering board, in old fur cap,
around big shoulders a black coat thrown askew,
black figure in a rough black coat at bay:
a single occupant, the captain is upright.
He grips the rudder and keeps it near his heart.
His eyes are angry as we come up near:
he gives a fierce wave to shoo us far away.
We ask him through the roar if he needs our help
and know as soon words said they deserve no answer.
He stares away, he grasps the rudder: he controls the storm.

And now a moment when the image sets
which lasts a lifetime and will not fade.
Half of him is cut away and lost;
his body ends in leather pads halfway up his thighs.
He seems to stand upright even when he sits.
A few words only he spares us in his rage:
'You are little boys. The river knows me well!

The river is my friend'. And turns away.
The tall black dwarf dismisses us,
his violent eyes are angrier than the storm.

'Stumpman of the river', fisherman with a dagger,
he's roamed the Essequibo sixty years.
In Bartica he's known in every bar and brothel:
drinks rum like water and screws pork-knockers' whores.
'His fingers iron and his temper bad:
in a fight don't let him get the throat'.
Sells produce from a farm and trades in gold,
owes no man a living, no woman dare give pity;
his real life is on the great river in his boat.
Not one day passes he does not set his sail
and take his blood-red paddle, settle in his place,
and hold the rudder tight beneath his heart.

No wild winds stop him, he likes the weather fierce;
in a boat he's easy without legs,
as dexterous as any man on earth:
hoists, unhoists, black sails in blackest weather.
The huge leverage in his arms gets him round at will,
his quickness awkward but quicker than a cat.
The great river soothes his soul and it is where
his unequal body shows unequalled skill.

Shocked as when a knife-slip cuts to bone
we fall slow astern, not wanting to be left,
silent, amazed, gripped by this black dramatic man.
At last the dark storm hides his scarlet boat.
The image is forever etched: he turns, salutes us,
a proud man in his boat, not less than any one.

CAIMAN FEVER

Cold wind creeping on the skin,
a shaking-ague deep in bone,
all night in and out of sleep,
fitful skin-damp wakings every hour
and a restless dream recurring:
huge caimans thrashing in the river,
tails beating the water egg-froth white,
eyes blazing as they struggle,
musky odour rising in the night.
I smelled and feared the grappling beasts.

Shivering in a misty river dawn,
I meet Majesta who minds this house,
ancient-slow but cooks a perfect pot.
She gives a look and knows the whole thing true.
'You have the caiman fever bad'.
(How can she know my deep-down dream?)
Her old bright eyes turn full on me:
'Caiman fever shake the bone'.
She has the cure for me she says:
cold water from a baked earth jar,
a pinch of golden powdering,
a dip of lemon grass put in.
Drink it off in one great gulp.
Taste of woodsmoke
and old nights,
moon in cloud-scud
red jasper round the throat.

The powder like a golden dust
she pinches carefully from a stone box
with sacred ointments and white spider cloth:
caiman's penis dried golden in the sun
scraped to powder on a fish's spine.

It's chased the fever
down a thousand years.
I will not dream the great beasts anymore.

ESSEQUIBO RIDDLE SONG

Bamboo hill is burning down.
Over the fiery trees
children of the moon are dancing.
The drumming is gold,
the drumming is silver.
Thunder in the high castles;
The copper sticks clatter.

Look at him, so sensible!
That fine river-man
handsome as a tall tree
passes the sleek girl
with bouncy-bottom walk.
The bird stays on the branch,
it does not wet its beak.

Fish-trap gleams with diamond.
Will the diamond stay?
Sell it and buy a woman.
Will the woman keep?
Morning-beauty.
What lasts forever?

LAST OF HER RACE

A walk in the morning:
sun burning off the early mist,
river-bank ablaze with Lady Slippers.

Old but in a green clearing:
no sign of fireside or children.
Friends who know the forest:
'Come and see this wonder,
maybe she's a hundred years.
Talk to her, see if you can get her story'.
Room is misty with strong tobacco smoke,
old woman in a corner croons and drools,
lifts up her terrible blue-stone eyes.

Miaha, 'last of her race',
frail, desolate, decayed,
Greets no one in the mornings,
relates no heroic deeds to anyone –
children, children's children, not there anymore.
All gone, all gone.
She wears one green stone of Amazon,
amulet against the snakebite threat,
the gaze of Spirits that accuse,
a trembling voice saying nothing.
Deer have grazed for long
over the rain-worn tribal mounds.
Her cloudy eyes skim past,
missing mine by centuries,
seeking something deep, eternal, lost.

I am shy, I am ashamed,
edge out into the sunlight
saying nothing to the picnickers,
breathe in the green deep forest air.

Old toothless woman comes and goes
in this forgotten place smelling of orchids.
Past and gone, the wind whispers,
past and gone, the forest hardly stirs.

A STOP BY COCOA YARD

A place called Cocoa Yard,
scattering of shelters
once was worth a name;
not now: cocoa orchards gone.
Stopped an hour to get cassava bread,
drink cold beers, prepare the guns.

Splendid things gleamed in the dusk:
mountains pink in the distance,
white-winged birds soaring in the last light.
Lamplight like a gold eel
squirmed across the river.

A pig's carcass chucked out by a bush,
guts exposed and oily black.
In the skinned, earless head
dead eyes are shining still.

RIVER GRAVE

Near giant bogwood that blunts axes,
half-buried in a moon-filled place
they dug up chanced-upon grey bones,
cluster of dog-grey bones, shining,
out of gold and river mud,
heavy, glittering, golden, clinging,
old as mountains, there, looming black,
far away, far in the mist,
the ominous, unsheltering sky.
Slippery as fish, silvery as river-fall,
in the bag that carried them to camp,
the grey bones sang and danced and clattered.
Men the colour of honey and black iron:

One man hung a grey bone on his chest;
one man carved a grey bone for a flute;
one man boiled a grey bone for his soup
to sup miracles, to gain the ancient thing;
one man with a grey bone called the rain
to rage, to scour the gold down quick;
and camp-men used the grey bones left,
made music with those clattering bones.
Hit hard at midnight, all together,
clack-clack, ringing, clack-clack, singing,
strange echo, clack-clack, strange floating moon.
Old gold men dance and dance and dance
and dance until, old bones all-a-tremble,
they fall down, watch the bones still clatter-sing.
Whose grave was dug a thousand years,
he must have been a music man.

LIFE AND DEATH TREE

Along the dark, lonely river
silent as leaf-drift
an opening in the cliff of white quartz;
a grove of dead-looking trees
stark in the burning sun.

Out of black, bare sticks
velvet-white blossoms spring:
the life-and-death tree.
Green leaves will sprout from it
as bright flowers die.
The scent of the gold-centred flowers
pours out of the live and dead grove.

Four girls from the yam farm,
they are preparing a sister's wedding,

they throw up stones in the branches,
accurately shaking down the blossoms.
Their clothes are coming down too.
The dips of their navels fill with sweat;
gleaming drops run down like diamonds.

Nearby, the stink of a killing place:
black flies, bright knives.
Gleaming with sweat, too,
three boys gutting fish
marvel and fidget.

CARIB BONES

Ten miles along a logger's trail,
greenheart in flower smelling rich and sweet,
a camp abandoned long ago
has nowadays a few huts rotted by the rain.
Enter the chief's hut by a slack-nail ladder;
three old men squatting down like stones
convey a welcome with their shrunken eyes.
We squat and take small gourds of drink,
brewed wild cashew and sapodilla skins.
The ramblings of the old men grow wild.
Soon others leave to hunt the angry pigs
and fish the clear, cold, black as satin streams.
The old men begin a chorused chant:
memories of remembering their fathers' fathers' tales.

The old men squat, scratching withered genitals,
sucking pipes of scented, strong tobacco.
Black tongues lick across half-blackened gums.
The chant rises, falls, whispers, shouts and ends
where it begins. And they are stone again.

The Caribs were the great ones,

greater than the tall trees;
no forest men could conquer them.
Out of the arm-bones of their enemies
they made flutes to sing their triumphs.
Courage was dear to them as life,
their war-songs sang of bravery alone,
no word for cruelty except for 'love of pain'.
Before they chose a warrior
they sliced his skin and rubbed in pepper bush,
tied him in a hammock filled with tiger ants,
and if he made a sound he failed.
Fear they did not know.
Death they despised, a puny thing.
Battle was good.
To feel the heart beat fast
was life itself,
the sweetness and the song of life.
The hearts of men they killed,
dried in fires made of wood and jaguar bone,
they pounded into 'chieftain's' dust
to drink with shining eyes like blood.
And when great warriors died,
their bodies, wrapped in snakeskin shrouds,
washed and watched by chosen women,
rotted slowly under suns and moons
until the flesh was ready to shred off.
Then women cleaned the bones as bright as dawn,
painted the clean bones gold of sun and earthen black
and placed them in honoured virgin-woven baskets
carried everywhere; more treasured than a home,
such great bones last longer than gold or settlements.

Kept forever, the old men chant,
forever kept, forever and forever,
forever to match their courage against foes
to guard the people against defeat,

to guard the people against all ill,
to guard against the giants of the dark,
forever guard, these strongest of the strong,
for however long forever ever lasts.

THE POISON-MAKER

Travelled miles that day,
gold savanna sun to shadows of darkest green.
A day of such beauty
I have not seen before,
the air gleaming like the start of the world.
On the edge of forest
hawks hanging in the blue heaven;
black wings beat once
and they are aloft forever.
They have always been in this great sky,
eyes scanning the long horizons
where suns have burnt to black the short-grass valley-fields.
Amidst orchid-covered granite blocks of white,
gold and scarlet cocks-of-the-rock sport and fight.
Then the dense-dark forest green;
in the cold creek canopied with branches
the bright, dark-red water runs like wine.
Mora-trees, breaking into new leaf everywhere,
white, liver-coloured, green, and deepest red
stand like huge chandeliers in ancient rooms.

Flashing messengers of light and swiftness,
grey-blue kingfishers lead downstream to a village.
Well-kept habitations in a green glade
bustle with life; women bake and cut;
children play with rolling balls of silverballi wood;
hunting dogs snooze amidst the cooking smoke;
red-stained hammocks swing in evening air,

strings of red beads are heaped for market day,
making mounds of brilliance on the brown earth floor.

Relaxed, at ease, on mats of yellow cloth,
chewing Indian corn parched white as jasmine buds,
the men extend an unsuspicious welcome,
offer pepper-hot iguana eggs and wild red cherries,
cool, week-old paiwari spiced with sugar-gum.
Their eyes are black and impenetrably bright.
It looks a place well-settled in good routines.

Alone, outside the evening light,
alone with black arrows,
who is that man, wrapped in black,
squatting in twin-circles of dropped black pods,
crouched like a crow, stirring a black pot
sizzling on red embers like a black cat spitting?
A chant of mourning comes from this figure of the night.
Why does no one approach him? Why so far removed?
Why will he never join the hum of life and light?
They shrug and smile like children who are happy:
'The poison-maker', they murmur, 'he is the poison-maker'.

DREAM ISLAND

Far up from the ocean coast,
green-deep in Essequibo forest,
for briefest season –
soon as fast-water comes, it will go –
the tides have tugged an island into being.
A blazing, bone-white beach
appears mid-river, sudden as a dream:
bank of sand and scoured stones,
pink shells from prehistoric seas.
Low-tide you can land

and own this silent, lovely place.
Clear, red water lapping past,
sea-birds alighting, preening:
the sounds of wings and water.
A great sky of piling clouds
and winds that are the breath of God –
wide, amazing, perfect stillness.
I come ashore through gleaming water,
bringing a feast of gold-red berries,
cassava bread, flowers for beauty
that will last an hour.
I come to read on this bright temporary island
the Overture to Proust's beloved book.
Heat-lightning flashes in far mountains;
storms will soon wash all this away.
Lost, lost in the great river of this book!
Clouds of fireflies burn as night begins.
No one will ever do what I have done.

A TRACE OF SUGAR

One day, hunting wild orchids
and wide-girthed trees for corrials,
deep in the thick, dripping forest
we came across strange machinery:
cylinders, wheels, a vine-entangled mill;
giant, iron, rare, calandria
half-sunk in black and drifted soil,
rusted nearly through and broken up;
a scattering of bricks that was a chimney once.
Black stubs of wharf-wood, useless and forlorn,
jut out few and rotting from the river-shore,
lost, lonely relics entombed in earth and forest.
And then, alerted, we found for miles around
tracings of the furrowed fields, row on row,
sugar's vanished, old plantations.

No one here knows anything of this.
No mystery why men gaze ahead,
show no interest in what once was done;
let the dead concern the dead.
It's simple to confront the new;
choice is bitter in remembrance.
Bad memories only hurt again,
good memories are forever gone;
history is soaked with sadness through and through.

Veiled through the tumultuous, sullen years
a vision of the past emerges.
For a blink of time the forest was defeated.
The bustle of a great estate arises:
cultured earth and commerce burgeoning
where silence has returned, melancholy, still.
For miles afar the cane-tops wave
shining, shaped, and folded green
along the contours of the winding banks
murmuring in the wind that gusts up river.
Thick cane-bundles, worth their weight in gold,
muscled in from sun-drenched miles aback.
Pure, clear juice spilling from the mills,
thick black-strap congealing in bright pans
to make at last the 'honey not of bees',
this ancient sweet grass crystalled in the cask.
The barges fill with dark-gold muscavado
loading out from jetties planked with ironwood,
tugged for miles down strong-running Essequibo,
across Caribbean and wide Atlantic seas.
You can smell it in the air
stronger than sweat, stronger than flowers;
wharves and storehouses, tall sheds filled with goods;
mule-stalls whose scent is sharp of shit and hay;
fiery blacksmith shops, forges, foundries;
whitewashed chapel, rose-windowed, blessed.

Empoldered river, canals cutting inland deep:
man's mastery for miles and miles around.

A narrowed eye which sees results
observes this alone: energy and man's creation,
the forest cut, thrown back and cleared,
river, sun, and the eternal wind
harnessed in their wildness for wealth and power.
The absolute beauty of nature tamed and used:
the earth providing for the good of man.

What good, what men?
The eye of history opens wider:
the serried cane, wounds striped and stitched:
man in agony, the coast enriched.

SCHOLAR

The forest clears, socket of silence
in the huge green shout of trees;
weather-greyed chapel, box-small, closed;
dogs snarl and snap on long ropes
round scarlet-blossomed trees.
My voice ripping the noonday air
summons the friar, frail as dried leaves.
Old age stoops him like a crescent,
one eye glass-white, skull clean-boned,
teeth broken-black, his robe of threadbare blue.
He has never come down river.

There is no greater mystery than any man.
I see the old books I have come to see –
shelves upon shelves in thousands once:
Latin histories, old maps, testaments and laws,
thick books of traveller's tales and governments.

They all were brought from Heidelburg and Rome:
'A wild, green place for books',
he gestures in the lustrous air.
'It seemed a good thing to be done.
I meant to write.' He shrugs it off.
The books are crumbling, tumbled out of place,
worm-holed, rat-eaten, damp-decayed.
They will go soon to dust like men.

I am allowed the old priest's journal:
ten marvellous notebooks two thousand pages long,
lined, yellowing paper half-a-century old.
I turn to April eighteenth, nineteen thirty-three:
'Rain fell nightlong and in the morning
gold-billed toucans skimmed the trees'.

The last note is five years back.
No more after. The old man shrugs again.
'To see the moon-blaze in the trees
perfect itself. A clearer sight of God'.
The entries end. The rest is blank.
Dust drifts in the warm, illumined air,
the shuttered room is still. He prays.

'HANGMAN' CORY

When the launch sank off Fort Island
people were drowning in the black mud,
bawling out, 'Oh God! Oh God!'
God did not come. It was like any day,
sun shining on wind-rippled river,
except men were struggling and dying,
women and children choking in the mangrove roots.
People were running on the shore and calling,
'Oh God! Oh God!' How God could come?

God can't mind everyone.
But look at this now! Look at story!
'Hangman' Cory arrive like God.
Let me tell you 'Hangman's' story.

Nathaniel Cory once loved a lady.
She was a wanton lady, she used him badly.
His mind stop work when he see her beauty;
he was a puppy-dog in her company.
People laugh at 'kiss-she-foot-bottom' Cory.
This wanton lady take another man one day;
open, brazen, she parade before Nathaniel Cory,
laugh and say for all to hear clearly
how this man was the sweetest man for she,
how Cory never, never could satisfy she.
Nathaniel Cory stay quiet all the long day.
Night came and when the man lay with the lady,
Cory walked in open so, easily, terribly,
lash both two with his sharp timber-axe fiercely,
cut them in pieces like red melons on a tray.
When judge-man say she provoke the jealousy
and Cory get only five years off his liberty,
'No! No! No! No!' shouted Nathaniel Cory,
'She be life, my love, my beauty,
I have to go to hell with she, my life, my beauty.
She only gone in front of me.
Hang me by the neck to die gladly.
Hang me high, high and quickly!'
The people whispering make it legendary;
is so he get the name of 'Hangman' Cory.

Off Fort Island that bright morning
was he who God send to save the people.
People bawling on the black stelling for a saviour,
they never expect to see 'Hangman' Cory come.
He live so quiet among them all the years,

minding a pumpkin patch behind the white Chapel,
he smoke his thorn pipe, never say one word.
There he stood on the black stelling like a God.
Bibi La Fontaine, ice-pick thin and hard,
fifty years trading plantain along the river coast,
recount what happen that bright morning in her life.
Launch just left the Fort to go Parika side,
deep inside boat-belly a thunder-sound was heard;
time flicker, in a second, in a cat-wink,
boat gone bottom. How quick it was!
She belched a warm beer she was drinking,
before the belch belch good, the boat capsize and gone.
'Under I go, the whole boat on top of me;
mud yellow dim my eyes, cold log brace my heart.
I see my little Fancy who die fifty years gone by,
and then I see for sure is the monster death that come.
And my mind saying why an old woman should struggle so,
let me go, and still I fighting not to go.
And there is Fancy, the little one, crying in my arms.
A rough hand come and choke me round the neck
and pull me where I done pin good in mud.
This man had come for me in the dark water,
he find me like a miracle and take me safe ashore.
Sun so bright, earth hard; I hear a singing bird.
Never morning wind feel so sweet, you hear, I give my word'.

'Hangman' dive and dive in the dark water.
Everyone like they turn to stone but he;
women bawling and running and pointing trembly,
big men shouting and doing nothing foolishly.
Only 'Hangman' Cory doing the work of God.

And every time he come up with another one
as if God guide him in the mangrove mud.
A score he save and still he went for more,
coming up with weed-tendrils round his head
and wound around his throat like gallow's rope.

He delivering up children from the river-womb,
his eyes staring red and cold and terrible;
not one word he said in all his glory.

These are the plain facts about 'Hangman' Cory,
his day of evil, his day of glory.
He cut his beauty up like a red melon in the market;
God send him one day to save the drowning people.
Time will sort the meaning of all this out;
the hunting moon will rise one last, appalling, time,
and he will come to rest like all men come to rest.
Though years pass, men should know his story.
'Oh God! Oh God!' the people call and God send 'Hangman' Cory.

THE SATIN PRINCESS

In the drear mist of Long Island Sound
I think of the Satin Princess.
Hearing the cold clang of the fog-bells
I see again her moon-walk on the river,
all around her from the forest
the warm breath of flowers.
This clammy morning
pale as ice seem the ladies'
wrapped, colourless faces;
their breath puffs white
and bitter are their eyes.
I recall the warm breathing
of the far Princess.
She dresses with jewels;
the river fills with night;
immense Van Gogh stars
shine on her black bosom.
This pallid, shining world
is bracing, bright, I know

but ah God! I shrivel in this land
where life's laced tight
and unburnished air congeals.
The cold throws a spear
through hearts here
across half the earth
the Satin Princess moves and loves.

THE FORCE AND BEAUTY OF WILD PIGS

Hunting night,
clear as once was crystal,
star-silvered forest.
Can life be ever better?
Luck with the quarry;
quiet tracking through the thorned boughs
and then the hot, fierce hours in the forest.
Five great pigs caught and charging,
crashing in anger through the wild-wood.
The temptation of those that chase
was ours as the black pigs ran.
When you have the upper hand
all danger is most sweet;
life racing in the blood
courses to its fullest tide.
They ran so near each bristle could be seen;
one eye close up glared red and gold.
We shared the killing all as one,
the blood and death of perfect things.

And then the good weariness.
Smeared with dirt and leaf-green,
sweating cold in thick khaki dress,
the warriors sit to joke and reminisce,
river coolness a hundred yards away.

Morning begins to clear the sky,
bird-sounds start up here and there.
Pitch-pine fire crackles in a round of stones,
curls of the pine-sweet smoke
join the mist drifting between the trees;
the fragrance makes breathing deep and good.
Coffee spiked with rum goes round;
a brother punches his brother's arm in joy.
One man does a leapfrog dance;
all are game, all is play.
Princes of the high forest,
princes of the crystal night.

Tough Indian men, guides for the hunting,
placid, squat, hard, contemptuous,
bring in the trophies speared from mouth to anus.
These pigs are named as ugly. Why so?
The lovely shape of the boar-tusks,
short, sharpened, white, and crescent,
curves in its own space: perfect tools.
Coarse, thick-bristled hide, undulled, alive,
powerful, short, dainty-trottered legs –
and the snout has its purpose like any snout.
These heavy beasts that stamped the night,
broke trees apart like thunder in their rut,
swing dead on sticks and cutlass-gutted.
Their force and beauty now are gone.
When they charged the forest shook.

DEATH AND BURIAL OF A CHIEF

The old chief is dead,
born before the tallest tree.
The village grew around him,
their great city rose and fell.

The names of everything were his;
the great river was not more important.
His anger was like a storm;
water singing in the streams
his voice when pleased and gentle.

The day he died he called sons near:
'I am gone so deep I can see the stars
at brightest noon'. The spirits closed his eyes.
Clouds darkened at his death;
a cold wind lashed the waters;
wild duck pierced the heavens with their shriek.
He had set aside a tall, straight tree
to make his coffin and its place
a hillside near the great river
past the ruined fort Kyk-Over-Al.

The great spirits of the Dark and Light
fight for the souls of men when they escape.
However good or bad the life,
the coward or the brave, the true or false,
the great heart or the meanest heart:
there is no certainty when life ends.
Eternity always is at stake;
nothing begins or ends for man.

The struggle starts again.
Great spirits, entwined, contend
and living men must see the signs
when chieftains are at risk.
The village fills with fear;
over the coffin the dawn-air shivers
as over a fire lit and burning.

Before night the whole sky flamed,
a dark red furnace lit the clouds.

Aloft the lightning is a fire-tree
growing in the night; river-thunder rolls afar.
The Spirit of the Dark retreats. By morning
he has risen to high glory,
he has passed to his burning;
as they say, all dross burnt away.
The seedcorn can again be strewn,
and pure water drawn,
and new village houses built.

PERFECT ROSES

The belching sawmill half-falling in the river
stinks of steam, pulped wood, and acrid smoke;
it's near the hut which sells the axe-helves.
Far and holy, the stars control our fate.
The full-bellied lumberman scratches at his balls.
The slattern woman by his side,
kimono slipping down a caved-in chest,
slings a snot-nosed infant on her hip.
The yard-space slops with mud and chicken shit.
A cur kicked half to death whines in a corner.
They walk me to where he carves the axes
and where it seems she tends a garden –
patch of ground, fenced with well-nailed wood,
black earth neatly forked, packed with shining blooms
sunset-red, and gold and white as quartz from Pomeroon.
The pattern of a life is fixed;
nothing prepared me for the perfect roses

DOROTHEA AT WORK AND WORSHIP

Dorothea, in plain black dress,
braceleted with black beads.

Beneath hair scraped back and grey
carved, still face
nothing gives away or back
except a child comes near,
and then it softens in a thousand smiles.
Spend a morning in her shadow,
you feel the plainess of her days,
days clean as sea-washed bone,
bare of beauty, bare with beauty.
Tuned to earth and sky and river,
as roots feel the wind that blows the trees;
town-convenience scraped away,
life scoured down to clarity.

Sun hardly risen she lights the morning fire,
pulls in and guts the spiney mud-fish.
She visits the crop patch two miles away
through dew-wet bush and hanging vines.
Amid butterflies like flying sunlit leaves
gathers the pale-green, silk-tasselled cobs
and violet-coloured eggplants, smooth and plump.
Returning, she grates cassava roots for flour,
chews joints of sugarcane for sweetness and strong teeth.
Batteau comes gliding under the huge sky,
skimming the river calm as mirror to the edge
where green dragonflies hover in a cloud.
She signals and the batteau-man lifts paddle,
comes in with sugar, salt, and lantern-oil and spice.

Old Dorothea unknots her coin-handkerchief to pay,
carefully knots it up again and puts it carefully away.
Next thing, to kill a tame duck from the pen:
wring the soft neck with a flick, cut off the head,
pluck the breast-down carefully to keep.

Noonday heat and stillness, storm-clouds pile afar;

time to lie down in the woven, handmade hammock.
Before, she shines a grandchild's hair
and cleans the pus from fly-infested sores.
Then briefly she purifies her body and her life.
She goes to the small room where she worships,
roof lined with parrot-plumes and nun-bird black.
From a gourd scooped out to hold pure water –
blood-drops put in from anything she's killed,
fish-blood, bird-blood drops she puts in it –
she touches lips, eyes, ears, and nose
to praise things as when God begot the world.

NIGHTSCAPE

Thin moon over water
far thunder on the breeze
eel-lights through river-mist
cassiopeia caught in the trees.

Another part of history
a mad prince ruled the age,
at night each star he counted
a throat was cut in rage.

In time the world turns over
See! The prince sinks on his knees;
the moon outlines his holy shape,
the star-entangled trees.

EXPLORER

Here men you meet are strange wayfarers:
  to find a tree that flowers blue in late October,
  grasshoppers thumbnail small and crimson-winged,

and ants that smell of citronella.
Track streams that spring from black-rock shelves
a-swim with parrot-eyed, ghost-white piranha.
Trade with men who make the stonewood boats
and carve amulets that look like pictures in a cave
that scholars say go back ten thousand years.
A day I saw king-vultures soar higher than the clouds
a man came by and stopped and told his story.
He searched for the lost Amazons.
Soft English life, brilliant time at University,
rich family, smooth progress to the top,
then he read about the Amazon,
the endless river and its secret tales.
A myth had now possessed him wholly.
Gaunt, charred-brown, eyes like blue stones in a river,
ten years he'd roamed in every Southern forest.
While the howler monkeys roared
like a wind through mountain passes,
he told the many tales he had pursued
to find the brave women without one breast.
'I heard this tale of men-despising women.
They danced their men asleep and flew away:
as they fly they clutch red peppers in their hands
and pelt blindness down as the men pursue.
Never to return,
never to return to their ancestral sway.
Never to return.
In a magic city they yearn and yearn forever.
They live a thousand years and one,
their vaginas turn to twittering birds.'
Next morning in a cold and crystal pool,
edged with flowing white mimosa,
drinking cashew juice and sucking bitter plums,
before departure when the sun was high and bright,
I asked him what the route was he would go.
'A white horse's tail has brushed my face;

it is a sign I will succeed one day.
Their sacred flutes will play for me
and I will come across their place.
Palms stand on guard with blackest thorns
long as a grandaunt's knitting needles.
A lake where all the gold veins run;
it is not near,
the Mirror of the Ancient Moon'.
Mad as a torn shoe on a burning road,
chaste as the stone I toss from hand to hand:
the beauty of God in every thing and man.
Gave him for his quest all he may ever need:
onions, sugar, salt, and fishing line and love.

INCIDENT PAST MIDNIGHT, BUCKSANDS

The house silent, lampless;
all close to me sleeping.
Deep in the night, alone
I go down to the edge of river.
It is a black night, velvet, no moon,
only the stars spread like panned gold.
In the middle of the vast darkness of the river
a batteau passes, paddle-chuckle just heard
and a song comes across the pitchy water,
one man singing, not loud, a clear voice:
'Holy is the wide river,
song of glory!
Holy is the forest tree,
hear the glory!
Holy is morning star,
song of glory!
Holy is the forest tree,
hear the glory!'
The batteau goes down river slowly,

Slowly the song of the man fades in the darkness.
I think of the huge river flowing to the sea
and the sea curled vast around the earth.
I think of the river coming from the great mountains
where it begins in small streams full of gold.
I look up at the black sky strewn with the incredible stars
and the bright net they cast on the water too.
At my back the immense forest presses
heavy with the weight of a continent of trees.
Like a dream that came suddenly
the song drifts to silence on the immense river:
the towering forest falls down towards me.
No one wakes and I know myself alone.
I want to talk, fill up time with noise,
speak with friends how we live everyday.
Something breaks in me, shakes me utterly:
to light the lamps, to regain the ordinary,
I utter oaths and sing and shout and pray,
cavort beneath the stars, anything to flee
the measureless absurdity of the glory of the world.

SNAIL PAINTING

Cold-pale eyes, pale hair, gold-pale skin:
he must have ventured from an icy land.
Once upon another time for Sven Neilson
a pure, freezing country in the North
must have been his stone-cold home.
Twenty years of wandering brought him far
to frontier river-town, deep in forest country,
mud-drowned in late December, dusty hot in May.
Down a side street off Bartica main square
he runs a rum-shop where bush-whores and gold-men come,
serves behind the counter and knows them all by name.
He likes customers to dance; claps his hands,

jumps and jigs and jives in his blue dungarees.
I've been there and suddenly he'll stop
to play Mahler and Walcott's 'Joker' on the box.
He keeps green leafy branches fresh all around the shop.

One night he closed the bar down early,
beckoned me to stay and led me in the back.
A long room lit by lanterns set on barrels down each side,
casting gold-black shadows on a strange display:
long, unrolled sheets of black cloth tacked on frames
nailed to rough gilt trestles four-feet tall.
Eagerly and soberly he explained it all to me:
it filled his inner life, it was important art.
From a jute sack, one of bundles in a corner,
soaked in water, earth-encrusted, tied with golden ribbon,
he dipped both hands in and pulled out a score of snails:
Gleamed white and pale blue in the lantern light.
He put them on the black cloth one by one
at all the corners, We watched their silver scrawls.
He demonstrates most carefully, anxious to explain.
The slow trails glow, meander, cross and multiply:
the tangled veins of silver make maps he can decipher.
The craft is where he spaces out the snails along the frames.
The largest works use up a hundred snails or more:
the black cloth glows in complex mastery.

At first he used to mark the movements on the cloth
to make precise record for painting on huge canvases
stored for years, vast elaborate scrolls slashed with all the colours.
His soul being not at rest, he destroyed them all;
the snails alone are now enough for him.
He sees no greater art or act than this,
such silver beauty, tracings straight from God.
Whole nights he sits and looks in wonder,
immortal patterns forming in his mind,
paths of peace and trackless wastes of war.

When daylight comes the silver marks are gone.
The day's first customers wait outside for rum.

THE CARD-PLAYERS

A paraffin lamp lights the play,
citron grass burns in a ring,
four men deal the greasy cards
passing rum to keep death away.

How much blood does a man hold?
He gives it all eventually.
Last year it was the curve of a belly,
this year it is for river-gold.

The stakes are high, certainly.
The drifting moon, how old is she?
The ancient river full of mystery,
and the forest, dark and mighty.

The card-players crouch in their play.
There is sadness in their eyes you can see.
They wipe their rum-wet lips avidly,
they want to keep death away.

One man beats his breastbone,
another lifts an axe:
the scorpion and the watersnake
leave them well alone.

DEEP POOL

Just past that boat-killer, Sansom's Cataract,
which boils the water white for half a mile

and takes the river ten levels down –
in a funnel of dark and green-mossed rock,
overhung with giant vine-entangled trees
so that no sun ever lights the gloom,
lies Deep Pool, cold and black as witches' bracelets.
A ledge of rock overlooks the still and crystal pool.
There's no hand-hold to be got down there
should you be thrown or dive. The rock is sheer,
slimed with water oozing like cold sweat
upon the slippery moss and lichen-covered walls.
The drip of water in that silent place is ominous;
sometimes you hear low sighs like women moaning.

A flower thrown in that water sinks like stone:
a skull will bob and float and grin.
From the tall ledge drop a severed jaguar's head,
it will descend the black depths for a day,
be cast up again with jewels in its fleshless eyes.
Let down a rope tall as all the forest's trees,
it will never plumb those hideous depths
that have no limits known to puny man.
The taste of its black water strangles cowards.
Bring maidens late in bleeding there,
they will gush blood like a fountain.
Before ever man wrote down his pain,
but carved it on enduring rock,
the purpose of this place was plain:
since angry Gods must be appeased,
here were they made promises and pleased.

A visiting scientist made precise surveys,
succinctly described the properties of the pool,
measured it exactly twenty fathoms deep,
which makes it deep, he wrote, but not mysterious.
Found nothing in it to account for miracles:
no dye, piranha, alkaline, or poison.

Strange sounds heard sometimes by the river-men –
explained by wind sighing through rock-fissures hidden near.
A plaintive noise, of course, but nature made it so.
He was content to note, in summimg up his paper,
that myths dismantled were his stock-in-trade;
he dealt in facts, not dreams and tales of men.

Deep Pool never gets the sun
and yet the moon is welcomed there.
The pale spectre of the moon is dear
to such places which shadows never leave,
shadows that are made by more than suns.
Agony, horror, hate, and fear,
not reached by measurement, are there.

MANATEUK FALLS

Jade-red stone below a sun-filled sky
colours the upper stream rich rose.
Steep walls of rearing granite rock
make a black and mossy gorge,
narrows the race of water,
makes it rush down fierce,
hurtling towards the edge of precipice.
The river looks as if it boils with blood
before it cascades down upon the empty air.
Rainbows flash in it,
the roar is mighty.
The forest round resounds to it.
Eagles mount the chasm's wind.

Here was fought a mighty battle;
above the gorge the warriors fought
the greatest battle of their tribal wars.
Heroes fell by hundreds night and day,

for days and nights no one can number.
Falling down towards the river's edge
the clash and shout and ring of conflict
made the black walls of granite tremble;
the echoes reached the roof of heaven.
The whole forest howled with rage,
vultures soared and shrieked below the sun;
the moon came up blood-red
and shone on blood-red death.
Bravery more golden than purest river-gold
shone on that field most brilliantly.
The Great Spirits looked down in wonder.
For this were men created,
to do their fathers honour,
and die in glory on the fields of war.
The Great Spirits would remember them.

Myriads fought the mighty battle.
Of all that number, noble rank on rank,
one hundred were led captive at the end.
They did not surrender; not one still stood
when wounded, senseless, on the ground
they were commanded bound, with arms behind them.
And when again they had recovered life,
taken to the blood-painted victorious King,
they asked for death:
'Not one of us must live to dishonour these that died'.
Their slavery would be the great King's triumph,
yet their demand was just.
He gave them death:
'Your glory shall live as long as mine,
longer than the stars that have been here forever'.
The hundred were unbound and spears put in their hands.
In the corrials carved with princely emblems,
those most treasured by the tribal fathers,
they took their honoured place, rank on noble rank.
The ropes that made the corrials fast were cut.

The river took them in its angry teeth
and shook them like a tiger with its prey
and carried them headlong in the boiling flood
towards the tumult at the edge of precipice.
The hundred lift their spears in grave salute:
a mighty shout ascends the red and darkening sky.

In the white tumult of the falling water down below,
you can see between the swirling mist,
the sun-flashed rainbows and the gleaming spray,
a line of jade-tipped granite spurs stand tall.
Like blood-dark javelin-blades prepared for war
these dark spears of rock look stained with blood
as if a hundred men falling through the roar of water
had dashed themselves in sacrifice upon a jagged altar.
Who knows how many thousand years will pass.
Still the forest echoes with the mighty shout.

LAST VOYAGE

Heaved up by the daily tidal push,
battered by storm-water and heavy wind,
the hulk has tilted on the beach of mud;
her rusted keel burns orange amid the green mangrove.
River-waves sprawl along the dead and gloomy flanks –
sucking, vicious noises, her dead dissatisfied.
The slanting deck has rotted black and grey;
mushrooms of fungus, white bird-droppings, stain the funnels.
Whatever din of passing traffic sounds,
or song of birds from the deep forest flying,
a heavy silence surrounds old wrecked ships,
a cone of loss and long-abandoned hopes.
Gulls hover, shrieking, as if above a death
or rotting food; their screech is ominous.
Each time I pass I cannot help but think
how once she shone at sea and came up river,

full of daring, to ply a precious trade
or seek some gold adventure far from ordinary coasts.
The mind's eye conjures up her spring time –
ambitious captains in starched and braided uniforms
and sheep-skinned jackets turned up to the ears;
sailors with fat bellies, sun-stained to mahogany,
cleaning the caked salt, caulking with aromatic tar,
the wind swaying, tumbling, the mass of midnight stars.

Her end grows nearer by infinitesimally slow disgrace.
Every month she sinks a little in the crab-holed mud.
She goes to her grave bitterly, pieces disappear,
mangrove wraps her closer in a stinking green embrace.
But last time I passed something had come over her.
Urchins ran up and down her crazy hull
and swung on yellow ropes they'd brought and hung,
saluting, firing guns, and raising steam,
reckless, fierce, as sailors surely are.
Somehow she seemed sprightly in a tilted way,
as if she might even right herself again,
come midnight glide out towards the Spanish Main
and, unfurling festivals of maiden flags once more,
sail one last voyage to one last triumphant shore.

FOREST PATH, NIGHTFALL

Paths cut last month to open up new timber
are lit with streams of late slanting sun.
Beneath a canopy of green crowns of mora trees
shadows gather except where float tall pillars
of thick golden light that sets the green dark shining.
So evening falls. I walk this forest path,
shadowy nave of an immense cathedral.
When Chartres is finest dust, this still will stand;
it stretches far, never-ending in its beauty,

shines with its own green and gold-stained glass.
When a wind comes, the stained windows shiver,
a myriad alternating, dark then gleaming, pieces
that never reach the floor but float suspended,
shimmering arcs of velvet-black and emerald.
One mile from here I found, below its cleansed white beak,
a swarm of ants eating the entrails of an eagle.
Night-shadows begin to rise, mist shaken
from hidden censers in this holy place.
Stars and fireflies, candles lit by ancient priests,
fill the huge cavern with glowing taper-lights.
In childhood, even joy seemed permanent.
I feel cold, as if earth was cathedral-stone
chilled for centuries before the age of man.
In this immense god-theatre, night after night brings on
a sense of never-ending mystery vast as time
that swallows man, all his art and legends.
You cannot walk in great forests without diminishment.

THE SUN PARROTS ARE LATE THIS YEAR

(for Chico Mendez, murdered Brazilian Environmentalist)

The great forests of the world are burning down;
far away in Amazon they burn,
far beyond our eyes the trees are cut
and cleared and heaped and fired.
Ashes fill the rivers for miles and miles;
the rivers are stained with the blood of mighty trees.
Great rivers are brothers of great forests
and immense clouds shadowing the rose-lit waters
are cousins of this tribe of the earth-gods.
Under the ancient watch of the stars
all should be secure and beautiful forever,
dwarfing man, generation after generation after generation,

inspiring man, feeding him with dreams and strength.
But over there it is not so; man is giant
and the forest dwindles; it will soon be nothing –
shrubs sprouting untidily in scorched black earth.
The sun will burn the earth, before now shadowed
for a hundred thousand years, dark and dripping,
hiding jewelled insects and thick-veined plants,
blue-black orchids with white hearts, red macaws,
the green lace of ferns, gold butterflies, opal snakes.
Everything shrivels and dust begins to blow;
it is as if acid was poured on the silken land.

It is far from here now, but it is coming nearer.
Those who love forests also are cut down.
This month, this year, we may not suffer;
the brutal way things are, it will come.
Already the cloud patterns are different each year,
the winds blow from new directions,
the rain comes earlier, beats down harder,
or it is dry when the pastures thirst.
In this dark, overarching Essequibo forest,
I walk near the shining river on the green paths
cool and green as melons laid in running streams.

I cannot imagine all the forests going down,
the great black hogs not snouting for the pulp of fruit,
all this beauty and power and shining life gone.
But in far, once emerald, Amazon the forest dies
by fire, fiercer than bright axes.
The roar of the wind in trees is sweet,
reassuring; the heavens stretch far and bright
above the loneliness of mist-shrouded forest trails,
and there is such a feel of softness in the evening air.
Can it be that all of this will go, leaving the clean-boned land?
I wonder if my children's children, come this way,
will see the great forest spread green and tall and far

as it spreads now far and green for me.
Is it my imagination that the days are furnace-hot,
the sun-parrots late or not come at all this year?

THE RIVER-CROSSING MOTHS

The sun rises on the silent river,
a few bird-calls haunt the morning air,
mist-tendrils drift among the tops of trees,
the batteau glides slow on the quiet, silver water;
it is a time of peace and solitude,
the dreaming hour before the world awakes.
In a flash, a cloud of velvet, shimmering moths,
black-shining, edged with emerald-white,
rise marvellously from the sun-touched bank.
They fly in thousands to the far shore.

The wild brilliance, the suddeness, the wonder –
fathomless parting from all that is secure!
Here the great river is miles wide;
in thousands the shining moths will die.
Their brave fragility cannot last for long.
Already scores have lost the way,
fall battered, gleaming, in the batteau
and flutter dying on the falling tide,
a destiny fulfilled to end without a trace.
The rising wind will tear their delicacy apart,
the sun will burn them in its great fire,
river-birds will spear them from the sky
for food or sport, or they at last will tire.
Their shredded velvet wings will strew the waters
for a moment, beautiful, then sink like sunburst bubbles.
Rare and distant from all it knew before,
will even one reach that green opposing shore?

Strange quest these velvet moths pursued
this silver morning on the great river,
dared to mount the dangerous, high air
and fly towards the rising flame of sun.
On that far shore for certain there must be
a perfect lure to justify such lunacy,
a trap more potent than any life-force sets,
a poison sweeter than moth-nectar ever gets.
Some fruit of love, some paradisal tree,
in the far forest they discover and are free.

BETWEEN SILENCE AND SILENCE

For my wife Mary and my sons Keith, Jamie and Darren

and my old friend Philip O'Meara

STILL...

Yes, it is as you say.
But let us get just one thing straight:
there is beauty in the world –
as when the hawk with sheathed wings
plummets in the morning air,
the child plays jumping in the ring,
the cloud-enshrouded sun descends in glory
in the river-mirror glowing
– yes, there is beauty in the world –
and the star-tree blossoms in the night,
night that will have an end.

IT PASSES

PRAISE SONG FOR MARY

Rounded
O of love
boon of heaven
heavy-looking now
birth soon to come
I celebrate the joy
beauty of body-swell
oval paradisal
proud miracle
I celebrate
all soft and circling forms
earth-root and flower
the golden pregnant moon
showers shadows
call-glory of carols
bowls of ripe oranges
rose mangoes full plums too
stuffed sweet melons
rotund sun-ball in the sky
fat cloud-bellies sailing
in looms and loops of light
smoke-mist over water
rain curves on river
ocean-swoops billows
roses pools of moon-water
home home home

Hollows look hallowed
they are the kin of hoops
fat loaves –
hot bounty
from old stoves
noontime and swallows
arcs of light

you are buoyant with becoming
a fountain
a meteor shower
flower-bloom
my burgeoning love
rock and cradling stars
in your belly-dark
time booms
and throbs and towers
life starts again
I hear the double-heart
that God made and me
and you will make me soon
a high-shining son

IT PASSES

Before the sun bursts upwards
pouring gold oil over the earth
darkness clings among the branches still.
In the quick-silver light
a humming-bird passes,
pierces bloom after bloom
for the hidden, cold syrup
clear as lit water.
Disturbed by the gleaming bird
flowers shiver down.
One gold petal falls shimmering
in a night-spun web:
quick, the spider glides to embrace
its gold and fluttering prey.
Thousands of years pass;
it happens again for me.
Murmuring, in the soft room,
my wife cradles a new-born child.

Night leaves behind a tender wind
like a song once heard.
I wish I did not have to die.

SHADOWS WILL HIDE THE SUN

(For Darren, at the ceremony of baptism)

Bathe him in light
I pray, bathe my son in light:
his be a good life's lustre.
Through a world growing dark
every passing hour
bathe him in light.
Let brightness gleam about him;
bitter will be days to come,
shadows will hide the sun.
Thus is the life of man,
but within him let brightness dwell.
Spare him dullness all his days,
defend him ever from despair.
From valley depths
let Heaven lead him;
never lose the mountain light.
Through gall and ash
a pearl will shine:
let his life gleam.
In the dark world
bathe him in light.

SMALL POEM FOR ALL FATHERS

To alarm their fathers half to death
new-born babies hold their breath
(mothers long by Nature schooled

rarely let themselves be fooled)
and gurgle when the jape succeeds:
attention is one of baby's needs.
By cavelight, since time began,
lumbering, lion-pelted man
bends to ensure his infant lives
(the babe, meanwhile, makes sure it gives
an imitation – and hides the grin –
of rigor mortis setting in),
bends lower still, in deep concern,
no sign of life he can discern,
'til bent as far as he can go
and frantic now to see life show
he jabs the baby in the side
to make quite sure it has not died,
and guiltily looks about
to see if anyone has found him out
in such foolishness, because, of course, he knows
the child is healthy as a budding rose.
And yet when night again descends
near baby's heart the father bends.
Despite himself he's never sure
whether baby's at death's accursed door,
through shadow stares and tries to see
on which side of eternity
the baby lingers. His panic grows
and grows, though well he knows
that babies are as tough as nails.
Night after night, it never fails:
he has to check the infant's breath:
sleep perhaps – but is it death?
So it has been since time began
and will be so until the end of man.

THAT MY SON BE KEPT SAFE

My small son burns with fever,
his whole body is furnace hot,
burning to death he seems.
'I'm so sick, Dad,' he'd said,
his eyes beseeching me to help.
Now his eyes are closed,
his dark lashes long like mine they say.
His breath rasps hard and dry;
it is agony to hear it.
To touch his brow stops the heart.
The doctor, stone-faced, stern-browed –
though we try to catch a saving glance –
will not look us in the eyes.
My wife, smoothing the bed, doing anything,
anything to help, to keep busy,
trembles with fear. I tremble equally.
It is the worst fear in the world,
fear of a sadness beyond all sadness:
God forbid this should befall.
All the years that pass
would not cancel out the hour.
Why are we constructed so?
were it not better to be a stone?

I remember times we watched him,
coming to his bed because we could not hear his breathing,
bending low and lower to catch the breath
just raising the small chest.
The slightest twitch of coverlet or ribbon
showing he was safe among the smothering pillows
was most sweet, most easing
of this fear we all have always
that they will die and leave us
No hope at all, the rest of life made senseless,
No ransom can ever meet this threat.

He burns to death
and my whole self cries to heaven.
For him to keep safe I would vow it now
to be good in God's sight always, always:
good father, good husband, good man,
Christ's good soldier even.
Though rum's still sweet
and friendship's fine, and laughter,
and a girl's walk catches the groin
and the world is so beautiful
and the wonder of every minute never ceases
I would give it all away forever
to let his eyes not close, my God,
that my son be kept safe.
And if God will not listen,
if God stops his ears,
so that my small son be saved,
I would make a pact
with the hobgoblin in Hell
who loves sudden misery,
who strikes when life is most fit,
to give all my gold,
give blood-health, body-tune, eyesight,
the touch of wind and water that I love,
memories I have of tenderest hours,
reason that controls all things
the life God gave me,
the immortal soul,
I would give all away
should my son be safe now:
safe now, my God, my God!

STAR OF LOVE

('At this time of the year in the early hours of the morning, Venus can be seen at its brightest in the Eastern sky.'
1988 Almanack: The Sky at Night for December)

My son cries out
and I am up to see him.
The sky is dark,
sea-wind blows in the rain;
there it blazes in the Eastern heavens,
the star of Love riding in the clouds alone,
gold ember burning tiger-bright.
Memory flies back
when I too was young:
my mother pointing
when I woke in tears,
voice gentle as a shepherd's flute:
'That is Christ's star,
star of love, my son.
It brings beauty to the earth,
blesses all of us.'
Now as I comfort him
I point again to the great star
blazing in the Eastern heavens;
my son looks in a wonder
that dries the tears in him.
And though the night is dark
and the hard rain blows in
my heart is filled again
with hope, the promise
that has lasted centuries.
'What is it?' my wife whispers,
our new child heavy in her.
'The Star of Love,' I say,
'The Christmas Star, my love.'

KITES, A TIGER FANG, A GOLDEN RING
(Silent's anagram is listen)

Morning broke clear across the sky,
water gleamed amidst the green glades.
A glorious chorus
of sweet birds sang.
I hugged my warm wife
and the children slept in safety.
Later we put up the kites
to sing in the high wind
across the sun.
With shouts of fear and excitement
the children found a tiger's fang
near the old engineer's tomb,
a giant tooth-claw on a bone.
I picked it up and told fearful tales
of the wild forest and the night.
When the stars appeared –
a black castle of such dazzling lights! –
my son and I sat under the sky
discussing mysteries.
Later, showering by lamplight,
my gold ring gleamed
– my grandmother's when I was young –
and I thought how it might end.
How long does gold last?
How long are rings kept?
Lost? Given to a careful son?
Sold if it comes to that?
Or on my bright bone still
in endless night?

WHITE CATHEDRALS

Five boys swim in the canal,
diving amid white lilies with golden hearts.
Water-shine gleams on their naked bodies,
eel-black beauty in the morning light.

No matter the weight
of the white cathedrals –
barns of heaven,
the massed shops full of goods,
the laugh-shatterers,
the exact and confident sciences,
the thud of marching feet,
nothing that the husked men say
can drown their joy.

SCORPION

(For Jamie)

Play in the sun, child,
play in the bright air,
run along the sweet wind
that has blown since time began.
Breathe the mango-scented air,
cast your kite into the high arching sky,
a brilliant bird upon the heavens.
Clasp me in your arms tight,
tight, until I feel the tears of joy.
Laugh, laugh in the glorious morning,
spin cartwheels on the grass,
shining somersaults of play;
in the kingdom of freedom take delight.
No time to warn you, no need:
the dry rustle in the dead leaves.

BEHIND THE RIB-CAGE LIES THE HEART

i

My six-year son is at my side
light-brown, glowing, olive-eyed,
he's precious beyond compare.
Certainly no gold or place of power
is worth hide or hair of him.
I would take unmeasured trouble
to keep him from a breaking heart.

Yet, unknowing, we cause agony.
He props a chin, intently reads,
then asks a question solemnly:
'Are bees made all of gold?
What is beeswax? Does it hurt?'
I make a tease of what he says,
throw the flowers in the flame.
His cheek tints rise in anger, shame,
he takes a swinging shot at me,
cracks me good and heavily
in my side, with all his force.
'Hey! young man! You're strong. That hurt.
You do not hurt the ones you love.
You broke my rib-cage right in two!'
That halts him most suddenly.
'Behind the rib-cage lies the heart,'
I tell it to him seriously.
The pale flash of a fearsome terror
wells up from his deepest being;
he confronts, alone, confused,
the mystery of a new-born word.
The wolf waits in the darkening wood
where spiders creep and prophesy.

'Please say I did not break it really.'
I laugh to put him at his ease,
show him what the rib-cage is;
he touches my still-beating heart.
I smile and tousle up his hair.
'Father, this is no laughing matter!'
I feel start up that timeless pain.
A great fool you are, I swear
I will not break his heart again.

ii *Mountains of the Moon*

Rapt in a book
about the desperate wars of men
I do not notice through the open window
the full moon rising
plump as a pumpkin;
golden calabash
pouring light across the heavens,
letting down its golden hair.
My son looks out in wonder
at the burning beauty of the night,
tugs my hand hard
to catch attention to this glory.
'Remember you said you love me
bigger than all the world,
all the rivers and huge forests –
all the tallest, most mighty things on earth,
the giant's palace built of gold.'
Grave and still, my hand caught tight,
he points, there, with a heart-rending wonder.
'Well, Dad, I love you too,
bigger than all the things you said,
far bigger. I love you more than anything,
bigger than all the seas and suns,

huger even than, you know what,
than the mountains of the moon!'
The moon rises in a perfect sky,
rides in all its mystery.
Nothing I can find to say.

MY SON SELECTS A STONE

When he was six and I was fifty-six
all that week-long holiday
my son brought stones from the sea.
What is this? A shark's tooth from the deep.
And these? Leaf of whitened coral.
Wave-worn bottle once held pirate rum.
Crystal from a drowned sailor's chain.
Magenta tile broken from a Great House floor,
a gleam of porcelain treasure-cup.
Snippet of glinting quartz we long pored over.
Are these valuable diamonds, Dad?
He lined them up to show his mother. Proud
cornucopia from the eternal sea. She praised him.

At the end he threw them all away,
kept none of the beautiful, the curious,
the sea-shaped wonders he had found
and brought for our appraisal,
but kept a solid, ordinary, small rock
no different from a scattered multitude
that I could see. He has it still.
He never told us why he kept it.

GREENEYES

By the green pool where the milk-bit cascadura is caught at morning
I meet my girl whose breasts have the scent of the sun-dried khuskhus grass.
I have nothing, greeneyes, better to say to you than this:
for me you are the last dimension in the touch of sense –
berry leaf, cocoa flower along its branch, white lilies near Easter River,
in them intricate as length and depth and colour,
as time they last, you are the binder of their form.
All my love you have brought them to the fullness of a season's rains
and now the balata tree has leaf falling to the stream-ferns
near this green and cascadura-haunted pool;
it is you who are its maker, meaner, who strips the tree to its diamond heart.
Come, greeneyes, feel the water like cold bracelets round your thighs.

BETROTHAL

Old story. Young girl getting bigger now:
fifteen, tender, good, submissive;
parents want the best for her:
pious, fierce for family and name,
and old traditions steeped in race and time.
Goldsmith's son is thirty-four:
had his days, boy, played an eager field,
wants to settle now and take a wife.
Offers house and future safe as gold,
cows and coconuts up Essequibo Coast.
The thing is done, families agree:
a marriage is arranged for all to see,
proud and suitable and good for all
except – she's irremediably locked in tears.
She will not talk to family or friends
except to say she does not wish to live
if this must be the burden of her days:
not furious but a quiet, downward look.

All are summoned against this stubbornness:
old, gentle uncles come, brothers hold her hands,
white-robed pandit shakes his head and warns.
They appeal to me: I see the girl
I knew since parents gave her birth.
She has her story when we sit alone.
Young man she saw once by the temple wall:
hardly speak though they meet at festivals.
Hands once touched, and held, and that's enough.
I say the sensible things I must
but eyes have blazed like that before,
storm-light on a sunless shore.
I meet my old, grey, saddened friends.
'She is young! What does she know of life!'
Yes, she is young as the new moon,
green as young grass after rain,
but what she now has is her heart –
hard as antique mountain stone
sleepless, ancient scythe of stars.
And, yes, she will kill herself
should you bring this goldsmith's son of yours.

WEDDING NIGHT

This cloudless night
stars crowd the sky,
a whirling bee-storm
glitters above the trees.
A table is alight with silver,
lustrous gifts presented
to shine with brilliant flowers.
The holy fire burns
amid murmuring of prayers.
Scarlet adorns her head,
sari of kindled flame.

Gold anklets shine on her feet
gold bracelets shine on her arms
a gold necklace gleams at her throat.
But brighter than all
burning with love
are her dark eyes
glowing in the lamplight.

II: MIDDLE AGE

MIDDLE AGE

i What Delighteth Me

A carnival of senses counted most:
it was drinking with the boys,
the marking down of women for pursuit
games of skill fought out on sunny courts,
the blaze of action in limbs or groin.
Tethered down at rest was like life lost,
passing time was ill spent with no company,
the itch of other people I had to scratch.
Candles guttering, dead flies in our wine-cups.

What a pleasure it is now
opening a new book I have wanted,
alone in a chair that fits my back,
anticipating delight, fingers cracking the pages,
the first sentences making the mind water,
no debts or business until tomorrow comes.
This is better than I ever thought:
pleasures quiet down, they simplify.

ii Dreams, Leave Me Alone

I am going along fine in the middle years.
I've left youth like a blazing fire
guttering out in albums, in old letters full of puzzles.
I am heavy with the stone of middle age,
the skin of all I touch is thickened,
a glaze on what I see,
sounds muffle like a pillow cuffed,
tastes fur like old peppers left in vinegar.
I smell the air; it has no smell at all.
I think the well-considered thoughts

that other men have thought before.
Unusual beauty I quite ignore or shun.
Like an old car on a cold morning,
I need a kick start.
But it's alright, lives find their level:
comfortable, not vivid, are the passing hours.
The joy of the world
is faded like a worn rug
in a sunny room.
It looks as if the time left
will be serviceable but not astonishing:
a walk, eyes down, through brilliant forests.

iii Tight Designer Jeans

The sun is shining and the girls are out,
walking two by two in full regalia
pretending not to notice what it's all about;
if men don't turn, reckon up a failure.
Breasts sun-silhouetted through silk-thin blouse:
the one intention is clearly to arouse.

From carnal prime observe a mighty fall!
I feel no prickling in the loins at all.
It is my middle age it seems.
This glorious girl in tight designer jeans
comes passing by in studied nonchalance
once I'd have grabbed at even half a chance.
Now no longer comes that yearning urge to watch
her sweetly grooved and clear dividing crotch.
Worse yet to 'fall in love' perhaps
and face the dreary, agonising lapse
into the unrewarding game of hot pursuit,
all because her perky breasts look cute!

Undoubtedly she sports a fine, upstanding bust,
but now I grudge the hours of such spectator lust,
imagining what might happen if one followed through –
and the worse waste by far if actually you do.
Count up the time, it fills one with dismay,
to think how many months and years are idly spent this way:
vast fractions of a lifetime absurdly spent
wistful, mindless, and concupiscent.

Asway they pass, I view the game with scorn.
Why does it hurt like this? They look at me and yawn.

iv Invitation to a Walk

The river gleams, the sun has burned all day.
'Come, take a walk and put your books away!'
I knew her kind, but she will never know –
such a girl, same sweet limbs, a long, long time ago.

So now I'll try my best, there's no one else to see,
but you and me, my soul, but you and me.
As life slides past, there's surely one relentless law:
getting old involves holding poses more.

Now confirmation comes how hard it is to lie
as looking out the corner of my slightly better eye
I try to make a judgment how she's judging me.
I force a virile-looking smile and leap up jauntily.

(Pretend for all you're worth the years have not departed
and feign a frantic sparkle now you've actually got started.)

Who said that youth, once gone, cannot return –
there's ways of seeming supple you can learn.
I ascertain my step looks full of spring –
bouncing on the toes is this man's thing.

There is an art in holding muscles tense
– the battle fought within is quite immense –
that makes the sag of stomach seem much less –
with care she'll never know my lungs' distress.

I flick away a longish curl of hair
which flops down, greying, out of place –
I well remember reading somewhere
such gestures hint a sort of awkward grace.

There is a knack of biting on the teeth
that sets the angle of the jaw just right
ensures the loosening jowls beneath
are not so unlustworthy to her sight.

There is a way of crinkling up the eyes
that makes the lines the years have scored
seem frank and humorous and wise
and not frustration's sad record.

I'm good at animated talk;
she doesn't need to talk at all –
there's quite sufficient in a young girl's walk
to hold such ancient flesh in thrall.

(The evening wind grows cold, I turn away.
I dream, I dream, and hurl my dreams away.)

My temper frays to see her youth.
Should I remind her of the truth:
beneath softest flesh the human bone
hides not even one erotic zone?

You miss a step, and catch my hands;
I see play-acting time is done.
My heart beats in forgotten lands
but you are only having fun.

Your flirting eyes cannot behold
my heart fill up with ageless pain.
In dreams my steps go striding as of old
and I am powerful and young again.

BREAD AND FISH HOOKS

A friend brought fat loaf-bread
crusty, straight from the oven;
I broke off a piece to eat,
taste of the first heat good.
He brought fish hooks, shining;
we followed a remote path, among stones,
dust gathering on our coats;
fished all day under a sulphur sky.
Returning, we ate a few small fish, roasted,
and the new bread he had given
and cold water from a plain jug.
We talked about the sea,
of other things too, like love,
but mostly about the sea which is large.
At night I had a vision of death:
a shore-line receding forever but always near
and a man walking there, gifts in his hands.

IRON POLE

The years wear all down.
Old men pass here
who were young,
strong and laughing,
walking on stone.

It tethered boats heavy with fish,

sea-wind, sea-wind,
blowing for fifty years,
rusts the iron pole
almost to nothing.

A remnant of it
juts from the stone sea-wall.
A fisher-boy,
fate-entangled,
stubs his toe
and his eyes are watering.

BURNING

Slowly, slowly my father shuffles to his rest,
my strong father whom I hugged for strength.
He sighs and settles; I kiss his stubbled cheek.
'I try to shave but now it takes up so much time.'
He rests. I lean upon the window-frame
and contemplate the night come on.
Moon-shadow of an antique tree
shapes slowly on the grass outside.
A candle near me sharply flares.
Wing of moth has caught the flame.
He rests. I hear the reddened sea-grapes drop.
Time's fire consumes us all.
As of old I take his hand. It's different now.
It burns. Eyes fill with tears to feel his grip.
Stars start to burn across the sky.

SIGNALLING

'After parties, in those courting days
He brought me safely to my door.

I could not bear to let him go,
Your handsome father – my young man.
He could not bear to leave me there:
When he left he turned and turned –
I see the stars above his head –
And tears of love came in my eyes.
A mile or so away he lived
Through trees, a tall apartment house:
We had a pact: when he got in
He lit his lamp, the window glowed,
He waved for me his silk-white scarf.
Heart raced to see that signalling.
My son, I feel my heart beat fast.'

The stars have burned for sixty years
The white scarf disappeared in dust.
My mother holds my father's hand;
Old and frail, he sinks to rest.

BEAUCAILLOU

The wind blows my mother's thin grey hair;
she speaks of Beaucaillou, her swift horse.
When she was a girl she recalls
the fine horse in his gleaming trap:
the snort and stamp and jingle
and her father laughing, clapping,
shouting, 'Home, Beaucaillou, home!'
And the wind blowing in her red, wild hair.

MY FATHER'S PRAYER BOOK, PAGE 44

Most life is ice-melt,
bells through sea-mist,

dark coming home and hurrying.
There are no exceptions.
Thoughtful men feeling
the stars' pull across half the world,
knowing coasts' thick rocks
vanish in the seas' wash finally –
these men too have urgent private business:
they deal in golden things and lures.

Faded writing in a prayer-book's margin –
this remedy for love affairs and projects:
'Stand under old trees in the wind'.
Heaven is huge then and not temporary.

ON THE HEADLAND

Where I stand on the bare, stone headland –
strong winds scouring the sky,
white gulls floating, falling over the heaving water,
drinking in draughts of stone-cold air –
at the mouth of the great river,
the tide is turning, huge and heavy,
crashing on the land everywhere,
leaning on it, pushing, tearing, wearing it away.
The sea's salvage butts inland;
the big pieces grinding and rolling,
driven on the frothing face of waters.
I stand and feel I have not lived before
and will not live again to be like this,
where beauty, changing utterly to mystery,
cannot be understood or learned or justified.

Yesterday, in the village by the headland,
a man howled like a maddened dog,
broke the bones of his treasured wife.

It happened. I saw it.
A branch of flowers
shaking in the wind.

I feel the need to go from here, this stumbling place,
this stone and furious threshold to the world,
to find a welcome, the certainty of grace,
warmness, mercy, meaning; to turn the old,
true key of love so often used before
the flawless bolt that shuts the heavy door.

THE SAND-TRUCK DRIVER

I take the Seawall's pleasant air;
fishing boats come in, grey sails snapping
under a peaceful sky.
A sand-truck hurtles down the public road.
A small dog, crossing, begins to hurry up.
The sand-truck driver, crouched intently down,
swings the wheel fast, swerving for the animal,
follows it, fleeing, to the utmost edge of curb,
crushes the puppy into squealing pulp and blood:
an entrail-vivid mess scatters on the stone.
I cannot believe my eyes; briefly glimpsed,
the sand-truck driver's shoulders give a shake
and, head nodding in a sort of satisfaction,
he settles in his seat again, steers a steady course.
The fading day congeals and people hurry home.

What piled frustrations haunted him that day?
Wife's nagging, kids' snot-nosed monotone?
Something impossible in how he had to live?
Money nut-hard to get, proud strength diminishing,
failed shining children, bailiffs at the unowned door,
a sour general hopelessness daily to endure?
Or something deeper: sick of a sick society,

the feel of being hounded down by gathering circumstance,
No hint of wherewithal to give yourself a chance?

Or did, at home, that driver sip his tea,
the conversation with his wife so eminently sane,
dandle young Johnny gurgling on his knee?
Outside his window you may think you see
– of evil's lurking kingdom one glimpse may suffice –
smokestacks of the Central European plain,
the killing-fields of Pol Pot's paradise.

WE DO NOT STOP FOR STRANGERS

We were taking a comfortable ride
to a convivial party up the East Coast –
four friends talking boisterously,
laughing on Friday, relating office anecdotes.
A moon sometimes appeared between clouds
but mostly it was dark and the rain spattering.
A man appeared in the headlights waving,
Probably wanting a lift out of the night-rain.
He held a child by the other hand,
a serious small girl in a pink dress, barefoot.
I simply accelerated past the waving man;
right not to stop was the general verdict.
'Late already for the party, man.'
'You want to bet the child's a lure.'
'Pass back for you another time, old boy.'
Only later in the chattering crowd,
stuffing barbecued lamb, swilling rum,
I thought of this terrible conduct.
What has happened to me?
What has happened to the wide world?

FRAGMENTS

The piercing sense how good to be alive
brings home to us the culminating truth
life will be as good, but not for us
soon. We turn our aging eyes away.
The clear, bright Andromedean stars
emphasise the blackness of the void.
The more brilliantly a man's life burns
colder are the ashes that are left.

The night has been hot, restless:
far rumble of thunder, hardly heard,
reminder of incurable wounds.
Getting up and lying down again,
ache of bone beneath the flesh.
Even the fresh words of poetry pall.
Morning. A grey mist on the river.
The passing shriek of one white gull.

TIME OUT OF TIME

Peace settles here,
beauty rests.
Blaze of blue
over black water:
spurwings totter on lilies,
fish burst and gleam,
bamboos grieve and rustle.
Hibiscus flames
by the old tomb.
White lilies on emerald salvers,
water orchids purple as bruises
on anaconda-haunted pools.
Green flights of parrots,

rasping gargle of the howling monkeys,
click of beetles, whistling frogs.
Smell of wood-smoke,
lukanini cooking in a pan,
sweet guavas in the sun,
red mangoes rotting,
and centuries of leaves.
The rub of silk and mosses
liquid, thick sound –
gold dripping on stone.
Stir of alligators.
Silence, the silence of undiscovered noises.
A bolt of evening cloud glows red
like iron in a fire:
the sun-disc descends –
gold wafer down the throat of God.
The wind sighs;
old ghosts walk about:
a water-engineer and fisherman.
The dark pond crumples in a sudden breeze.
Silver ripples,
the wind in the throats of birds,
swamp grasses in the night wind.
Slim dark boats
slide past at midnight.
Where are they escaping?
Here is love, balance, ease,
context and perspective,
certainly in valuable things,
long, unflustered, thinking time,
a chance of choosing perfectly.

Morning comes –
suddenly a shining:
a bird skims down;
the silver surface breaks.
In life elsewhere the vital lies await.

LOOKING INTO THE EYE OF A HAWK

Hours travelling
the dazzling river;
the black creek
is welcoming now;
shadows shivering cool,
tree-green overhanging.
Sudden as its scream
I look in a hawk's eye.
Young in a nest near,
it will not flinch
from the low branch.
Again, again the screech
its battle cry;
the hawk defies me.
Try gesture imperial
– Man is master of all –
fails, unmoves it.
Lustrous wings arise
in combat, not in flight,
even if it dies.
The inflexible beauty
stops me.
Icy agate eyes'
fire of anger and love
pierces me.
It was here before me,
that scream, that ancient eye.
Pass by.

AT THE CREATION

This is a place of arid, enclosed rock
where the storm's thunder is heard best,

cannoning and echoing, reverberating, rumbling,
rolling tremendously down the gulch-land
when clouds mount the heavens in black battlements.
Valleys, walled with hard, forbidding stone
high as eagles hanging on the sky,
hold bare shattered slate and ruined granite blocks.
A few trees stand in pools of dry earth,
stunted, hunched sideways by the wind
that whistles full of heat down narrow gullies.
Earth crumbles under the harsh beat of sun;
falls of rubble lie beneath these valley cliffs;
the sound of small, far avalanches
threaten and alert the wanderer.
There is no sign of man, nothing
man-made, man-handled, man-kept,
nothing soiled or greasy or disposable,
not even a carved rock or bright pennant in the wind
to show the history of man or man's mastery,
only the litter of wind, sun and beating rain
over ten thousand thousand years, and old debris
thrown out by the great earth shaking;
only the storm-shifting sentinels of stone,
crusty vomit of age succeeding age succeeding age.

Why have I climbed here utterly alone,
setting out from others with only water flask
and bread and a few plums in a back-bag,
without a watch to make a sound
or show that man has put a grip on nature?
It is not for wisdom that I venture here:
the bleak perfection, the empty, stone-filled scene,
adds not a thing to the mind's essential imagery.
It is not to trawl for beauty in this turbulent high air:
for me no beauty in what's so austerely stripped,
gaunt, burnt-out, dull, lustreless and bare.
Not for testing bravery I climb the stone-filled valley:

I am careful, steady, test each step I take
and others are not too far away for shouted help.
It is not to get an inkling of how saints feel
that I have come: such purity is quite beyond
a short, unpleasant walk in this mountain place.
It is not because it's there, that I have climbed:
that proud, ironic challenge was not meant for me.

Trouble in defining? Look close for sentiment:
it wells up an endless spring, a great torrent,
a teeming source of reams of inspiration,
agonies, ecstasies, incoherent, ill-expressed –
discipline flies weeping out the blood-red casement.
Fuelled by yearnings vague as hope and glory,
a dazzling summit beckons; we slither
on its slopes, struggle with the craft of poetry,
until dust brushed aside, clear rock, gold-gleaming,
shines under it and shines forever.

Such shaping of the formless stone beyond
the shadow fall may come once only,
may never come, a flash, a blast of light,
blood shot through Christ's shroud, at death,
who knows how. And we are there at last:
the reason why we climb
empty valleys filled with stone
and thunder from the sky.

SEEN THROUGH CLOSED EYES

Mountains hung with dreams;
from the caves, whispers of healing.
Across the onion field
bright berries glow in green trees,
flights of birds

soar below the thunderhead –
sudden circles of light.
Remember how love burns
before flesh and bone are parted.
Faraway, tipsy as Pharoahs,
children shriek with joy.
The noise of time fills my ears
endless as the air.
Fire-falls, the dying of the day,
and then the intensity of the night.

HURRYING NEAR

'Now death could come,' said one.
'Life has nothing left;
the hours are filled with pain.
Let sweet death come.'

'No,' said the other.
'If every century past
a bird wing brushed a stone
big as Hog Island
and death would not come
until the wing wore out the stone,
still death would be too soon,
still death would come too soon.'

RAIN

No rain for months, sky hard blue,
ground hardening like iron,
earth hot to shod feet,
smoke-shawls from bush-fires;
sun glares red before night falls.

White the worst colour, bright as bone.
Time soon coming when the oxen starve;
grass turns to ash, savannahs
send up clouds of burning dust.
Green is a colour gentle and forgotten
like blood gone from a dead face.
Mud cracks in pools once sweet with lilies.

Old men, who have known
the hard seasons, say
water would be the best gift
if it could be wrapped.

And so it comes, a fundamental beauty,
a simple thing not often counted –
like love; when it's there life balances,
though we do not feel the balancing,
until departure leaves us husked and dry.
It comes again and steadies us,
soothing, far away, a noise in the clouds,
a summoning freshness in everything.
An arid heartland springs alive;
water is love; it clears and shines:
clemency for a wracked land.

CHERRYBAGS

Rain in the marketplace,
black night falls,
glittering, dripping night.
I wander among the bags of red cherries.

Why did the world begin,
where will it end?

Books are written,
but nobody knows.

Only these three bags of cherries,
plump and rich,
stand in the market stall:
one bag leans to the side,
spills twelve red cherries.

A blackbird flies down,
beads-of-gold-eyed,
steals a red cherry;
red-pearl beaked,
proudly looks around.

It begins and ends,
balanced amidst the stars.

III: ARCHIVE

ARCHIVE

One by one the old men die:
the libraries are burning down.
On Lombard Street near Ma Belle's parlour
in a high and rotting house
greyed by time and fungus weather
I find one of the last ones,
a century old, and half alert.
He inhabits a bare, discarded room;
greets me sitting on a single bed.
A quarter candle gives him light;
enamel basins catch the rain.
The food is peppery, the rum is strong.

In a cracked mirror hung askew
I catch sight of my own lines of age.
The shadows carve them dark and deep:
shocked to think I'll follow him so fast.
Nothing keeps; the years defeat us all.
Framed in silver on the bedside table
a picture set to seize the eye:
Sunday dressed and stiffly posed
a small boy holds his father's hand.
When the city tidies up this life,
the silver frame but not the picture
is all that will remain of both.
Decades too late our heroes are acknowledged,
names announced in unattended stations.

Gnarled fingers like black twisted roots
now clutch an ancient bamboo flute.
He plays a twittering, faltering tune;
it peters out and leaves him sad:
'Oh lawd, brain get hard like bone!
Pickle to stone, pickle to stone!'

Stored in his memory are a thousand songs,
now and then he finds them still –
thumps his hand and shouts them out –
and stories for ten shelves of books,
gold chants, cures past numbering,
tinctures from the sap of plants,
lotions, balms from crushed green leaves.
He tells tall tales from Pomeroon:
charms, hunting signs, bull-monsters
from the dark forest, fires witches hung
from starry heavens, tribal flags, and waterfalls –
why they hacked the head off the bone-white ram…

But things are fading fast for him:
recalls exactly how the century turned,
he can't remember yesterday.
I take some notes. But it is sad.
Nobody keeps old bibles any more.
The old man sighs and shakes his head,
hums when he forgets the words.
The young men do not want to learn
and old men do not live forever.

MACARTHUR'S LIFE

What happen to old MacArthur
I wonder. They call he Barnyard
when he young, Slim Boy, Hot Cock.
All about town he run, crowing, mounting,
sunlight and morning, stain-sky and night.
It so sweet, why he should bother about anything else?
How a man like he could always find women?
He never pay but he always get. Something, boy,
something in this world; people don't want lonely.
But he get old and begin to fall in trenches.

Women ease he for a while, then drink.
Like he could always find women, he could always find drink.

He eye soft, people like he,
he never pick up a stone to pelt.
The years go by so quick, life waste, life done.
The last I see Slim Boy he look groggy
and like he trying something new, I don't know.
Mass finish at Sacred Heart, I see he in a pew
sink on the knee, head bend, one hand shaking.
But that was years ago; I don't know after.

SING-SONG'S PLACE

Sing-Song work forty year in Parkview Club.
Everyone know Sing-Song; he rum-punch famous.
He humming happily when he make the drinks;
everyone know he style, he take good care.
He bother how much ice, perfect measure,
he proudly bring the drinks, as if it matter.
He like to hear compliment; it is he life you know.
He don't know nothing else, he don't want to know.
He share a lifetime with a God he love.
They come with slide-rule and computer, the new people.
Parkview Club change hands; they measuring money.
Sing-Song spilling a few drinks now, he old,
and how he could learn to put a pinch less
when he know the taste going change with that?
Better you put out light in he life.
So he have to go. They knock he off. Who sad?
Redundancy nothing much when dollar value gone.
Well, I hear they closing Parkview down:
computer working good, customer leaving fast.
Why they could never learn true cost?
Sing-Song take it easy, he humming still.

He gone by squatting fields to get a lot.
He build a shanty; it is Sing-Song Place.
Poor people also drink, now they have their prince.

CANTICLE OF THE MAIN STREET MADMAN

The old man blesses stones and men,
a supermarket clerk for years,
they say he has gone mad.
All day he signs the cross on things:
food, trees, earth, and the rubbish trucks.
He stands in Main Street blessing men.
He lifts his eyes towards the sun
blessing that great medallion too.
All night heaven's holy stars are blessed.
I've seen him bend down very low,
give benediction to a lump of shit.

He kneels in rainstorms, blesses them;
bliss lights his mild and streaming face.
Trench lilies red as blood he blesses;
he wades up to his waist in mud.
Birds! Takes a special joy in birds;
they perch or soar, he blesses them
with gestures wide that tell his love.
Stands by the churches during Mass
and signs the cross on celebrants.
Perhaps he means some irony;
he does the same thing at the banks.

What harm does this man do?
All he does is bless the world –
more sane than me or you.
They say he troubles normal men;
it interrupts the train of thought
of busy men, of serious men,

to have this peculiar man intrude
and sign the cross on their backsides.
Degrades the human race, they say.
Who will forgive our sanity?

The only men he will not bless
are policemen. They treat him rough,
come for him, 'Main Street disgrace',
cart him off like roadside rubbish,
bundle him into Brickdam station.
'Cool your blasted arse in there!'
But inside he starts again;
the four walls of his cell are blessed
and any inmates that are near.

He has never tired in his work –
must have blessed the whole of town.
Shakes with age now, soon will die.
Wonder who will take his place?
Who will bless us down the years?
Who will bless the men and stones?
No one will be mad enough to try.
Bless us, Lord, when he has gone.

THE MAN WHO TOOK THE PLACE OF GOD

Beyond the sea-endangered coast,
interior-deep, where rivers spring,
past white quartz outcrops shining in the sun,
green trees clinging on the steep slope downwards
to the burnished foot of the silver cliff,
trees, orchid-studded, swaying in the wind
the mountains make all day,
I visit the black doctor of the tribes –
'Protector from calamities', they call him.

Forty years have passed since he was rich in town,
his practice built with money-conscious skill –
society buzzed around his Brickdam home.
One day he packed a small bag, left,
aimed for the deep forest, met Potaro men,
never came out to the coast again.

He discovers herbs, cultivates his garden,
dreams brimming past the edge of time.
In a plum tree's shade he rests, swaying
in a swinging hammock, greets me with grace.
Light on the wind, hawks soar above us.
He speaks of the salves he makes,
the teas and ointments, bandages of leaves
to suck the bad blood out, root cultures,
aromatic balms, gut-soups of bark and buds
from plants no man before him ever saw.
His eyes are clear, his fingers rub an ancient stone,
cleansing aloes on a sour-wood plate.
'I've side-stepped death a thousand times.'
He keeps a room where spiders float,
spinning webs for wounds that tigers make.
The cracks in tortoise shells tell him of the future.
'They say, far off, there is a vine
wrapped around a solitary tree
four centuries old.
The vine has blossomed only once
and will blossom soon again.
Its fruit will make my old skin smooth.'
He shakes his head and laughs, ha-ha,
slaps his hands above his head.
'Tomorrow I will search for it:
I want to live forever and be young,
peach-skin shining, young as morning,
all my work to do.'

MR. PERFECTION

His name was actually that, Manuel Perfection.
The certificate in a slim dossier sets it out:
born in Bartica, Good Friday, nineteen twenty-four,
son of Theodore Perfection and his wife Mathilda.
Schooled by Catholics until the age of twelve –
'A bright boy but rebellious and does not love the Lord'.
Then he left 'to seek his fortune in the bush'.
Laconically a priest records the facts.
The vast forest swallows him for fifty years
and the time has passed like the wind
and the time has passed like a flying cloud
and candle-flies have winked ten times
and soon enough time brought him here.
He died this morning, not pleasantly,
a long time struggling to take a breath
until I, beside him, grew breathless too.

Before me rests the brown folder with his life.
Certificate of birth, baptism card, a school report, a letter.
That's all, except the page that ends the file –
sparse list of all he brought in here: bloodstone, knife,
old clothes, a cap; Matron countersigned the list.
The letter dated from thirty years ago,
dirty, scorched with fire, water-marked,
crumpled, it seems, once in an angry fist,
creased so many times it tore in half,
fixed, refixed, with transparent strips of tape.
I read the lines between the scorched-out parts,
guessing words but the sense is plain:
'You deserve the praise of this community
and its children most of all, who thank you.'
A village schoolmaster writes the thank-you note.
Such notes in thousands make up our lives
and some keep many and most keep none at all.

'You did the job well, all of us are pleased.
The desks and chairs you constructed to perfection.'
I'm sure that word was not deliberate –
the note looks hurried, there are words misspelt.

We all keep things whose value others miss,
shadows of hands that have caressed us.
This is what he culled and kept
and I will keep it too, to remember
how the wind changes and the centuries go
full of meanings we can never know.

A SIMPLE MAN

The garden needed more attention
we had decided. A man was at the gate,
slow-witted, surely; the first time that he spoke:
small vocabulary, stuttering words,
hesitating diction and a frightened look.
'Ah want the job. Ah could work mo' hard.'
A froth of spit lightly lined his lips.
What made us let him stay I do not know.
The routines explained, it took him long,
but gradually he learnt the daily rules
of cutting, clearing, digging, planting,
the right amount of watering, mould to be applied.
Learning all this slowly strengthened pride
and self-assurance grew as flowers bloomed
beneath his fingers, trees came to blossoming
and trellised vines shaded paths he cut.
A day came when he could take steps himself
to make more beautiful without instruction –
what he had begun and now had got to know
in his heart's root through utter dedication.
He just did small things very well –

repeated and repeated day by day by day
never letting his attentive eye divert,
not letting love withdraw at all from work,
until the year's end saw the good results:
a tended patch of earth transformed, green,
serenely ordered, shining with the fruits of care.

As the great plots of the world unfold
my thoughts drift often to this simple man.
There are few that catch the eye of history
and those that do, break the world or save it,
discover truths that none have found before,
find the fires that make the stories ring
and art shine for centuries, make timeless song.
All others born are lost beyond their deaths.
A man at peace who tries his best
and gives his share of love and work
but knows no dimension but the ordinary
is forgotten quickly in the seethe of time.

He has been with us for many peaceful years,
daily has he filled our lives with good.
We wake at mornings and hear the sounds of work,
the sweep of broom, earth being dug and placed,
water filling and the clean chop of wood,
the tuneless whistle which tells his peace of mind.
The house will fill with flowers and green leaves.
I know that this is good. It holds the sense
of work fulfilled and certainty and grace
enduring beyond the purposed hour.
It's said that nothing lasts,
but if what's good keeps,
then this, I know, will keep forever.

DEATH OF AN OLD WOMAN

She was eighty-five. Death came for her
without fuss, walked in quietly,
nodded to us all and took her hand
as if to say, 'Come now, it is time,
it will not be hard' – which she agreed
and lulled into the sleep that will not end.
She had been preparing, a quiet came on her,
and then she wanted one last thing:
the summoning of a son she had not seen
for many, many years and wanted now to hold,
touch his face, remembering where that scar runs,
how he fell and cut a child's brow fifty years before.
She waited for that, his summoning, his tears,
put up her frail arms to be embraced,
sighed and touched his face again.
Wanting nothing more, she closed her eyes
and welcomed patient Death, the comforter.

With pride she'd kept the small and spotless house
she and her husband owned for fifty years;
when he died she followed old routines
that he had known and she would not forget.
In their corner room that catches the sea-wind
each morning, she cleaned out floor and cupboards,
aired the clothes, made beds smooth and fresh,
then, as the sun rose, or rain perhaps swept in,
always she must spend time at her window-sill
breathing in sea-wind and the smell of pomegranates,
looking out on what was hers and, further out,
far sky spreading and the sea, on what was God's.
This morning scene she knew by heart and loved
as men love things they make, like bread in their
own homes, earth daily dug, chairs and tables
not moved for generations
and seasons' chores that children teach their children.

The morning of the day she came to die
she could not reach the window from her bed,
asked those who waited there to carry her
again to breathe the salt sea-wind, that
all those fifty years smelled gentle, sweet,
and come next sun rise would not feel again.

As the day wore on, silence lengthened
in the air, and she got clear of things.
At evening time when dark had not quite come
she died so soft one hardly knew,
and the stars shone brighter and the night went on.

She'd begged her sons that holy fire
should take her to eternal rest;
no dark and lonely earth should rot her bones,
or worms creep into flesh that once was sweet.
But fire! Fire she loved, the purity of fire.
'Entirely I am burned away,
I die and then I cease to die.'

She lay in white cloth, pure as light,
her white hair braided, limbs composed for sleep;
a husband-given bracelet from their courting days –
she loved this more than anything she owned –
hung on her fragile wrist, no other ornament
except clear lines of peace and beauty on her face.
Those she loved gathered where she lay,
they closed the casket at the last,
threw flowers in and fragrant herbs,
and heard the pandit speak the ancient words of hope:

'Life lasts a moment,
yet it does not end.
Even as a jewelled drop
returning to the sea

is this woman's life:
the sea is measurelessly deep;
even as a spark
from the great fire
is this woman's life:
the fire burns forever;
even as a single blossom
falling from the tree
is this woman's life:
the tree does not cease to bear.
Yesterday she was born,
tomorrow she is born again.
Entirely she is burned away;
the fire only mounts the higher.
If you shed tears
it is not for her they fall.
Does one sorrow for the boundless sea?
Does one sorrow for the great fire?
Does one sorrow for the blossoming tree?
Though darkness seems the lot of man,
all the universe is radiant light.'

We walked the enamelled fields of green –
ox-eyed flowers lined the way,
grasshoppers brushed against our feet –
and reached the place where she would burn
in brilliance in the flame she sought:
clear sky, oiled bier of wood, bright evening sun,
sea-wind to make the fire blaze and leap
heavenwards with the anointed soul.
There, on cleared ground, near the lapping waves,
we brought her, said the last farewells,
heaped aromatic wood around her like a house
where she would live a moment, bathed in fire,
until the flames consumed her utterly,
even the bones made ash as light as petals.

At the far corners of the holy bier
Pandit directed where the sons should set the fire.
Slowly it caught the oiled wood, coiled, and grew;
soon flames were tall and climbing clear,
bright pennants in the evening air.
For her no sinking in dark earth
but a leap lightwards, a resurrection
made of burning light, the deepest caverns
of her soul made marvellously bright.
For an hour the clear flames leaped and soared,
then sank to glowing red, a flower in the night.

The chosen son walked lonely to the wall
at morning's flush of pear-pink light,
gathered the ashes in a blessed white cloth.
Fishermen took them on this journey
under a sky now bathed again in light,
and then he cast the ashes wide upon
the sacred bosom of the sea, and threw
a solitary flower from the garden
she had loved so well, and watched
it float far, far upon wave succeeding wave
until it too was lost in blinding light.

HISTORY

History is
a drift of dust
the wind blows away
and forgets.
Gold and stone,
gossamer,
the mountains
of the setting moon,
Egypt's thrones,

old Aztec altars,
Rome's high tombs,
are dust.
Saints' blood dries,
empires end:
they are dust.
Walls that kept out
infinite armies:
a child steps softly
on the dust of them.
The horn of plenty
of love and art
lasts for a time,
is dust too at last.
Man's rights strong
as sacred marble,
the trumpets of justice,
are dust.
The grey walls of Auschwitz
are dust,
and the rose of mercy,
dust.

IV: THE BIRTH OF POETRY

SPINSTER GANTEAUME AND THE BIRTH OF POETRY

Close neighbour of the first home I knew,
gaunt spinster, Bernadette Ganteaume
('On the morrow God will rise again'),
I remember her always in long green dresses,
face bumpy with rosy unerupted boils.
Thick lenses made her pupils hugely bulge:
eternal gargoyle to a little boy.
Cats followed her and she was kind to them.
Lives like hers are blurs of memories like these,
except once – remembered like a bright wing
caught in ancient amber shining like the sun –
when poetry transfigured memory.

One dark night, she woke in fear;
drops, thick and slow, not water, fell on her.
With light she found them golden-red,
oozing spider-webs of gold, dripping
luscious oils from ceiling cracks,
bright honey from the dark attic of her house,
rain of strangeness smearing her white sheets –
generations old and proudly kept – embroidered
with the blood of night-birds in old heraldic tales,
pearls hanging from the open wounds of Saints.

She was a keeper-to-herself,
did not interfere with others' lives
nor wished others to interfere with hers.
But now, the sun just up with singing birds,
she fled her dark and golden house
and came to us to calm her heart,
to tell her story with dramatic hands.
A small boy sat and rubbed his eyes in wonder.
My father acted with concerned despatch.
Mid-morning the bee-catchers came sternly in;

children gathered round in awe
to watch heroic men in masks of black,
stiff yellow canvas suits and leather gloves –
like falconers playing with enormous hawks –
tramp bravely into old Ganteaume's tidy house,
ascend the dark attic to the golden hordes.
There they caught the Queen of the great honey-hive
that all the bright long days had built and burnished.
Then descended, with due ceremony –
to me, transfixed, it seemed with princely step –
casket before them, careful not to let it fall,
(memory tells me it was all of shining gold)
encrusted with golden bees at worship still,
that held the Queen in living, jewelled thrall.
The attic's abandoned bees they smoked to death
in black-winged thousands and swept them out in heaps.
For months old Ganteaume's house with strangeness shone,
fragrance drifting as from the caves of Gods.

A wheelbarrow came over to our house –
somewhere I still hear the axle creak –
filled with cakes of honey-comb,
dripping red, thick heavy drops.
I ate the crisply shining gift of cakes,
heaven's food, sweetness lacing the tongue.
Later huge stars came out in thousands,
seemed to fill the arching sky with light
golden rivers streaming in the night,
stretching without end, a pulsing beauty,
heaven's nearness blazing on the world.

What transmutes the ordinary to other,
as the host-bread baked by sweating men
becomes the living flesh of God?
Men transfixed by poetry,
what first transfixes them?

Memories of love, pain and mind's awakening,
the various beauties that overflow the years,
are not so strong for me as that attic full
of golden bees, the extraordinary honey-spill
the ropes of sweet, pearled honey-drops,
the bee-encrusted casket of the Queen,
a wheelbarrow arriving at our gate,
creaking, filled with honey-comb –
the golden hives that dripped on old Ganteaume.

AN OFFERING OF STONES

He got to know his only son,
He had just time enough for that.
In the small time he lived
he looked into his dark eyes,
he kissed his cheeks a hundred times.

A twelve-day lifetime,
all of it a struggle of breathing,
fists of such smallness, such delicacy,
desperately clasping, unclasping, clasping,
timed to each breath, rise and fall,
as if reaching, grasping, reaching,
grasping for the great gift
being slowly pulled away;
the gift given for twelve days,
and then no more.

Wandering along a stony way
he chose a few unusual stones
hard and smooth to the touch.
He scraped them clear of all earth,
scoured their surfaces, sluiced them
with water again and yet again

until they shone, until they were beautiful,
scorched them in a careful fire
of shaved samaan and jasmine leaves,
burnt them in this small fire,
held fast to them when they cooled.

He walked twenty miles carrying the stones,
stones of water, stones of flame,
forever beautiful, holy, true, and strong.
At Parika he took a slim boat, slid
with a dark ferryman up far Essequibo,
came to a place of ancient suns,
where the river makes a dancing pool,
the forest's thick, and rare birds sing.
The stones like silvery plums
he offers to the Gods with courtesy,
lays them exactly in the hunting pattern
he would have taught his son to use.

Cold! He found the heavens cold!
Never will the fresh shoots by the river spring,
the winds whispering, the moon cascading down.
Thick tears brim the circles of his eyes,
the salt of horror clogs his throat.
Though breath was sweet and beauty all around,
nothing that makes a difference ever can take place –
no sense in anything, the emptiness that waits.
He knows his fate, the endless fate of man,
no matter what creation he perfects
never to reach a limit to his longing
never to find a meaning for his loss
never to get the attention of the stars
shining beyond the end of their own ending.

TREE OF DREAMS

I went out and bought a cabbage for supper.
Fire shone in the night.
We bad-talked Dolores and her brood
then I climbed in my tree of dreams.
I got up early and went to work as usual:
golden decisions, morsels of wisdom all day.
At home the left-overs are thrown out
and for all eternity evil is redressed.

MASSA DAY DONE

Viv in a mood today, you only have to watch,
see the jaw grinding, he stabbing the pitch, back-lift big.
Look how he stare down the wicket, spear in he eye,
he going to start sudden, violent, a thunder shock.
Man, this could be an innings! This could make life good.

You see how he coming in, how he shoulder relax,
how he spin the bat, how he look up at the sun,
how he seem to breathe deep, how he swing the bat, swing,
how he look around like a lord, how he chest expan'.
You ever see the man wear helmet? Tell me?
They say he too proud an' foolish.
Nah! He know he worth, boy;
the bowler should wear helmet, not he.
Remember long this day, holy to be here.
See him stalk the high altar o' the mornin' air.

You ever see such mastery in this world?
You ever see a man who dominate so?
This man don't know forbearance,
he don't know surrender or forgive,
he lash the ball like something anger him.

Look how the man torment today!
He holding the bat, it could be a axe.
Look how he grinding he jaw again, boy,
how he head hold cock an' high
and he smile, he gleam, like a jaguar.
Don't bring no flighty finery here; it gone!
Bring the mightiest man, Viv husk he.
He always so, he stay best fo' the best.

I tell you, he smile like he hungry;
you ever see this man caress?
That mood hold he, it bite he!
He pound the ball, look at that, aha!
Like he vex, he slash, he pull, he hook,
he blast a way through the cover, man,
he hoist the ball like cannon ball
gone far and wild, scattering the enemy,
and foe turn tremble, danger all about.
It's butchery today; bat spill blood
and he cut like he cutting hog on a block;
nobody could stop he in that mood.

Almighty love be there! Almighty love, boy.
We know from the start, he one o' we.
Something hurt he bad, you could see,
as if heself alone could end we slavery!

MEETING ONCE A YEAR AT BRITNELLS

Which book will I find you browsing in?
'There', you will say, finding the page,
as if no time had passed at all
to wear away life's bright-edged blade a little more.
'When Isaac Singer died he said,
"What the earth swallows is soon forgotten".

Wrong. "Like moonlight on whitest sand
we use that dark to gleam, to shimmer".'

Following a plough through ancient fields
we turn up treasures:
sun-varnished plums that sweeten to the taste.
A Cypriot proverb:
our history is a black stone carved with wings.
Swords shine in Agamemnon's cupboard:
a traveller's fire lit by Gibbon's noble prose.

Still virgin, Newton died at eighty-five.
Was it worth it to discover
the laws of all the universe?
Ah, we have long loved books together
but Walcott's Homer says it well:
'A girl smells better than a book'.
No, the poet stands himself corrected,
'A girl smells better than whole libraries'.

We have gone long ways apart.
After ferocious evil in the gentle land –
throats gashed to make second mouths of screams,
eyes coldly savaged out of still-fleshed skulls
(Oh, what a work of hate is man!) –
snowfall in Kathmandu;
in that far world where mountains climb
gleaming, that age-old, god-filled bastion,
you're safe with love and books and the high stars.

A world away in dark, dazed Guyana,
I settle for the comfortableness of love,
a good wife's caring, the miracle of sons,
a sea-wind murmuring in green trees.
There's well-drawn tea on the veranda,
delicious meat patties melting on the tongue,
jobs to do for money, men from Porlock –
the poetry later, should there still be time.

Let us choose together the spirit's victories:
Mandlestam's widow counting out like gold
word by word his poems in her head –
'The strength of men against cruelty and power
is memory's victory over man's forgetting';
and wisdom's final lesson, and most true –
'He only merits freedom, merits life,
who daily has to conquer them anew.'

You told me once:
'We think we are immortal
And we are.' It is so still.
Truth does not die and we have savoured it.
The morning's beauty lasts for all its time.

What shall I say, old friend?
Distance, time, still brings no rift.
We sail our separate seas
but when the sea tracks cross
the bright sails unfurled still flash
as I remember, and feel no loss;
the lines that tighten round the mooring post
are strong and taut against the ocean's drift.

THE WEATHER IN SHANTY TOWN

The poets sing, the sweet words gleam like shining laces:
'When the sun harnesses the earth like a goldsmith,
praise the rain, praise the cold lady rain!
When the black storm throws pelting rain down in spears,
praise the fire of the sun, praise the gold wand of the sun!
This land is land of big weathers, black and gold;
storms and fierce heat descend like cruel princes,
black warlords in their thunder palaces.
Under the new moon sometimes there is peace of weather,

rain falling like white lilies on the iron streets:
praise, praise the convenor of the dark winds, the bright airs!'

No poets' words for shanty town: the weather kills and cankers every day.
The black storm in the morning shakes the tilting huts.
Women stuff the cracked walls full with rags against the pour of rain.
Their children play in drowning pools, laughing in the sudden mud.
The black rain and the flail of storm is horrible:
the sodden damp stinking, cess pits overflowing, dryness nowhere.
The water pearls on black tin walls in sweating dews of filth.
The wet air swims like slime in every space and lung.
The rain is piss in shanty town, it brings no grace of silver.

Another day the avid sun hammers the hard earth gold.
Flies blacken the silver eyes of dead pigs in the dumping grounds.
Dust stuffs the bright air streaming from the sky.
It is hot as ovens, hot as engines, hot as deserts.
The heat simmers, the sun sings in the air, torpor everywhere.
The scums of old rain crack like scabs on beggars' sores.
The brass of sunlight poisons shanty town, the hot air fumes with shame.
The smell rises in a shimmering fog, a smell of death and guts.
Black vultures land with dusty wings to browse on heated filth;
the children blaze with joy and race to catch them on the carrion grounds.

Men in good clothes do not feel the weather.
Men sweet with food do not fear the weather.
Men in shining cars glide easy through all weather.
Paper-mighty men at desks do not hate the weather.
Men in strong houses do not know the weather of this world.
Such men, such cocooned men, they do not live in shanty town.
The weather in their hearts is mild, they have not lived in shanty town.
In shanty town the anger hangs like smoke, like fire.
The weather in those hearts is storm, the weather in those hearts is hate.

ON READING BIOGRAPHIES OF ROBERT LOWELL, SYLVIA PLATH, JOHN BERRYMAN AND ANNE SEXTON IN RAPID SUCCESSION

I see there is not much to tell
in a life if it goes well,
but it goes bad, well then, hooray,
there is always much to say.
Hideous lives these great ones live:
forever take, and never give –
but then allowance must be given
to the soul that's sick and driven.
Cruel fighting, knives unsheathed,
thorns around the laurels wreathed;
desperate loves, antic madness,
fits of ecstasy 'midst sadness;
moods and alcoholic tantrums,
the boom and bash of beaten drums
sounding out the loud despairs
of re-reiterated fears.
Descents repeated into Hell
where agony and anguish dwell
is the story of their lives:
art on madness ever thrives.
Self-flagellating lash and groan
lend a rich compelling tone
to each self-exculpating tale
and every self-confessing wail.
Others, of course, have lives as well
and didn't volunteer for hell:
no matter, the non-creative other,
be it spouse, or child, or mother,
or friend, or lover, who had the luck
to touch or even chance to be in suck-
ing distance of that heroic taint
enrols to play the willing role of saint

and put up with each desperate trick,
accept in full what's deeply sick,
issuing from the one appointed
from on high, the Muse-anointed.
It matters not what others bear –
the poet's duty is quite clear,
the lesson is as plain as day:
'Let others suffer, I go my way
in fulfillment of the Olympian plot:
The work's important, lives are not.'

Or, not to make such a song and dance about it:

God save you, should you cross the path
of Robert Lowell or Sylvia Plath.

THE PEAR-WOOD CUP

Carved pear-wood:
golden as if filled with sun,
cleaned to a shone perfection,
handled to fit a big and battered knuckle,
simple, ordinary, well-proportioned shape,
deep-bowled for a deep thirstiness.
In it the deep, long wear of usefulness,
entering, lasting, then transforming,
has engraved a beauty without passion:
there is no harm in this good thing.
The man who made it lived when times were slow,
knew old occupations that start at morning light.
This cup has no comparison,
no others match it on the kitchen shelf.
In it the touch of generations
joins the taste of everyday:
cold, clear water gets colder, clearer.

The trouble is with us:
too few good things kept safe
come down from the ancestors
to teach us what is past and prized.

GIFTS FOR A FAREWELL

Koetsu, famous for his tea-bowls,
mainly black, others rufous or turkey-wattle red,
some splashed with white as from an eagle's droppings:
his glazing holds a brightness like fireflies.
Eighteen tea-bowls that he made are left.
All the rest are gone, thousands they say;
the centuries have stamped them all to pieces.
I wish you this gift, a bowl so baked and spun.

Farmers in vivid scarlet clothes
till strawberry fields in Pougastel.
A wild wind haunts that Breton coast
where fish-boats bring in their silver catch.
Honoured for beauty, I have read,
you must walk in Pougastel.

In Mexico the Tarascans long ago
made mosaics from the wings of birds.
Most famous of all villages in this art
Tzintzuntzan on a golden lake –
in Mayan meaning 'tresses of the day-star'.
They worked thus: drop by drop an orchid's glue
bound gold-green feathers into tapestry.
May you seek and love such wonders all your life.

These gifts for you, Philip O'Meara,
friend of the good hours, you would like to know
these things and you will treasure them

and yet reflect how simply beauty falls
and the dark comes and hearts slow.
You who dance upon the ice
have always known what dwells below.

POEM

(for Arthur Seymour)

One night your poems were in my hands
when sudden as blindness in the dark
the lamplight in the room went out
and I was sightless in the poem's heart.
I sat there in the deepening night
your poems held upon my knees;
the sea-wind made its quiet sound,
a half-moon slowly etched the trees.
In my mind their cadence grew
like waves that run against a far-off shore,
that restless whisper from the world begun,
that eternal sound men have hungered for.

CANDLESTICK MAKER

Beneath the ox-tail, shit bubbles and descends;
peasant fare, smell of cake-stalls in the air.
At last he wakes, bolt-straight,
eyes afire, from his complex sleep,
throws off the embroidered heavy clothes,
sets about the task, self-given;
matches the multiplying suns,
the green glaze of leaves, the Plato cave,
the bears, the waterfall, the galleries of love.
He makes the single candlestick
golden, polished, perfect, sure;

sets in it one perfect candle
and lights it to light the world.
Though the taper's frail
and the wind a-howl,
full of the hiss of serpents,
blows the flame flat
and the flame flutters, fails,
nothing can be put out again,
far darkness is illumined.
The candlestick maker:
ah, his craft is needed.
Nothing ceases when he begins
the sift and seethe of endless time;
light will last forever now
radiance in every tumbled grave.

BETWEEN SILENCE AND SILENCE THERE SHOULD BE ONLY PRAISE

Should there be a great flood
whole cities would be cast on the fierce water,
floating, drifting, down to an ancient sea;
men and women shouting at the windows,
carrying children to the rooftops,
whimpering in the bleak wind's fury.
Desperate swimming as the houses sink;
life's comfortable arrangements awry and lost.
That slender-waisted girl, sure of her beauty,
she is gone too, with the despots and clowns.
Under the vast sky, much pointless activity –
as well a skull pick its nose and snort
to breathe the evening air.

On the black creek a man's at work;
a fisherman sets a nest of ants afloat,

clump of twigs and green leaves clotted
so intricately to make this insect home,
neat, entangled, well-planned habitation,
now, suddenly adrift, the ant-swarm circles,
tests the water's edge, retreats,
all safety ended.

The impassive fisher sits above;
the floating nest, his subtle bait,
spills ants amidst the swirling flood;
fish flash, gather for the living feast.
He takes his time to flick the rod
assured of victims as the ants drop off
the sinking nest, efficient lure.
The ants' nest drowns and sinks
and bubbles rise like pearls and burst.

Man need not have been. No one knows why
God maintains his kingdom without persuasion:
the dark world of the forest and the river stirs,
intricate catacomb, the grub-furrow under earth
leading to stone, the sun-soar over clouds,
mud caked Johnny Smallfoot, the bent idiot,
whose pleasant laughter maddens those who sorely hurt him.
Shadows pass, empires are cast down.
Friend, it is past the time when tears matter:
between silence and silence, there should be only praise.

THE COMFORT OF ALL THINGS

ANGER

I mistook the falling moon
for a white hawk in the night
aloft amid the splintering cloud;
it screamed but it was only the harsh wind.
Storm-bursts of light cracked the heavens,
dark-wrapped glittering darts of gold
changed utterly the gentle passions of the day,
the patterned peace of quiet routines:
caverns of fire, a wheel of iron turning,
the wild wind screaming like a hawk.

ANY POEM

You can make a poem about anything.
In fact, that would be the first line of it:
about life, how it passes,
about death, how it comes,
about beauty, how it lasts
while it lasts,
about love, which is a strong thing
but strong things break,
about the old lady in lace
who lived a hundred years
and is forgotten,
about great men, who wear out
quicker than stones,
about truth which is fidgety
and will not stand still,
about eternity, which time contains,
about God, who invented Himself
like a poem.

DE RERUM NATURA

I took my garden seat
to read Lucretius's great poem,
eat white-kernelled almonds,
watch life wakening on the shores of light,
birds shimmering amid the green leaves,
flower to flower flashing
incandescent blessings on the wing.
You cannot cage their fire
they drop and drably die.
Aeons ago they skimmed the trees
their inch-long skeletons
bound in age-old crystal rock
and still they fly this very day,
their shoulders miniature as watch-gems
rotate the hurry of their humming wings'
incomparable intricacies of flight.
The sun goes down beneath the sea;
their wondrous flight precedes
the corn-scatter sweep of stars.

THE GOLDEN BARNS OF GOD

Life has been long and good
but it is not forever.
I will not come again to the savannahs,
past the green, beloved trees,
the root-red streams, the silvered banks.
I will not see again this far horizon
where the great rock silos rise,
thunder of the gods around them.
Is there meaning in what we are and do?
Ah, the end and purpose of all creation!
Endless time has brought this to my eyes:

the wild winds throwing the birds,
the air becoming marvellously bright,
the large sun sinking to the very edge
and end of the world,
the golden barns of God ablaze.

THE UNIVERSE ILLUSTRATED BY HUBBLE

Godlike are the great valleys of the sky.
The immense and glowing spires of heaven
soar upwards in gold and purple masses.
Endless voids pricked with starry worlds
extend beyond time in marvellous successions
of bright stone-encrusted bottomless abysses.
Explosions vast as half of space are frozen
in all the colours of a billion sunsets,
cargoes of jewels spilled down precipices
collect in heaped and brilliant treasure piles.
Fruits of a million stars stain and ripple
the sheer sides of green pavilions built
on perilous black cliffs above deep seas of blue.
Vaulted heavens writhe with cloths of gold,
waterfalls of silver and blaze of comet tails.
See shining deserts of cold white ice reflect
Mexican gardens of burning yellow blooms,
pooled molasses all a-swirl with mercury drops
and sumptuous leaves of gilt. Beyond the climb
of chasms curtains of rain ascend,
and hallways shadowed by tall fretwork arches
march in tremendous ranks towards the end of time.
Sudden blaze of cathedral colours in the night;
out of nothingness, endless purity of white.

WALTER RALEGH'S POLICE DOSSIER
10TH AUGUST, 1618

Failed, his last adventure to the fabled land,
"Guiana, whose rich feet are mines of gold,
whose forehead knocks against the roof of stars".
Returning to a king's wrath, he tried escape.
His heart was hardly in it. Tricked and trapped,
remembering much of love and seas of storm and treasure,
weary, old, fate beckoned and he surrendered.
The scaffold may have seemed the last brave thing to do.
Held his elbow roughly – he stumbled, almost fell.
His person gave up all the Indies:

£50 in gold coin
A wedge of 22-carat gold
A stobb of coarser gold
A chain of gold with diamond sparks
Sixty-three gold buttons with diamond sparks
A diamond ring of nine sparks
A naval officer's whistle set around with small diamonds
An ancient silver seal bearing roebucks from Ralegh's coat-of-arms
A few leaves of poetry, written in his hand
A Symson stone set in gold
A sprig jewel mounted with soft stones and a ruby
One ounce of ambergris, pungent flotsam of warm oceans
One spleen stone from Guiana for the cure of melancholy
A lodestone in a scarlet purse
A diamond finger-ring given him by Elizabeth the Queen
A gold-cased miniature of the Lady Elizabeth, his wife,
its frame set fair with diamonds
Three sea cards or charts of the West Indies which,
out of everything, he was most reluctant to hand over
One plott or map of Guiana and the New Kingdom
Another plott and description of the river Orinoco
Five silver-mine samples

One jacinth seal engraved with Neptune's figure,
tied to it with string a specimen of Guiana ore
An idol from Guiana made of copper and gold.

He got one ring to keep, deep ocean blue.
Marvel, dream: centuries pass,
the shaken loom of history gleams.

A GATHERING AT THE WORLD'S END

It was a bad year for the people.
A comet set trees blazing far and wide;
the rivers rose past history's highest mark
drowning the most solid encampments;
a swarm of eagles completely hid the sun
with their flashing talons and burnished wings;
at the foot of a far mountain
a giant was unearthed, eye-sockets filled with gold.
In such times what could be foretold
except mysteries and death?
Yet here was a child whispering to its mother,
a man embracing his kin,
sounds that seemed like music,
a sword set aside in a corner,
and the warmth of roasted loaves
bringing the message of endless blessings.

AT THE END,

the path not cleared, steep and wild,
thorn bush and small birds beaked like eagles,
rock-scuttling spiders small as berries,
twelve wolf-teeth white as a hill of chalk
gleaming to a snarl on the vined bridge,

barring the way to heaven – no going there,
the scent of smoky candles, the endless
accordion whine of green and delicate crickets
under grey cloud shot with red,
the rainbow-caverned, swallow-haunted gulf,
din not dimmed by distance now, an altar's rising mist.
I cannot reach the end of words,
I cannot fix a tether on the truth –
the archive still to come of newer meanings.
I should go back before it is too late,
before the fall-in to forever and fierce final rush of wind,
the blue light of void, endless and content.

SPEAKING TO THE GODS

On the village outskirts, by the water's edge,
where great disaster struck, a new church stands,
white, wooden, built on sacred ground.
In that place before were modest habitations
in which no one escaped the killing sea
when it rose up one night, cascading in
to smash and drown every single soul,
corpses torn and withered by the sea.
As memorial, the village fathers built a church
to honour the dead with prayers and song
so they be not forgotten and the sea not rise again,
did this to get the gods to listen. Collected randomly,
as Fate is random in what it saves,
remembrances that survived the mortal wreck
are blessed, anointed, placed to fill
an excavated space beneath a simple altar.
There they rest forever, speaking to the gods:
tables, kitchen pots, portraits, a fishing spear,
an intact necklace of great beauty, an axe, a bucket,
school uniforms and dresses, caps and shawls,

a fat carved owl which was a toy or amulet,
Christmas balloons of red and green –
miscellany of living before sudden death.
And bells, bells which a few households kept,
which whisper still for those who come to mourn
and forever will when all are gone to dust.

SILENCE

I walk alone among sea-birds
in this graveyard sloping to the sea –
a sheet of gold at sunset.
Mahogany trees set against the sun-gold,
small green leaves appearing after last week's rain
overhang moss-mottled gravestones
fearsome in their silence.
It is a long time since I spoke with those I loved.

DREAM HERON

The great white bird tugs itself to heaven,
steps upwards in the morning air.
In memory, my eyes are clear
as when I was a boy, all days before me,
time still in the shadow of green trees,
flowers pouring from the freshened earth,
a froth of colours, a cauldron rush of brightness,
that white ascension! Life intact and new
summoned from an empty season.

I LEARNED IT ALL IN ONE KIND MEETING

(for Frank Collymore)

I learned it all in one kind meeting;
he praised a small thing I had sent,
young and eager to make an instant mark.
He showed me how it could be done better,
important to get it absolutely right;
he smiled, so much at stake, so much at stake.

He walked quietly in the history of his people,
pointing out this matters, this is good.
Write words carefully, they will last
longer than empire, they will shake our world.
Cultivation of language is an equal craft
ancient and useful as the farmer's trade.
Constructions of the mind bequeath the most;
tales told well are told for evermore.

What he meant and wanted us to do:
hourly practise the measurement of truth;
sort out the saying of good stories;
set forth as daily food the privileges of art.
Build him a monument of a green tree growing
with fruit to pick for generations to come.

THE COMFORT OF ALL THINGS

I went out for an evening swim alone.
A perfect pendant of lightning blazed
deep in a far thunder-head as I walked.
I was astonished how it lit the world,
revealing smallest details I would have missed.
I pick a stone up, feel it, smell the wet dirt,
rub it clean – its shape marvellously unique.

I wrap it in a gold leaf I also noticed,
walk on, wind rising over the wide water,
the ancient lantern of the moon aloft
for aeons gone and to come, the river washing
and retreating, swaying in the vertigo of time.
Immensities surround me, infinity of sky,
swimming a long way out, full of peace
I think how old I am compared with the stars.

HOMECOMING

(for young Brian Lara)

There was such a mass of people
there was so much joy.
We stood in the sun for hours,
sweat-soaked, hungry, happy.
A gust of rain came; we exulted.

At first there was a barrier
but that broke; a surge of people
flooded to the platform's foot.
I was carried in that surge
jostling for position, good-humoured
police just part of the crowd.

The whole world echoed with his fame;
he was ours: we waited to consume him,
feed on his glory in those thin times.
We roared when the young prince came
we threw our hands high in praise:
the crowd had a full throat!
Everyone was in good voice, some singing,
everything vivid, a bird soaring, black ant on the skin.

He said a few simple words:
It was from God the runs came,
it was for everybody, not him alone,
that he was glad he had done it
for his father, for his mother, for us.
He waved the bat, it was a blessing
full of the sweetness of those runs!

What a glory to be there!
We drifted away in our sodden clothes
heavy with tiredness, satisfied
we were walking into our other lives.

THE EDGE OF NIGHT

Watchman by the seawall koker –
twenty years I met him on my walks.
Smoked his curly pipe; we talked,
fireflies sparking in the low, protected fields.
He was old when he began this job,
guardian of the tidal gates of town.
Got away from a rum-soaked father's home,
wandered to other lands then home again.
He never built a home or had a woman
or concerned himself with God.
"Ah live from then to now an' don' remember how."
Long ago he was a forest guide,
went with museum teams in Essequibo
and made a name for his strange collections.
One day he brought for their inspection
a black and shiny scorpion whose helmet-head was gold.
They honoured him, named him discoverer,
the keepsake plaque engraved in Latin script.
I tell him it is beautifully done.
He gestures, an old man stranded on the edge of night.
The sea in tumult rises at our feet.

THE BONE-TRIP

Bone-trip, he called it, his brutal name
for dying: "The bone-trip is always hard."
I remember his face lit by fire,
cracked into a thousand creases
as he bent over, hardening nails –
he repaired boots for working men in Gentle Street.
One day his smiling partner wasn't there.
"Well, bruds gone to make his bone-trip now."
Wiped his sweaty face with rag,
went on nailing the rough, strong boots.

TESTIMONY

I saw a child, a thin girl, about six,
carrying a weight of water, two pails on a stick.
She made staggering, small steps; the water splashed
and wasted in the burning sun.
I could not bring myself to run to her,
I told myself it would do no good;
the child would be frightened, drop the pails.
I remembered urchins in bustling Regent Street,
long ago, dancing for money, stern thin faces
and sad old eyes. I flung money and hurried by.
Once, at a restaurant's fancy door
children accosted me, uttering not a word.
They felt too near, hustling me,
putting out their hands, almost touching me.
I offered them nothing with an ugly face;
they were disturbing my peace of mind.
Whatever good I did in my life is cancelled
by such deeds, these anguished memories.
Time is just. This night seems long.

LISTEN TO THE WOLVES

From the peaceful forest
a disturbance of kings.
Nothing is rightfully ours.
The Monastery's fine crop of sorrel
will not be reaped this year.
There is hardly one child left in the settlements.
Walls with strong foundations have been built
against the tall seas that are coming;
the thunder of horses
across the sunlit heavens;
avalanches of ice descending.
Deeper than that, newly discovered atoms
swerve and weave through restless time.
Everywhere the wreckage of stars.
Listen to the wolves;
their strange music comes on the wind;
splinters of gold fall from their coats.
My heart drums against my side
in my dreams lately.
I hear voices call for healing.

STRANGE PLOT

Strange fellowship of the earth,
stones in the graveyard side by side.
The new one brightly cut for Meg Longstreet,
died at ninety-three. And one, time-darkened,
cracked and crooked, inscribed for Meg
who died at six months old, who never
heard the drum of life go rat-a-tat-tat.
Through long and faithful years the joy,
the love, the hope, the good times passing,
the first-born's never-ending loss endures.
"Lay me to rest by my beloved daughter Meg."

ON BEING SHOWN ROUND HIS ROOM BY THE POET

A bedchamber full of mirrors
awash with moons that fly between the clouds,
an open drawer dusty with half-made poems –
"Do not go near water
if you want to see the moon."
Slowly he shakes his head,
finger to his lips as if for silence,
his eyes lit with fire.
He rocks an empty chair
he says he never sits in,
offers a few plums on a plate.
I am trying to remember exactly
as I can what that room was like
and what he said – "what the thing is,
not what it should be",
"the beauty of doors that never open",
"tear-stains on a poem, throw it in the fire!"

THE RED CRYSTAL NECKLACE

Blankness now, lips slightly agape,
vacancy of eyes that shone,
heavy length of body sags.
I sit beside her in despair.
She speaks of what was long ago,
asks for help to dab her eyes
with linen laid to wipe the tears.
The colours of the world are gone.

A portrait fixed above her bed
near seventy years ago
was her husband's favourite picture
of his bride. It shone for him

throughout their time.
As I look up her eyes catch mine.

The portrait is in black and white
necklace of black stars chained on glowing white.
She turns to give a lover's glance,
his heart forever stopped in wonder.

"It is as if it's happening now.
He asks me first to close my eyes,
places it round my bare neck gently.
I feel them fall upon my breast,
red crystals with their weight of love.
I knew my world would end with him."

She sighs and slowly turns her face away.

LIGHTNING IN THE FALL

From morning I stayed out in the fall air,
not wanting to come in, to miss anything –
how the sun shone, how the clouds travelled
across the cold land and the golden trees,
green pastures of quiet. I walked abroad
as far as I could, surprised at the calmness of people
in this sepulchre of bright days. Everything was ordinary,
only a murmur on the wind and two strangers,
bent old women, walking slowly, who raised thin hands
in triumphant style. All the day long history
had cleared its throat, preparing at last to cough out
long-collected phlegm. I stayed outside to wander
in the night, to see what beauty might still be hidden
after the day had gathered in its toll of deaths,
marvelling, marvelling at the jagged stars.

LAST DAYS

I cannot walk without stumbling
in the unlit garden. The showers of gold
in its beauty dismays me. I remember
children crying in a stranger's arms.
I am always reminded of death. Everything
reminds me of death, the frequency of flowers,
the sharpness of knives. I rise again.
The moon is a badly shaped heart.

GEOMETRY OF THE DYING MIND

These are bad days now,
geometry of the dying mind decrees.
Zero makes into zero
the enduring primes of life.
It is not the mournful rain
or the cough deep in the chest
or the cracks widening in the wall
that must be given serious attention,
or the unmown grass, or golden flowers
going brown. Such defects again appearing
as ever are willingly corrected.
It is not the income and the bills,
their measurement and balancing,
the habit of dealing with matters as they arise,
the responsibility of getting things done for others –
all that wondrous maze of problems and of joys.
It's that the doing and the doing over
will not have to be done again.

ZEROIC

Still alive
at seventy-five?
Do not wait
eliminate,
put an end
to ever more.
Lovely thought
nothing sought
no excuse
reduce, reduce
life's store
to the core.
How you came
leave the same
the enemy is clutter.
Every day
throw away,
aim to be
completely free.
Simplify
to zero.

MARIGOLDS

Walked out of a bower of green trees,
and there was a whole field of marigolds
set fire by the wind.
The path between that leaping gold
led down to a dancing edge of sea
blue as a child's imaginings.
I walked laughing, exulting, praising,
remembering the whole field of marigolds,
the multitude of birds coasting and swerving.
Should there be a world of gods,
those gods took care today.

LEGACY

Our garden grew an old, gnarled orange tree
when I was young; its fruits were sugar-sweet.
Spent hours in its branchy shade, reading,
picking, peeling, sucking fruit,
thinking how good life is, how sweet,
shaded from the bright sun, a wind blowing
and the book falling open at beloved passages.
I searched the sky for hawks, coasting on air,
high messages of strength and grace.
In such a perfect day, boyhood is summed up.
What I speak of, though sixty years past and more,
is so alive I hear the gold wasps buzz,
feel the squeezed juice drip upon my fingertips –
licked, to get the last full drops of sweetness.
And every page so good to read and think about,
I savoured all, then returned to savour all again.
I did not want their end to come,
I did not want the day to end.

MULE

Texan mule, big strong fella,
I rode him in the sugar fields
long, I tell you, long ago –
my ancient hands could not guide him now.
To this day I hold him dear,
rough hide of hair beneath my touch,
gold-flecked eyes – I see them still.
Shook his brute head when I came
with sliced mangoes mixed with nuts.
I fed him by hand until he loved me.
Blossoming immortelle was the order point
near chuckling pigeons pecking corn;
from there we walked the long backdam,

glints of sun, wildflowers in the path,
high-standing cane, white-tasselled ripe,
storm and wild winds in the sky,
hooves sucking when the dam was mud,
but mostly sun, sun stove-wood hot,
red heart glowing after brilliant dawns,
sweat smearing cane ash on the skin.
Brought up soft, I suffered,
yearned to get back to cooling water.
He had sure and steady steps until
I slapped his neck and he went fast.
I put my hand along his brow
to feel the tremble between his eyes;
he was a living glory in my youth.
I left. The big fella nudged my chest.
I thought he tossed his head in grief,
but it was me, for only men are sad.
I had a hard-stone keepsake carved;
gold-pebbled eyes still punch my heart.

WHAT IT WAS LIKE ONCE FOREVER

I wake to see the gleaming salmon
spring in the dark river of the morning,
the wind full of sea-salt and garden-flower,
the trees brimming slowly with green.
Mongoose, snake-catcher, sleek as a seal,
darts out of sight; I give him a sharp salute.
The day goes well. People are well-disposed,
what is owed to business is efficiently transacted.
Back home I leap heavenwards as high as I can,
not far, but bravely done. My wife smiles,
she shakes her head, after all I am close to seventy-five.
There is no limit to our love,
even death will set no limit.
Our sons are content, healthy as snorting horses;

they will be coming soon.
I write this absurdly happy verse
to tell what it was like once, forever.

IDEA INTO WORD

Resting between red flowers
green leaves glistening
heron perched on a flamboyant tree.
Strange and graceful silhouette
silver water still beneath
sun-pierced rain-cloud over all
sky-dark and honey fall.
The gleaming cut
and polish of creation.

PAINTING THE WIND

"Poetry should reproduce the qualities of painting"
— Horace, *Ars Poetica*

The brooding clouds of Essequibo,
brewing squalls and thunder,
march up the river-reaches.
The winds of Essequibo coloured by the sun
push strongly on these caravans of cloud,
rough up the shining coat of evening-water,
make a green tumult of the forest trees.
See the high birds ride the heavens on them,
see them veil the full moon with their silk.
Please God, if I am born again an artist,
let me go far up Essequibo again
and this time paint its soft and hurtling winds.

GARDEN POEMS

The garden created by Mary, my wife,
over thirty years is a continual joy.
These fragments have been chipped from her creation.

The Great Trees

I doubt there is anything
more beautiful than the flying moon
between the branches of great trees
clouds obscuring
then revealing
leaf-entangled stars
night after night
the great trees stand.

Tree Orchids

Sumptuous cape
of purple orchids
thrown overnight
across the boles
of mottled bark
flourish in the wind
wrap of kings.

Orchid Mobile

Balanced spring
in the open balcony
poised coil of cobra
violet – hued curl of flower

green-stemmed orchid
quivers in the wind
perfect mobile.

Sky Flowers

Heart-shaped vine leaves
half-cover sky-blue blossoms
shaking in the wind
on a white wall
curtain incomparably woven
honeyguide for hummingbirds.

Shower of Gold

Sun flags
fall among the leaves
sudden fans of gold
wind-waved
along black boughs
drip brightness
the old tree
radiant again.

Flamboyant

Gnarled tree
blackened branches
wind-awry
death coming
this year for sure
sudden green filigree
bursts of red
rush of blood.

Plumbago

Quiet evening light
shadows shed gold
willow-pattern blue
blossoming
entangled in emerald
flower of peace.

Frangipani

Intense white
without flaw
pennants flying
in the sun
spears aloft
amid the green
sharp fragrance.

Poinsettia

Peacock flowers
flame and glow
bright fire-coal
red bleeds into green
home decorations
for a sunlit Christmas.

Bluebells

Blue as eyes
sun bright
jewels strung

in a nymph's hair
sapphire sparks
bride's joy

Almond

Glossy green leaves
age to gold
lovely to read below
green overhang
where green parrots
hide and throw
bitten seeds down
look up delighted
shake my fist.

Crown of Thorns

On show
in bright sunlight
red blossoms
fire-lit on spikey branches
blood wounds
of Christ

Easter Lilies

Carpet of white trumpets
lustrous in sunlight
nestled in green sleeves
cool and glistening
earth song.

Water Coconut

Cutlass on high
brings down the ripened fruit
lop its green head off
white pith and shell
sip sweet and cool
what God called water
scoop soft jelly
eat and live forever.

Cherry Ripe

Abundant in green branches
picked red cherries
plump tart swallows
in a white pail
juice in a stone jar
for old friends.

Pak choi and Lettuce

Picked dew-fresh
tender leaves of green
chopped and mixed
beans and sweet peppers
in a plain bowl
for good friends

Sweet Pepper

Rich profusion
garden food all week
plump peppers red and sweet

cut in salads
bedded in dark green
or lightly roasted
to go with choicest meats.

Rosemary and Thyme

Crushed rosemary
chipped thyme
aromatic walk
daybreak sun
breathe deep
fresh morning air
in my pocket
a handful of fragrance.

Lime Tree

Time-laden branches
shelter me
from noon blaze
what a blessing
cut limes
a sweetened pitcher
crack of ice.

Rose of Gold

Pure gold could not
possess this gleam
sun enters
every sovereign bloom
day is dark

leaves are dull
these petals pull
all gold all light
to show us all
what gold is really like.

Midnight Rose

Rose bred
to such red darkness
blood of centuries
gathers at its heart
moon crescent gleams
above this bed
of wild black leaves
thorn and dark rose
a deeper shade
of night.

The Day Begins With Beauty

Gold-tendrilled dawn
dew-beads glisten
in the risen sun
rain far away
brings a cool wind
ruffling my blue shirt.

Matins

Quiet morning
the garden gently prays
except one bed a-froth with colour

never seen such blossoming
praise-shout
ascending to heaven.

Firecrackers

Shimmering of green
green-gold sparks
hummingbirds skip
among the firecrackers
darts of coral
sips of syrup

Paradise

Morning walk
found a long red feather
vivid as a wound
macaws fly here
multicoloured in the sky
when I was a child
they flew from paradise.

Mussaenda

Among green foliage
rain-jewelled
chandeliers of light
hang by the jasper walks
pass them every day
hooked by beauty
however far I wander.

Venus

Day-long rain
scoured the air
clear evening light
for our garden walk
in the cleaned sky
a droplet of night-fire.

Sunset

Flowers in the sky
light blues and yellows
mild as peaceful meadows
soon blackest clouds
edged by molten gold
heavenly shipwrecks glow
purple drapes of night.

Night Choir

Darkness descends
out of sky
out of earth
cacophony of silver
frog calls creak
crickets sing
lone cicada hums
throaty songs of night.

Moonrise

Day burned bright
coloured by the sun
shaped by shadows now
trees palely robed
dark world washed with silver
spilled from a golden moon.

Hawk at Rest

Glides tree to tree
all day long in green shadows
rested for hours
this cloud-ascender
so still so quiet
garden talisman

Hawk on High

Sun-burnished
sky-soarer
in a dive
beauty   and death.

Lightning

Went out to see
what red is like
at midnight
flash of bright
red not red
strange flowering.

Volcano

Heaven's oceanic winds
blew ash from Montserrat
mists of olive
underwater colour of the sky
never-seen-before rose tendrils
disaster far away
lands strange beauty here.

Woodsmoke

Grass-crisping sun burns
the garden drought-brown
fires nearby swirl smoke
scent of cinnamon
black wood-grit
and flower-ash
plum tree aflame.

Garden Storm

Tempest in the trees
a savage rain
wind-whipped flower-fall
it softly ends
silver patterning
and nothing greener
than drenched green.

Sea Wind

Hot stillness ends
winds from the sea
murmurous and fragrant
hustle plants
toss the tops of trees
blossoms fall
leaves scatter on the grass
in dancing disarray.

Death

In a dream
a vast salt sea
climbs the gold barred heaven
mountain of night
the world over
forever

Flood

Sky-tarpaulin fills and slits
grey water-weight for weeks
the garden gone
swamp of silver
black ashes of dead grass
a water-fire

Start again.

The Overwhelming Sea

Beyond the saving wall
ships sail above our heads
spring tides rage
higher than the garden
the rising sea
inches up the sky
this beauty all will end.

Remembering

Everything purposed
weave of sun
and shadow
wind and leaves
she remembers
how every flower grew.

Mongoose

Seal-sleek
silken movement in the high grass
quick snake-killer
so finely tuned
unimaginable miracle
in a random universe.

Grass

New cut lawn
sun's oxygen
fill the lungs

breathe deep
again and again
smell of health
and homecoming.

Ants

A billion spots of life
multitudinous unseen
drip of syrup
meat-morsel dropped
bend to watch them
scurry in the grass
ceaseless seethe of being

Butterflies

Orchid-lovers
sip and kiss
wings of marigold
dance in a twirl
playing in the air
just for joy.

Bees

Black-gold swarm
in a dark tree-notch
forage dangerously
smoke and masks
remove the queen
sweet comb
drips honey-gold.

Web

baskets of ferns
drip spider garlands
dew glistening
black beetles trapped
furiously scrambling
in silver gossamer.

Water Lily

Soft evening light
sun dance of birds
they skip and peck
bright and joyous
leaf to leaf
green to green
float on silver
white blossoms
beneath their feet.

Water Hyacinth

Such lithe growth
slithering green
alive as eels
bubbles bursting
and blossoming
this sun-tangled
frog-heaven
emerald abundance.

Reading

Books and a garden-seat
brightening gold of evening
lamplight colours
green shadows lengthening
the pages turned 'til dark
clamour of marvels
oh what exquisite times
we are given in this life.

The White Chairs

Two empty chairs
side by side
white in shadow
canopied by orchids
why do they
sadden me so?

The Orchid House

Where we take tea
tasty meat patties
see the burnished sky departing
where variously beautiful
the hummingbirds
come out at six o'clock
surrounded by flowers
and peace.

Ground Orchid

Rare blossoming
garland of silver
dropped overnight
on the dark green
one day a year
and gone.

Lilies of the Field

Half a field
of beauty
blowing in the wind
white carpet
lustrous as Persia
age-old poetry
breaks my heart.

Fern

Fountain's edge
fern tendrils
creep deep green
mosses underneath
slipperiness of rocks
water gleams in the sun
bright fan
blows in the wind.

Fountain

Green leaves drip
into clear cool water
ixora banks of red
ring the quiet pond
spears of silver
arc and glisten
in the wind.

The Cassias

Four cassias
mounting to heaven
give blessings
of their shade
yet April comes
they rain down sun.

Solace

News of a death
walk hand in hand
under whispering trees
amidst orchids
the colour of tears
the kindness of the garden.

Ash

Fire
and hummingbirds
utterly, utterly
different
dead

Egrets

Sun-shimmering ponds
of morning rain
gold-eyed egrets
motionless
side by side
old as centuries.

Bougainvillea

Throw of red
against the wall
bougainvillea a-bloom
shouts of colour
joy of children
phagwah in the garden.

Marigolds

Struck by brilliance
intensity of gold
in a small space
no one looking
covered my face
in soft blooms

able to say
I bathed in marigold.

Hibiscus

Garden's glory
hundreds all a-bloom
wind awakes them
I walk amidst
the fire of their colours
thanking and praising
my wife my beauty.

Hedges

Hibiscus all aflame
crimson and soft ochre
patches of ixora red
and green ficus
creamed with white
years have built
these walls of peace.

Sunday

Cut dew-fresh
flowers fill the home
glow on white cloths
green ferns
in brick-red pots
garden work is love

QED

What is this garden
but light
rainbow of colours
alpha's beat of life
the scale of nature set
all we see and sense
all we know of god.

RIVER DANCER

I

EVERYWHERE THE LAND TURNING GREEN

"Well, eighty years to choose from, tell me quick –
don't think – the happiest moment of your life?"
My father's land, Antigua, our holiday home each year.
Antigua was like burnt bread; for two years drought
parched the land, water giving out everywhere,
the stone cisterns emptying in the house, boats
bringing water from Dominica. How long
could that go on? Whispers of an abandoned
island. Day after day the sun blazed in an arc
of blue heat haze and smell of smoke. Perhaps
the cossi green would be all that's left –
a burned crisp in the ocean.

One morning black clouds piled, heavy storm-towers
in heaven. Pray, our parents said, pray pray.
When the rain came hard on the roof, I went out
with my small sisters. Yes, you go, our parents said.
We danced wild dances in the rain – what would
have been forbidden – we danced and laughed again.
Our parents came and we were lifted up.
Next day the rain came hard again, everywhere
the land turning green

I REMEMBER DYING

At six at night the doctor came, gold watch
swinging to distract me. *Get him to hospital now.*
They took me from my mother there, masked me
with stifling chloroform – my breath still stops to
think of it. They were killing me, I knew.
Waking later in the night, my mother sang me
lullabies, *Golden slumber kiss your eyes*,
touched my lips with glittering ice and never

left my side again. I begged her with such
desperation to give me sleep instead of death.
This I remember, and her tears.

STILL LIFE

My father ran estates in Trinidad,
open trays of coffee drying in the sun.
Green-gold grapefruit cannon balls
fell in high wind on the iron roof
of low, unpainted agricultural sheds –
scents and sounds of childhood never lost.
I see old woodchoppers bend,
cutting cocoa wood in sweaty vests.
I see a big man wave and shout,
The boys gone on a parrot hunt!
The overseer lifts me on his shoulder
to get ripe Governor plums from high.
Shadow of rainfall in the far hills.
How do such images last forever?
The coffee beans are fragrant still;
the gold-green grapefruit fall and clang;
I reach up high for purple plums.

HERMIT OF THE CLEAR TORRENTS

It was a place where birds congregate,
songs in every tree, not far from ponds
scooped from rocks, where the river falls
in green tiers quiet over moss, then wild descent –
Caura Valley river, beloved boyhood haunt,
clear crystal springs to sport in with my friends,
catch butterflies to add to our collections.
An old man had made his home in a makeshift

shelter, blue-gowned, bearded, hairpin thin and bent,
the earth a rolling pearl beneath his sandalled feet.
Inquisitive, we heard him playing a flute;
he pelted us with bottles, laughing madly,
so he did not seem a threat. In time we gave him
due respect. Once, I saw him ride a horse,
withered in the shank, white hooves, yellow saddle
hung with sunflowers. It seemed a dream. Still I
hear him playing flute, see vultures hanging in the sky.

BUT NOT ONLY THAT

Planning tomorrow's things to do – nothing special –
paying bills, visiting an old retainer, sending emails,
one to a friend with stage four cancer – what to say? –
collecting a package of car parts you can't get here.
Out of the roar and glare of the world, there's my
grandmother showing me a wall-covering –
white silk, black pelicans gliding over a golden sea –
then in a flash, there's Alice, the tall, dark woman,
Carib slant of cheek, who cooked for us on Sundays
seventy years ago. I see her by the fireside
with her box of spices – even the smoke smelled tasty –
and I find myself suddenly wondering if hummingbirds
sing or is it the thrum of their brilliant wings.

CEREMONY

Walking one morning years ago, along
an Antiguan coral path, I came across
a black dog's corpse, not long dead,
but smelling, emerald flies buzzing at his eyes,
black fur still quite beautifully shining.
A lorry must have hit him not far away;

he crawled here to get away from death.
All around the cossi bushes grew
yellow-flowered and thick along the path.
I would have liked to burn or bury him,
place the white coral all around him;
when life ends there should be ceremony.
I broke off handfuls of golden blossom
from the cossi bushes and heaped them up,
going back many times, enough to cover him
until he had a coat of flowers. Then I got
some bright corals and placed them in a crooked cross,
feeling I had done something, though not enough.

RITE OF PASSAGE

One morning in school holidays, myself and Marcus –
his brother famously to be Carnival Minshall –
went up Mount Tucuche, just the two of us,
sun on our backs, at first feeling the heat,
then shadow of trees on the green tangled path.
A rainstorm came in the afternoon,
soaking us cold, already soaked with sweat.
It was good slogging to the top,
the trees dripping, the slush of black mud,
huge crapauds hopping in the pools,
wild orchids leaping in the branches,
a rotten stump of tree pouring out red
bajac ants in angry hunting streams, lady
slippers amid ground-creeping emerald vines.
everything seemed good and memorable.
Our muscles aching when the way got steeper;
it was harder than we thought it would be.
At last we sat on a mossy rock and ate
to the last ham-crumb the soaked sandwiches
from our knapsacks, and drank cold water

from the carafe. Coming down, tired,
we exulted, laughed together, slapped hands,
ran, slipped and fell, and shouted loud
on the green paths of the mountain.
Far from us were the years to come, our sense
the evermore of youth and comradeship.
It was very late. Our families sent out a search
for us, and that, in the reckoning, was also fine.

A PURCHASE LONG AGO

Out hunting butterflies in the mist-filled valleys
around Mount St. Benedict, our band of friends,
thirsty after hours and hours of exhilarating chase,
walked in the monastery on the green and windy hill
whose angelus of bells we heard at evening six o'clock;
a choir practising was so pure of voice;
an old retainer of sweet kindness brought cups,
pouring cool water from a red stone jar.
And I remember getting a pot of honey
to bring back home to surprise my mother.

HOSANNA IN EXCELSIS

Furious wind savaged the green forest;
in the night the tall trees' calm has gone. Early
morning boat to the monastery, light
just breaking in the far sky, river dark still,
fog rising, drifting; a small rain far off
dancing the water; on the approach, sound
of a solitary bell. We mount the steep
hillside stairs, baskets of picked sorrel resting
by the path. Golden blossoms fall from a tree;
the plucked notes of a lone guitar drift down

to us – both a blessing. Peace, the river
stretching eternally, the sky to match
with red sailing clouds, a garland touching
heaven's brow. A brother comes to greet us
on the hill, his smile wide, embraces everyone,
full of gaiety and joy. *I have been adoring God*, he says,
his arms outstretched, *adoring God and all His works*.

TENNIS

Feeling the joy of immortal youth,
being healthy and wanting to run, leap,
feel fresh air and golden sun scorch
face and back, on afternoons of dark clouds
gathering, I prayed rain would stay away
so tennis could be played. I would
get faster, better, stronger, fitter,
getting the body ready to win.
I pounded the ball against a wooden wall,
until the rhythm entered me, hour
after hour until dizzy I almost fell.
I risked sunstroke, my mother scolded.
Too much of a good thing. Go and rest.
She sopped my head, kissed and hugged me
with a worried look. Once I found
blister blood, hid the socks from her.
My father told me when alone, *Get a hat, son.*
Apply sunscreen, take a jug of sweetened lemonade.
Gradually I got better hitting at the wall,
never lonely – the game was my companion.
Then getting on the competition ladder –
first time I knew I would be good, hit a backhand volley
with perfect timing, to the inch I aimed at,
against Darnley Scandella, a good strong journeyman
whom I never beat and now I beat him easily.

He praised me and took my hand in his.
Such a delight to feel the body muscling up,
movements swifter, reflexes sharp, balance more assured,
breathing after hard running, easier and easier,
heart coming to rest so quickly after exertion;
how to make the right shots embedded in the brain.
Felt invincible, marched to inner exultation;
days were not long enough to contain the victories.
Once I saw a tiger lash its tail – that was me.
When I think of being young, fit, striving
with the flourish of good health, mind desiring
rivalry and winning, ready for glory
on the courts and honouring the body trained
in a sort of perfection – well, all this,
I think, is to describe happiness.

RIVER STATION

Down river, our boat stops for gas.
A mango tree with red-cheeked fruit
fat in the branches overhangs a little hut.
Her belly big, a girl comes out to greet us.
A slow and smiling joy adorns her
plain, flat-cheeked face, eyes alight.
Now and then she feels her belly, secretly;
she is so certain in her calm and happiness.
We get the gas and pay and wish her well.
Who going drop first? Our captain smiles.
Dem rosy mango there or you? She laughs.
Due any mornin, me mother say. Me first.
She say, *Stay good and blessings in the river.*
The captain calls, *Amen!* On our way again,
What weariness betrayed old men has gone.

WHITE ORCHIDS IN THE NIGHT

Dim light leaking from the start of time,
grains of pearl in a moonless night,
a venture into caverned rustling darkness.
Want to show you something I can't believe.
Deep forest at the edge of Essequibo,
river deluge aeons, flooding to the sea,
my friend the bushman leads me in,
along trails overgrown, two hundred yards
or so deep black. Suddenly I see,
in hundreds, sprays of orchids growing on
the bark of immense forest trees in total night
hung with tendrils of perfect white,
candles without flame but purely bright
arrayed in timeless halls of splendour
displayed for us alone to see. Even
for a bushman forest wonders never cease;
I cannot believe how privileged I am.

RED MOON

Long days of unclouded sun,
smoke all over the savannahs
blurring the brightness of the land,
streams down to trickle or to stone.
Tremendous moon rises in the night,
blood red as it soars aloft.
Because of beauty I remember this.
Also it was the vivid time
the ranchers showed us how to ride –
it's hard to ride a horse first time.
I remember the ranchmen, matter of fact,
riding with me on their safest horse.
Afterwards I shone his trembling coat,

fed him oats and chopped star-apple.
How can I forget the red moon
in the sky and the big horse nuzzling
my hand for star-apple in the night,
the red moon rising above the vast savannah.

THE FOUR-POSTER

The old house stands on black granite rock;
a bend in the immense river commands the view.
Wind rattles the shuttered window slats.
Century gone, vast shadowy groves of cocoa grew –
see the stelling skeleton where they shipped it out –
private plots of rice and corn and sugarcane
(handmade crystals), goats for milk and cheese,
blacksmith's forge, chapel with stained glass –
shards still found up to the other day.
On the beach below, an old man ties up his boat,
comes to chase ghosts from empty cobwebbed rooms –
his weekly chore to poison the wood-ant nests,
clear leaves blowing in the long balcony,
check water in the pipes. He remembers when
he was a little boy: in old wardrobes froth
of white lace dresses, white weave of dancers
as accordions played, kitchen feasts steaming
from the fireside. One day they came to move
the big four-poster from the master bedroom,
complete with all its drapes. A special boat
came to take it into town; the people hushed –
it was a sort of sign. Past midnight, rivermen,
hurrying by, heard faint strains of ancient
music come across the silver paths of night.

CANE CUTTING GANG

Low clouds, black hawks in the sky, sun hardly up,
dull silver light; I came back from the cane fields
far aback, soaked with sweat, sore backside,
unused to the mule I rode in state, straw hat's
elastic strap stinging round my throat – a week
as an overseer to see how it was done.
Could be as yesterday I felt it, insects a-whirl,
leaping grasshoppers in the dew-bright grass.
A month earlier I was saying goodbye
to Cambridge smelling of apples and linseed oil,
to young friends in the Seeley Library of History,
pouring wine to toast the promise of our futures.
Now here I was, destined to run a sugar industry,
but first get to know the growing cane, the stalks
of sugar fired to burn bare for reaping,
leaf-ash mixing with my body sweat; while
the men who cut and load and carry, who
swarmed around my stalled and stolid mule saying:
Wuk hard hard, money too little, crop bonus
paying late. What did I know? They were right.
Manager by my side chased them back to work.
The student in me thought of slave revolts;
their thirty cane knives cutting us into pieces.
Poor me returned to quarters dog-tired, fed up,
smelly with smoke-stains and dried body sweat.
How could I do this even for a few days more?
The cold sweet dousing from a rain-fed shower
was a blessed thing; I feel the beauty to this day.
The old overseer assigned to teach me served up
breakfast eggs and peppery salted fish, slapped me
on the back, a grin and whistle, and poured
us out a brace of rums and ginger.

BETTY

The most terrible conversation I ever had –
the one that hurt my heart the most –
an old woman from a rundown logie
visited to get details for estate resettlement.
Her eyes were filmed with sickness,
said her life was nothing to her,
said all women's lives were as nothing.
No one had been pleased when she was born.
Boys were princes. Always she was hiding in corners,
hiding her face, hiding. She had tried to help
by working hard. One time only she knew
some happiness. A man come and take she
to marry, and she belong to him and she
get to love him and for a while she was
a flower in his sun, but he find someone else.
No tears could come, she as dry as husk. She had
a child, a boy; he was hate and fire. They had
put her with old women in this place. It was
what she knew; she didn't want to move.
She told me again of the man she loved
and how he loved her for a little while.

REUNION

I was at the old club playing tennis again,
friends at a reunion – fifty years we hadn't met –
the tree raining down gold blossom on the court,
just as I remembered. It was like yesterday,
exulting in our memories, recalling days of triumph,
laughing at the ineptitude time brings to old sportsmen.
I embraced the rivals I fought so often
long ago, so swift before our frailties.
Afterwards we showered, changed, still laughing,

went for beers and Chinese at an eating place
I did not know from the old slow days.
Then, just before we reached, I saw the church.
Surprised to see the place where once I worshipped
in new surroundings, the memory shocked me.
I said I would be a moment and left them
to go in the church, dark and empty, old
echoes in the silence, though still much the same,
except for new stained-wood Stations of the Cross,
the same confession stall vivid in my memory.
All that time ago, there were people at prayer;
a young girl stumbled out of the stall,
fumbling, took a gun from a purse she had,
shot herself through her opened mouth.
A young priest, screaming, followed her,
took her in his arms shaking and crying,
still embracing her when the police came,
a little swamp of blood beneath them.
I know I was telling about a reunion –
fifty years we hadn't met and played –
but this seems more important,
which is what happens, so I will stop.

THE POTATO FARMER

Coming away from a parliamentary session,
there to advise a minister at question time,
I turned to a friend: *Why is this so important?*
A man selling potatoes is more important.
We decided I should follow through that claim.
Found an old veteran who sold sweet potatoes
at Bourda, got him to take me to his farm,
hours in the sun sharing what he did –
helped him dig, weed, plant and water,
dug the potatoes out of manured beds;

saw how he graded them and bagged them,
the feel of dirt and dung in the hands,
the purple-skinned produce in the golden sun.
Drink of water in the hot sun tasted
so sweet; sweat of the brow stinging my eyes,
soaking through my clothes. One time, working late,
fireflies swarmed around us. All those things –
going to market, seeing the potatoes sold –
once meant nothing. I only spent a week
with the old man who had a stall at Bourda,
and he was nothing special – cursed his wife
when she nagged him about drinking rum.
Well? my friend asked. I said, *Yes, I was right*.

AT A DEATH BED

Shining with sweet youth,
when I saw old people
I did not think of love –
they were not beautiful enough for love –
skin pillaged by the years,
hair loose and scant and grey,
limbs bent and withered.
Love was for bodies in their glory,
matching curves in hot embrace.
In age there could be nothing of desire;
love must be something else, not love.
At his death bed, I saw for myself
how she held his hand, so crabbed
and marbled. For hours they could
not move her. What was I to think?

FATHER

He weakened in his final days,
Too tired to listen to the radio,
too tired, he smiled, *to stay alive*.
He rubbed his grey and stubbled face,
said sorry that he couldn't shave,
he who'd kept himself so well.
I sit close and grasp his mottled hand;
the liver spots have multiplied.
My sadness makes it hard to breathe.
Calm grey eyes once steadied me,
young and lithe on court and field,
taught me so much I came to love;
his love and confidence in me
meant nothing really could go wrong.
Way, way back, suddenly I see him
stride toward me with a bound of joy,
take and lift me to the heavens high,
soaring laughing – again! again!
Puts me down and hugs me hard.
Oh how I loved him then forever.
Forever my heart could burst.
He asks me how I'm doing now.
His free hand takes out a handkerchief,
dabs the lids – *Not tears you know,*
just an old man's rheumy eyes.
Wants me so bad to smile with him.
You have always made me proud.
The wind blows off the green-blue sea
that he has known for thirty years.
Son, get me up. I half-carry him
to look down on the beloved sea
where years ago we swam and sported.
He leaned on me; we watched together
where far far out the green and blue
fades to grey and then to nothingness.

II

DUDLEY

Goggled-eyed through thick pebble glasses,
bulbous nose tacked on a fat and owlish face;
lisp pronounced it "Lishen to me" as he spoke –
all the prompts for nicknames and ribaldry.
No. Dudley Issac, master, was revered in his time,
classicist from Ireland who long adopted us.
At Queens Royal College in its glory years,
he taught language to boys who wanted to know
excellence in life. Learning was his chief concern,
but he instilled his special hatred of cruelty
and lies. Head erect and rule-straight stiffened back,
vividly, I see him now, near seventy years gone by,
striding tall in tall socks and khaki shirt,
turbo-charged god-horse in his beloved classes,
strict enforcer of discipline and standards.
He lit creative fires when he pursued a thought,
yet minds set free must know the boundaries
beyond which it was false and brute to stray.
New discoveries need not trample on tradition;
fresh blossoming could grow from earth well-tended.
He loved his tennis, clumped about the court,
magisterially curshed his indomitable miscues.
The years will melt away his name – and all
the others – as the ten thousand minds he taught
wink out one by one.

RORAIMA CLOUDS

I pay a duty visit delivering a package
and some US dollars to a home up
the Mahaica Creek. At the gateway
to his bottom-house, an old man in a turban
greets me where pomegranates ripen on a tree.

Black-skinned, golden-eyed old man,
he almost bows in courtesy, takes me in.
Scripture texts are pinned up on the walls.
He stands with jaguar-headed cane in hand,
brings out honey in small ceramic jars
and begins to talk in cultivated tones.
I find he's travelled half the globe,
lived in Egypt more than twenty years,
roamed all about in Africa and India,
found himself in Europe as tourist guide
for years, chuckling how he made up most of it.
Then he returned, he tells me, to his "little niche".
He takes me to the back to see the garden;
it stretches far along the shining creek,
huge sunflowers in a row of scarlet pots,
a grove of avocado, pawpaw in abundance,
five pools in which sleek tilapia swim,
huge bell cages with blue beady-eyed macaws.
We sit inside. He offers me Havanas
and a clear liqueur he says he brews from rice.
You is a words man. I see you in the paper.
I pass school children in a back street here,
and I wonder if you know the line come in my head:
'in their gambols they sweeten all the day'?
No I do not, but I will surely look it up.
His grand-grand-grand father was a rebel slave.
They hang them up in netting rope
and soak them down in thick molasses
and lef dem to the bird and beast and sun.
On and on the stories go. I wait bemused.
For years back home he joined surveying teams,
found a new route to get up Mount Roraima,
recalled the crooked fleshy trees, the prehistoric rock
and scorpions they said were like no other.
He best remembered how the shifting shapes of clouds
hid them in white shadows, wet them down with mist.

He takes me to the gate and thanks me warmly,
gives me ripe pomegranates in a canvas bag.
After these few hours I am home again.
Expect anything from an ordinary day.

BLESSING FOR A SON

For years courtesies exchanged, I had become
a welcome guest in the old pandit's simple home.
His wife serves me sweetmeats and tea; he speaks
of his people's customs, sings songs and translates
the words. *My wife is soon to bear a child,*
our first-born, I proudly tell them. He smiles
and gazes in my eyes. *I bring you blessings*
for a son, the mangal song the women sing:
"My life is fulfilled, oh friend, today my life is fulfilled.
I served my husband in a golden plate and he ate
with great dignity; in a golden jug
I served him Ganges water which he drank
with great dignity; *I gave him betel leaves*
with cardamon, which he chewed with great dignity;
I prepared his bed with flowers; with great dignity
he slept. Oh friend, today my life is fulfilled."
His wife smiles nearby, shaking her head.

TOWN PLANNER

It makes me think of my own ordinary life:
no wars, near martyrdoms, no arctic adventuring;
my encounters calculated, experience gained with care,
storm warnings noted, meticulously obeyed –
a quiet creek under bamboo sighing, if you like.
A man I met said he fought a tiger
going along a Mazaruni forest trail.

Cat came at him, sprang and clawed him.
May not have been mature. The man survived;
showed me the scars of his adventure.
Important to him, he hadn't much else to say,
he was in town planning all his life – though
nothing wrong with that. He and his quiet family
grew old in peace and the conventions.
Except one other thing out of the blue, he said:
Sometimes I think my body is a dream
someone else is dreaming and soon will wake.
He says it matter of fact, a coffee in his hand.
What lies within the claw-tracks livid on the neck?

PLANTING

After December rain, the planting of rice:
girl in a red skirt shies the rice seed
until the cool of evening. Waiting,
a boy joins her under a rising moon,
offers her a sweet – suck slowly, girl –
throws the rice with her until darkness
claims them in its embrace.

A MORNING FISHING WITH AUBREY WILLIAMS IN THE LAMA CONSERVANCY

Casting in the rose-lit water, he had luck,
but the brilliance of the fish he caught,
rainbow colours of the lukanani,
faded in the bottom of the boat.
Death put out the gleaming on the hook.
He shakes his head, *Just so, just so.*
He grips my arm hard, points down.
Look, the heaven-colour in my mind,

it shines with such inspired beauty;
I land it on the canvas dead!

RAM

A lifetime ago, I noticed Ram grafting lemons
in deep shade below our big samaan tree,
deep shade, cool as water, out of the blazing sun.
I asked him what of all things in the world
he liked to do, thinking he might say,
Grafting lemons, since he did that so well,
his fingers green and dexterous.
But no, he said, it was milking the cows he loved.
Another morning I went to watch him in his yard,
barnyard smelling of old grass and fresh manure,
and I remember the milk spurts ringing in the pail
and the clear bubbles in the rising milk.
He tugged the teats rhythmically, but very hard.
I thought the cow might kick him in his face,
but it stood still and was easy in contentment.
At intervals, they return to me these marvellous
fragments, shining clear as the bright wings
of a flying bird, and they fill my mind with love.

BOY AT PLAY AMONG GOATS

Are not goats stubborn and unschoolable?
How account for the joy of this small boy
who herds them by the busy public road.
I slow the car to watch. He guides the troop
with whistles, and flicks their flanks lightly
with a green and gentle switch, running beside
them barefoot and deft. Not flustered at all,
he has them do his bidding. Some prance but

none get out of line. This boy, light on his feet,
skipping by their side, adroitly turns them
into a field of sweet grass, dances among them,
flicks one or two in play, their coats glossy.
In his harsh world, I think he must love them.
I have not made this routine drive for nothing.

IN INCOME TAX ONE MORNING

I was in the Inland Revenue office
waiting to sort out a tax return.
The place had a bad reputation –
delay, incompetence, bullying, corruption.
I could see a young man at his desk
dealing with people. I watched carefully.
An old Indian woman was called –
white sari, white hair tied with white,
looked frightened, took a long time to get up.
The young man in crisp blue shirt and tie
came round to help, pulled out the chair for her.
She took out some papers from an old envelope;
hands shaking badly, she presented them.
The young man studied them as she explained.
Mother, I heard him say, *don't bother yourself.*
I going solve everything, ease your mind.
Have you seen fear go out of a face?
It is a lovely thing, eyes suddenly calm.
She didn't thank, she blessed him.
He took her to the door with that smile.
Go safe now, he said. You too, young man, go safe.

GIRL IN A RED DRESS

Slow music playing in the smoky room,
she comes in from a mist of rain,
girl in red-brocaded dress, slender
but big-breasted, beautiful; she looks
prepared to party. Young men rush around
to help; old men hurt their yearning hearts.
She puts a hand to her flushed face, dismayed.
I thought this was the place they told me. I'm
so embarrassed. Certainly she need not be;
wherever she finds herself will be the party.

THOUGHTS AT A FUNERAL

Early in the century, he cut cane;
later, for thirty years, boiled cane juice
into liquid sugar – an important skill
in the old Antigua sugar factory plant.
I knew him in his retirement;
thirty years he worked for the family,
cut the grass, cleaned the drains,
trimmed the trees and bougainvillea hedges,
repaired the damages of home,
hard-working in his daily tasks.
I do not know what family he had,
what wives he might have loved and lost,
what children he begat and cared.
When he retired from his retirement job
a nephew helped him build a home,
a single room where curtains made the spaces,
bright and well-kept near the shining sea.
Lamplight gave him golden light to see
and barrelled water to wash and drink and clean.
Church work was his life every day.

He loved cricket – his other God was Viv.
Most nights he played at dominoes,
a few old friends as decent-old as he.

How measure praise for a man's whole life?
The six old men who bore his casket in and out
the little, well-attended church he served,
blessed by the wind breathing in old trees,
blessed by the sea within our hearing,
the six of them in suits, the cloth worn
threadbare shining, all six of them –
and not for show – tough old faces creased with hurt,
their eyes were streaming tears as they walked
their old companion to his resting place.

HANGED BY THE NECK

Driving near the city centre,
you can see the death house,
a wooden turret higher than the rest.
There hasn't been a hanging
for decades at the Camp Street jail;
still, cars slow down take a look.
Why is there always a light there,
cold and unnecessary in the day?

THE GRACE OF GOD

Tried snatching a costume bangle
worth nothing in the world,
cornered in the marketplace,
shot dead among sides of beef,
sacks of onions, golden oranges
scattered among trays of broken eggs,

table overturned where he jumped,
young carcass bleeding in the gutter.
Next morning's headline picture
blanked out the spilt guts;
only the eyes open in wonder.

THE BLUE GO-CART

A cruel birth dwarfed him, made his skull
a cavern where winds blew, a little useless man
gaped at on the streets of this indecipherable world.
Only his mother loved him, sang lullabies,
sopped up his dribblings, hugged him to sleep,
She got him a go-cart, a blue and gold wonder
he frolicked in, peddling it furiously,
rounding wild corners, skidding to marvellous stops.
His lips opened wide, his throat made cries of wonder,
strangled, eerie animal cries that made her tears fall.
She begged God not to die before her dwarf-man went.
God declined the plea.
They put him in a home as tenderly as they could,
with charity fed, clothed, cared. Devoted men,
within the rules, warm as they could be,
measured all the pros and cons, then quietly
took away the thing he loved – not done idly,
you appreciate, supervision could not
be guaranteed to watch him ride his blue steed
all the day. Trembling like a dog, for long
he screamed, longer than it takes a heart to
harden, then he was quiet. That became a silence.
He crept within the hollow of his soul,
lived on for fifty years, never made a sound again.

CARTS

Woman pushes a broken child in a cart,
limbs bent all ways and eyes askew;
the woman herself is thin and desperate.
Soon after – God cannot be serious – an old man
passes, tired beyond reckoning, pushing
and pushing a charcoal cart. Nothing protects
them from sun or sorrow. Such encounters
in one disturbing hour! How can my good fate
afflict me so? It makes me want to shout and throw
my wealth in fury at them. The privileges
of life haunt me, yet I will do nothing.
If I changed my life completely, what good
would that do? The age-old justification
relieves me. But this brutal hour chanced upon
has brought a sort of death to me.

THE MATCHBOX

A small girl, smaller than her age in years,
eyes astonished at the window ablaze,
the star-strewn tree, gifts glittering, haul of toys,
dolls so beautiful, dressed in lovely lace,
heaven-fall of pleasure, moves her hand,
touches the cold and bitter glass. In the other,
a little box is clutched – matchbox painted red
her mother made for her, tied with golden thread
to make it special. It is what she has
and she'll get nothing more except this visit
to the shining windows in the night.

Now beneath our tree, full garlanded and lit,
the grandchildren play in tangled toyland glory,
be-ribboned merchandise stuffed in Santa socks,

their shining eyes darting here and there –
what they love best they hardly know,
happy in the rubbish of bright wrappings,
discarded boxes – *What else, what else to open?*
On this enchanted day, what else, what else to see?
Faded picture of a solemn girl, matchbox –
you can just see the golden thread –
held tight tight tight against her breast,
preserved against all fading Christmases, long ago.

THE WINTRY ROAD

(For Barbara Callender)

The family should prepare – come soon.
And so the sons and daughters came.
In bitter cold the roads are white,
they gleam like bone in winter light,
low horizon sun displays
bare, black-clawed silent trees.
Underfoot stone struck by boot
hard as chilled antarctic ice;
bells ring silver in the frozen air,
plead to save her in our chapel prayer.

So far from the hot-dust, donkey roads in Industry,
where, young, she walked to sell in morning markets,
weary hours in the brazen sun. She alone at work
for them – rent, food, clothes and books – for fatherless
years, counting the long years until they got the education
for which she yearned. On her deathbed now, from near
and far they gather and mourn, to thank and honour
she who created them and built good lives around
her sacrifice, families flourishing as she grew old.

Now snow hangs in the trees like dressings,
an extraordinary weight of silence
on the wintry road to her last resting place.
Ah what reaches the heart from the far stars,
to remind them forever of roughened hands
and tired eyes, night after night, when alone
she kept them safe from peril.

III

WILD HORSES

She remembers wild horses in the morning,
slim child, walking miles to school.
She remembers early light above the cane field,
what the light does in the morning.
She walks between them on the stony path,
coats burnished by the rising sun.
One wilder than the rest rises up,
stamps his metalled hooves down hard.
She fears them, fears him most of all,
passes them – no other path to take.
What fearsome thoughts possess their turning heads?
She passes them but does not run.
They toss their heads, their eyes are bright.

She dreams their dancing steps,
their glaring eyes bigger than the stars of morning.
Weeks go by; she walks by them in peace,
the demons faded in her mind.
She thinks they greet her, ducking down their heads.
Now she lingers before she passes on,
moves among them, feels their trembling,
their coats ablaze with morning light.
She dares to face their shining eyes,
feel their power with her touch.

One morning they were gone for good
an empty path, an emptiness.
All her life she remembers.
Who would not be a tamer of wild horses?

THE STRUGGLE

Dark night on the river, water agleam,
moon climbing the storm-black stairs of heaven,
her sudden shout: *Got a tiger on the line,*
big big one, cannot handle, help me here!
But it is yours, you caught it good and strong.
You will not own it if you bring it in with help.
She doesn't answer; she struggles in the river,
knee-deep in moon-water churning,
the tiger pulling her this way and that,
shoulder joint wrenched out of line,
her cry says the pain must be intense.
Remorseful, I go to help her. *No no no no,*
I've got it. The fight goes on and on
and the rod bends to breaking,
but she knows the exact time to relax it.
Gradually she beats the great fish on the line;
strong and dangerous, but it lost to her.
She brings it thrashing on the spit of sand,
hand-palm blister-bloody at the grip.
Moon was higher now, great tiger fish gleaming,
thumping at her feet, standing skin-soaked,
gloriously small and pretty. I go to hug her.
Sorry, are you hurt, my love?
No you were right, of course. Why did I ask?
I think she's thinking of the long long years.
I know the look. Her eyes are bright with victory.

35TH ANNIVERSARY

I found my wife secretly crying.
What had happened, what sadness had come
upon her? Not long before I'd embraced
her, said how much I loved her. *Life is good;*

you make it good, my love. Talked about our
children's children for a while and she smiled,
squeezed my hand by the kitchen door. *Join me
in the garden when you're done; there's a poem
I want to read to you*. She was late coming
to me, said, *I cannot bear the thought,
I grow cold as death, I cannot bear the thought
there will come a day…*
I held her close, close as I could.

REMINDER

In the time before hint of morning light,
I cannot find sleep in deepest silence;
stirring of a leaf is loud, pale owl-flutter,
whisper of wings somewhere out of sight.
On the veranda the orchids shine,
garden's well-remembered fragrance in the air.
I am looking at the strewn and random stars,
breathing a soft wind off the sea.
Choking sorrow comes over me.
I cannot explain the sadness, the tears.
No complaints, the world is a good place;
there is love and delight in my home.
I am expecting great personal success.
I go back in where I cannot count the stars.

GIFTS

I was coming home from the office;
it had been quite a good day –
finished a paper on markets overseas,
selling sacks of speciality muscovado
in the islands – good profit margin;

decided to bring home gifts for my wife,
not a birthday, not an anniversary,
just a sudden thought: why not?
I love her. She is good to me every day.
A simple dark-blue ceramic bowl,
red anthurium lilies in an earthen pot,
a wrap of green cloth with silver threads;
I loved this one, imagining it around her.
All this may seem extravagant, so many
sudden gifts, a whim. But what's
proportionate in the measurement of love?
I ran upstairs to bring them to her,
and she was astonished and hugged me
warm and close. No, *You shouldn't have.*
No, *What is this? The cost, why now?*
No explanation. She used the gifts right there:
red lilies near the place we always sit,
threw the green wrap around her neck
twirled to show me how lovely she found it.
Joyously my gifts were gifted back to me.

HOW HANDSOME YOU LOOK!

Age fetters as surely as iron cuffs, hog-ties
the arms, legs, sinews to a felon's walk –
this slow decline from supple youth, light of foot,
turning on a penny, ardent every move
in course of games and love. Straight grows crooked
into hunch, light entering eyes grows dull,
every inch a hero becomes a joke. Who then
prays for more of time's dreadful work?
A mind lit by lightning and the world it still
can savour: birds over the shining river,
radiant in their homing flight; this stranger
with a tale to tell – talks wildly all the night;

growing a good crop of garden vegetables;
and the woman I have loved so many years –
her smile delights me. She trims my hair, says,
How handsome you look! Who would not miss
the children laughing as they rush towards your arms?
Add it all up, it's life; we cling to it
despite the body finished by the years.

THE CASE AGAINST SLEEP

I wake from sleep in the afternoon and think
what a waste it's been to miss the rain
leaving gleaming pools and the man selling
green coconuts and, of all things, bubble gum.
I could have asked him why and heard the story
of a life. I'd missed the shapes of clouds –
they will never come again like that –
and somewhere far a star exploding,
and my shining grandson, Jacob,
whom they hushed, told I was sleeping.
I will not see him today, his eyes dark
and beautiful. Full of new words and abilities.

EVENING WALK

Houses of God, four in a stately row,
Mosque, Jehovah, Temple and the Risen Christ;
dilapidated buildings spaced with empty lots,
chaos of vines, weeds and wild-wind flowers;
girl by a standpipe, singing sweet Hallelujah,
moves back her hair with languid grace.
Long avenue past green playing fields,
old solitary man, pipe drooping in his mouth,
sits watching boys in a football game,

boisterous and golden in the setting sun.
A sudden darkening and a storm of wind,
cannon fire far away, getting closer.
Thank God, I think, weather not war.
Have to hurry now past the lily pond –
red blossoms floating on green umbrella leaves –
past Brutus's workshop where my car gets fixed.
See a scurry of ants and stop to take a look.
Run, now under big pearls of silver rain,
stumble on the driveway home, on my knees,
handkerchief's beautiful bloodied silk.

LIFE GOES OFF IN ALL DIRECTIONS

Last night, bathed in the wind off the moon,
my wife brought glasses of chilled white wine
to the orchid house. We laughed,
exchanging stories about the grandchildren,
every day blossoming in love and promise.
Now, up early, computing letters –
Water Board about wrong-read meters,
beloved sister healing from surgery,
poet who astonishes and hurts me,
dear friend about the art of batting,
breathless phone call from St. Petersburg –
excitement at the Hermitage I will never know.
Front gate rattles, old man selling plantains.
Dog barks loud. I shout down: *Don't want any*.
He walks on, right arm severed at the shoulder.
Later, I ask my wife if we needed plantains.

THE BILLION THINGS OF LIFE

I imagine I would remember a knife at the throat,
wall of drowning brown water, in tsunami-struck
Sri Lanka; pearl at my beloved's ear; red Essequiban
dawns, Rilke's panther pacing with misted, desperate eyes –
but why do I recall, sixty years gone by,
in corner of a nursing home, three old ladies
sitting huddled with knitting in their hands?

WHILE GLACIERS MELT

First thing I read this morning
how unfathomable glaciers melt
and tigers in India near extinction.
Dawn sun blesses the rain-fresh grass,
parrots caterwaul in the almond tree.
My wife puts out marigolds in vases.
I go about the business of the day.
I eat a delicious cheese omelette.
A friend calls me about the football,
and did I know the Rolling Stones'
manager was a Bavarian aristocrat?
Young man visits – we knew him from
swaddling clothes days – showing us
phone-photos of his baby son.
Where I go to pay the water rates,
an old lady carefully unties a handkerchief of coins.
Walking in the garden, counting hibiscus,
I realise how much my gait has changed;
I once was lithe and never stumbled.
I take down Keats' letters from a shelf.
I have heard that John Milton,
ere he wrote his Answer to Salmasius,
for one whole month rolled himself

for three whole hours in a certain meadow
where the mark of his nose
at equidistances is still shown.
Night comes again,
a blackbird with golden eyes.
When it is over, it will be over.

THE THOUSANDTH GLORY

(For Philip O'Meara)

Well, my friend, you've lived so long a life,
what among the thousand glories of your days
was most beautiful to your yearning inner eye,
so keyed to find a heaven in all things?

Three little sparrows fat as dimpled cherubs,
floating in a birdbath made of olden iron.
Each weighed four-tenths of a single ounce,
no more than the talons of a hawk.

Not floating, surely? Swimming, dipping wings?

No floating on three big autumnal leaves,
light tiny saucers from the lilac tree,
sharing happiness in their joyous game,
side by side as dancers might gyrate,
and so they balanced and did not sink.
Suddenly another miracle came. The sun
emerged and through the leaves above
threw gold-dappled patterns on the dancing birds
whose wings, flirting with the shining surface,
sent chips of diamond flashing in the air.
You asked. Yes, that for sure was beauty
I won't forget; it overturned my heart.

THROWING A HUMMINGBIRD

My study window overlooks the garden,
a branch of bougainvillea trails upwards –
within my reach this last month.
This morning, a hummingbird tangled in it,
fluttered and fell onto the desk,
stunned and still. I seized it quick.
I swear I felt its beating heart,
saw closer than I ever will again
the soft green feathers at its breast.
Threw that green-gold shred of light
soaring flashing heavenwards again.
This happened once in eighty years.
These lines make no particular point.
Just if any reader sees them,
they might suggest that everything
is miracle and mystery all one's life.

WEST INDIES HAVE JUST WON THE CRICKET

There's the always extraordinary moment
my wife is pleased with the new orchids;
there are cakes and meat patties for tea
in the white chairs by the mossy fountain,
the sky stained with astonishing colours;
a new book on Walcott is in the post;
rain sweetens the earth, good indeed for the newly-
planted herbs; my son is coming with his friends
and their laughter, and I will discuss his plans
stretching far into the future and give my opinion;
my taxes are done and I have enough money;
an old friend sends a bottle of good wine,
to toast a success in his life;
and West Indies have just won the cricket!

THE SEA-CAPTAIN VISITS

For forty years we've sat out here,
on the verandah looking out to the sea,
entertained the best of friends,
seen ten thousand sunsets blaze
above the sea-defying wall.
Sea-captain Horace Sally comes
every time he is in port.
Decades have dignified his figure,
salted his abundant beard.
Now our talk grows very troubled.
My friends, the ocean's rising fast.
No no, the reports say inches.
Believe me, friends, it heaves beneath me
bigger, heavier. Brimmer, fiercer
towering waves I never saw.
The immense worldwide swell and tumult
will sweep whole island-worlds away.
Silence as he shakes his head.
He does not wish to catch our eye.
We contemplate our garden's beauty;
sweet sea-winds touch the flowers,
hibiscus and blood-red crown of thorns,
gold-threaded orchids delicate as lace.
We drink a rum for old times' sake.

RAGE

A high sea is raging at the wall,
water and black clouds everywhere,
green sails the old trees in our garden.
That high sea raging in our ears
will make tossed blossoms of our homes.
Will they go down in decades or in years?
We'd hoped generations would pass,

this peace and beauty would last a century,
passed on beyond our yearly reckonings,
many old endings and new entrances,
grandchildren and their children's children
to watch the crescent moon in cloud,
as now we watch it fleeing in this storm.
We will the sea be beaten back as long it has been,
the earth protected and habitations safe,
forever white egrets lighting on the lawn
at dawn amid the dew-fresh marigolds.
After one time it is another.
Unspoken fear and anger in our eyes,
on the veranda sharing wine together,
ocean spray crashing through the rain;
can we survive the night at least?

ON AN OLD FRIEND SUNK IN DEMENTIA

Old friend mumbles about the ripeness of red
mangoes; eyes are vacant when I hold his hand.
I remember how alert he was, mind alight,
talk spiced with a hundred speculations.
What is he thinking now, I wonder,
as when I go he half-raises a salute.

I take my own route to the madhouse door.
Halfway through an ordinary day,
I set out to write down every single thing
I have done or sensed, not leaving out teeth brushed,
time spent on the toilet seat; scattered dreams
trespassing on my conscious mind; first sight
of morning sun, birdsong in the air,
men with fishing nets passing on the road;
breakfast details – eggs and cheese and cherries –
what's in the newspapers and on the BBC;

computer checked and the first phone calls;
lizards scuttling on the high white wall –
but you see what I am getting at:
an exact record of every single thing the brain
processes – and then I think about my haircut –
a big event, complicated goings-on –
scissors, razor, shaped eyebrows, barber conversation.
After three hours careful application,
I had forty pages of foolscap paper filled.
Got to 9.00 a.m. and knew, of course,
infinities of data escaped recording. I was lost.
Memory is mostly silence, else we all go mad.

MAKING SENSE OF THINGS

Night clothes sour, drenched with sweat,
bitter blasts of cold shake my frame.
I dream of locusts in a field of corn,
a bird singing on a branch of blossom,
of walking on paths of glittering glass,
orchids overhanging a green lake,
spikes of iron in a marble ruin.
Nothing makes sense, in and out of sleep.
Wolves with blue eyes howl in my head.
Days ago I was playing tennis, banking money,
friends visited, slapping fives and tens.
In my hollow skull a golden bell
clangs on a mountain far away.
I try counting the thousand things that happen
in a single moment of my life;
I consider being born a century hence.
My heart stops thudding grievously. I am well.
I can imagine necklaces and Orion.

MOON IN OLD AGE

A night full of beauty, moon ascending
in a scarf of cloud, throwing nets of light
to catch the huge whale of the river. Came here
in a lonely boat, an old man with pain
in the gut, fearing this may mean death.
It is the same beauty so many years ago
when I sat with my sweet love, and we smiled,
drew close and said we would never forget.

DAWN BREAKING ON THE RIVER

I want to find true words, the truest words,
to say what I see and think when seeing.
I go out before dawn on the great river;
wind is sharp; I am waiting on the sun,
the biggest stars still seen in the far quarter
fading as light invades the sky.
Blaze of gold now on the horizon;
lights fire in the clouds. I can see the birds
flying, flashing over the wind-rippled water,
tangles of silk mist caught in the green trees.
I'd bite my lip until the blood comes
tasting in my mouth if only I could make
these images in song or paint or better words
than these, distil them to perfection, so I
could share them like fruit or cake or wine
when next I see my dearest friends.
How fortunate I can at least write this,
as the sun rises in its vast river glory.

CUTTING ORANGES

Every religious Sunday morning
I cut oranges for our breakfast meal –
baked bread, coffee, the cut oranges.
Wife and I sit talking daily life,
children, what matters in the world.
I perform the cutting of oranges:
first peel, in spirals, the mottled skin –
takes time, takes great attention –
not peeled in a single spiralling,
bad things are bound to happen.
Then precisely cut the naked pieces –
check two-thirds remaining sliver –
oblong core where all the seeds are left,
served on a blue, bird-patterned platter,
the same for all our married years;
each sweet piece sucked to pith.
Would have to be a deathbed case
not to cut the Sunday oranges.
In high Himalayan snows, I read,
monks save the world by murmuring
their single prayer of prayers,
twisting worn beads on a silver cord.

THE ALMOND TREE

Beneath this old beloved tree I sit and rest,
golden leaves falling from its shadowed green,
beautiful shining in the setting sun.
I am alone; tea brewed perfectly, salmon cakes
crisply made an hour past and pepper-seasoned
to my taste. A book I've brought with me.
The wind is sweet and cool; aloft the branches sway.
I do not see how I could be more content.

The book is Pascal. He tells me a little earth
is thrown upon one's head and that's the end forever,
thud of dirt thrown in an open grave.

My wife, granddaughter to look after,
joins me late. Smiling in the telling,
The bright child, she said as her hair was combed,
'You're shining me, Grandma.' Yes, my shining one,
that's so lovely. She sits beside me now;
thirty years we've spent such afternoons together;
the woodpecker chatters; hawks hang in the air;
hummingbirds gleam amidst the orchid vines.
Almond tree has grown from when she planted it;
green canopy now gives us this shadowed ease,
embraced by growing beauty through the years.
Night comes on, dousing red embers in the sky;
the white hare chases down the sloping field of heaven;
the spaces between the stars do not frighten me.

SHOPPING

My wife is Friday shopping late.
I ask her to get Lindt Swiss chocolates,
smoked oysters – we are out of them.
Park the car and decide to wait.
Blue sky at evening breaks a rainbow into halves;
dead leaves are falling from a dying tree
between the grocery and a hardware store.
An old man in dirty singlet, white stubbled
cheeks, eyes a-swim in blood, chewing his gums,
bends collecting at the rubbish dump: bottles,
half-toothless garden rake, tattered bunch
of artificial roses, unopened tin of food.
This he holds up – cannot believe – bags it in a hurry.
I go to help wheel out the shopping cart.
Will he or I face death with calmer heart?

MASTERPIECE

Today mid-morning in Mary's kitchen,
all the ingredients: branch of red cherries,
lettuce on a plate, wedge of yellow cheese,
shoulder of lamb, cutting board with bread,
jug of cold water, and lady in a flowered apron;
all it needs now is Matisse.

FLOWERS FOR THE HOME

Another time I watched her cutting flowers,
how she leaned low sometimes with the grace
women have. She looked so young. Watched
how she looked for the best, not clipping
in bunches, looked at each hibiscus, rose,
sunflower, orchid, matching in her mind
vases for our breakfast room.

EPIPHANY

By Hedley Simpson's house in Sheriff Street,
a cut coconut gleams green and white in a drain
where mottled frogs flop from leaf to lily leaf.
Years ago, when I was a boy, I recall seeing
mother-of-pearl on a beach and thought the world
revealed in it, nothing more real in the universe.
Years later a Jesuit priest told me that
Thomas Merton wrote in his daily journal
of gold cheese on a white plate, a goose feather
floating in a mountain pool – God's beauty in those
ordinary things. Now this sliced coconut in the gutter
summons me in old age to see everything afresh.

TIGER FLOWERS

What was it like, Granddad, when you were little?
Ah, the world was greener then, and I was closer to the stars.
I walked barefoot in mud puddles. I had a pet goat;
he nibbled cauliflowers. Tell me, tell me about the goat?
Yes, he had a silken coat, so beautiful, the colour of sun
and fierce tiger lilies. Tiger lilies? What are those, Granddad?
The flowers tigers eat; it makes them good. We had them
in this garden to keep us safe from all the tigers,
long ago. Let's go pick some now, Granddad. Quick!
Make Mama, Dada safe. Eyes solemn, he tugs
my hand. I smile, hug him hard.

JACOB

Today he wants to know about whales.
He saw a Great Blue on a TV programme,
their hearts as big as limousines.
In his third year of life's astonishments,
wonder is everything. What is the circling moon,
flowers, the quickest bird, why hummingbird?
What is that on my desk? *It's my Kaieteur stone.*
Easy replying when what is there is simply there.
What is blood, how rain falls from heaven
are possible to explain. The darkness of night,
swords and castles, how fires burn – easy.
Beloved grandson, you will not stop there long.
It won't be only how planes stay in the sky,
how we breathe air into our beating hearts,
it will get harder. I must prepare myself.
It will not be long before you want to learn
what is fear and pain and cruelty and age.
Why death will be the hardest one of all –
to tell the truth but soothe his heart.

Still hard, but first I'll chose to tell you
of love and joy and tenderness and pity,
the great things, the beauty of the world.

ZOEY SLEEPING

She breathes lightly as silvery webs are weaved.
Time thicker than a mountain passes slowly,
baby-watched granddaughter in the depth of night.
Outside the darkened room, whispers in the trees,
stars, tips of arrows aimed beyond the Milky Way.
Cradled in the universe's impossible terrain,
I struggle to describe the meaning in these hours,
she under the protection of my arms. All I know
is she is nothing more than herself, and much
more than what is known so far. For two hours
while she slept in peace, I was astonished, prayed
and praised her complex beauty, my mind wandering
down a thousand paths, thinking of what might last
through all eternity. She stirs and sighs; I bend
to see her breathe. There must be something
instilled in everything that transfigures and brings love
and joy into life like hers. My random mind blanks
and overflows a hundred times. She wakes.
It no longer matters what I think.

WALL OF GOLD

My sleep is inhabited by an emperor –
Aurelius – he stands tall, directing the traffic
of the world, sending riverboats full of casks
of wine to French encampments, bidding
forests cut to build temples and academies.
He has gentle eyes, he gives strong guidance,

specifies the design of a set of silver goblets,
sets aside a place where eagles can't be hunted,
talks to old men to comfort them,
talks to young boys to urge them on.
Heaven overarching us all is bleak.
Life is good. Come on, come on.
Ants swarm, spots of black on a gold wall.

THE SILVER BROOCH

My wife does not catch me looking at her;
she is combing out her hair, pinning it with
a silver brooch, putting on lipstick, bougainvillea red;
she appraises herself, she seems half-satisfied.
I think she should stop now, she is beautiful enough.
She pins the brooch another way. I see what she means.
Every moment of life I love her more. I go away
without her seeing me, to wait until she is perfection.

GOING AWAY

Where my life has been most sweetly centred,
this garden is wildfire, sometimes hot and gold,
ripe-sun-lit blaze of flowers, sky aflame.
This evening colour calmed to mists of lightest blue;
I sit alone in this green and quiet place.
Over the seawall, far-out grey clouds
merge with silver blush-smudged sea,
white-winged birds, pale shadows,
weave patterns in the darkening air.
Tomorrow I leave here for a while.
Fine drops of rain begin to fall. I won't move
until the hummingbirds appear,
bright jewels gleaming in the dying light,

branch of crystals shaking in the gloom.
When will I return? These days nothing is certain.

RIVER DANCER

Night is cold; she has gone a while.
The white smoke of age gets in my eyes,
but still I see her as she always was,
young and fearless and I in love with her.
Dirt poor made childhood bare as bone,
made her strong. She enriched me.
I see her brushing her long long hair –
all these years I have seen that –
and tears come in my eyes, so young again,
calling out to me her joy in creation:
a sudden decoration of orchids on the old tree,
a bank of vegetables and table greens.
See where I've got the sweet herbs now.

When I had cancer, fifty days hard treatment,
half my strength gone, not much left to love,
every day, every single day, she was by my side.
There is a picture of her dancing by the river,
turning to smile at me, hair swaying past her waist.

NEW POEMS

1: ANNALS

KINDERGARTEN

Wet windy afternoon. My first school sports
a race for six-year-olds. Desperate to win,
ahead, struggling – mother, father supporting,
waving by the side – at the very end I slip,
sprawl headlong, no hope of winning, but on the ground
made one last lunge for the line, stretched out in the mud.
I cried so hard a special prize was found for me;
I knew it meant nothing, despite my parents' hugs.

Surgery scheduled tomorrow, right maxillary sinus
filled with hyper-intense material bulging in the cavity;
cancer in the growing mass seems likely –
facial bone may have to be reconstructed.
The many threats involved have been unfolded –
the anaesthesia danger for a heart now eighty-two.
Well, I've come a long way; it's been very good.
I've known heartbreak more than match for this.

NORTH STAR

Mornings, I tiptoed in my parent's bedroom,
but mostly found them in bed awake.
My mother snuggled me, my father smiled;
felt loved, the day well begun.
Once I entered they were still asleep,
barely dawn. Went out on their balcony,
looked up at the Abbey on the hill.
In the clear morning, the Northern Star
was a thorn of light balanced on the mountain;
it never moved at all, my father told me.
Light swerves through the universe, he said,
deflected by great suns and invisible material.
Ever since, the stars have danced for me

in heaven's wonder, except the Northern Star
which shines above the Abbey Hill unchanging.
When I see it, through all my life since then,
I think of love which does not change or bend.

THE FLIGHT OF BIRDS

I recall when I was very young
my old nanny would point at birds
and tell me men and animals left marks,
but birds left no footprints in the air.
Now I am so ancient, I look up
at birds flying in the heavens
and think how they leave no footprints,
how they step hard nowhere,
but know exactly where to go.

STAR TAUGHT

My father liked to show me stars
on clear nights, pointed out Orion,
his golden belt with sharpened sword,
silver cluster of the Pleiades safe forever
from the Boethian hunter; and, from the veranda
of my parents' room, the North Star shining
over Mount St. Benedict. Pictures in the night
he drew for me of glory, bravery and myth,
the abiding beauty of the steadfast star.

STARRY NIGHT

When I was little, no more than ten years old,
Van Gogh's huge and blazing stars alarmed me.

Stars were not like that, golden tips of pins,
yet there they were, Van Gogh's stars in books,
mysteriously wrong, beautiful beyond compare,
dripping fire in blue-black skies at night,
bowls of flame spilled across the heavens,
incandescent globes – not little gleams of light
unworthy to illuminate God's unending universe.
In so much else Van Gogh's world prevailed –
cypresses making seawaves leap upon the air,
gash and scar of blackbirds in spreading fields of green,
sun-saturated meadows below a piercing blue,
shivering of silver gleams on harbour waves,
crooked chairs more real than my own furniture.
His golden cornfields filled my dreams at night,
purple valleys and shining immortal hills,
but always the stars, the gold and blaze of comets
splashing a sacred sky I thought the most about.
I saw life should be lived like that, in discontent
with given worlds of comfortable perception,
not satisfied with pallid daily replicas
of what we can conceive to be, if we look deep,
see things as no one else ever dares to see.

COLOUR OF TEARS

My sweet sister, in her childhood, asked our mother
the colour of the tears she sometimes shed.
Different every one, our mother said. *Depends,*
my little one, on what tears are for: joy and sadness,
fear and love and laughter – all the colours
of the rainbow flow – blue and grey and red
and dancing silver. I remember the tender look of love.
May yours dance with silver always. She hugged
and hugged my little sister.
My own tears gleaming see-through colour mostly,

spring-clear as water in a Mazaruni creek.
But many tears are grey with bitterness and grief,
or whitened tears misted in ancient eyes,
or hate-red in armed and angered men.
I read how an Emperor's sacred tears for soft young
Tai Chen the Beautiful were amethystine blue.
A philosopher once set himself to harvest tears
a thousand acolytes let fall in vials thumbnail small
and delicate. They vanished utterly as soon as they
were shed, not like blood which can easily be collected.

BARRACUDAS

In Antigua, on that lovely coast, I remember
I was ten years old, one night my father
showed me the smudged white carpet
of the Milky Way, told me tales of how
it came to be. Later, he took me fishing
in the night beyond the glittering reef,
let me help him pull in two fierce and gleaming
barracudas. The heroes in the stars looked down.
Home I raced into my mother's arms;
she smelled of blossom and sea-wind.
She laughed and hugged me out of breath.

CLIMBING

When I was a daring boy
trying things on the bike
rushing into the waves
my mother hugged me hard,
said, *Look before you leap*.
My father taught me about climbing trees:
Test the branches are strong enough –

experiment on one, holding another.
Slip – you can still hold on.
He showed me how in the big orange tree.
I think of them now so long ago.
Always had fall-back.

ADVICE

The greatest batsman who ever lived –
white Headley – they say had poor eyesight.
Fierce concentration more than made up for that.
Other greatest batsman of them all –
black Bradman – he had the same intensity;
he walked to wicket seeing nothing
but the score he compelled himself to make –
he would have gone straight past his beloved.
And the great Federer – watch him well,
apart from the grace, the lovely ease of shot,
look how he concentrates, only the game in his eyes.
I was a boy just learning, about twelve or so,
my father of the far-grey eyes, my calm wise father –
always remember him telling me,
Son, play the game as if every single point in the match
is the turning point, and that goes for life as well.

MOUNT PELÉE

Old beloved aunt – I was the son she never had –
adored by her, she made me feel supreme;
she knew I would be a wonder of the ages.
I never ventured anything she did not bless.
She said the chaplet beads and rocked
in her chair of wickerwork and oak,
with prayers for victories in all I did.

Her gnarled and ancient hands, rosary-entwined,
told stories too by lamplight before sleep,
of how she lived in years gone by, how once
strange sunsets gleamed in the skies
of Port of Spain for months, a blaze of crimson,
as if the sailing clouds were stained with blood.
She told me of the great volcano that blazed the doom
of forty thousand souls in Martinique's St. Pierre; how
the smoke of death arose and hung a shroud around the sun
for months on end. It was so beautiful that arching sky
of blood, she never saw red sunsets and did not think of death.
Seventy years have flown. My great-aunt's chaplet
still winds protection round my adult years
and blood-red sunsets signify the sword of death.

BLUE BIRD

In a workshop in Tunapuna, Constantine's
shop – like the cricketer – my father was getting
a cabinet repaired. I saw a young man shaping
a bird, handling what looked like blue mud
coming to life under his fingers, the bird with wings
outstretched. He smoothed and smoothed, perfection
it seemed to me, countable blue feathers, a white
white beak, a dust of yellow at the throat. My father
let us stay until the bird seemed ready to fly.

KISKADEE

He did not think for a moment he might be accurate
at such a distance – crude sling-shot, the yellow bird far,
singing in upper branches of a breadfruit tree.
He aimed, yes – so he meant it – but what were the chances?
He would surely miss the mark. The thought of killing

beauty never entered his head. When it was
on the ground, perhaps stunned only, its feathers
ruffling in the wind, he very gently picked it up,
felt its softness, its brown and yellow feathers,
but one eye was cut, head crushed and bloody.
It had been singing its song, slung stone had
cut the singing short, the singing which he loved.
What he aimed at was not that, of course,
what he hoped for was the perfect shot,
not thinking what perfection might achieve.
Covered the bird with dirt, never would boast
of his amazing feat, never used a catapult again,
aware of what the bird's song asked.
Sorry sorry sorry forever, he replied.

SPILT MILK

On an Antiguan road, metal containers full of milk
fell off a lorry in front of us on the way to Shirley Heights.
It was just beyond a church built in green stone,
women in white dresses with black bibles going in.
My father stopped, our car wheels wet with milk.
No one was hurt. The driver scratched his head.
"Good thing it wasn't honey," my father said.
The driver liked that; they laughed together.
I am clear in my mind about this
when so much else has faded.

A HOUSE BURNS TO THE GROUND

I was watching a hawk chased by small birds
when a friend came running and excited.
Let's go, let's go, big house on fire!
When we got there it was blazing,
poor people's house I could see –

weeds, thorns, glass bottles in the front yard.
Water had given out in the fire tender;
the house well ablaze, crackling
flower of flames beautiful in the sky.
Not much saved, not much to save,
except lives, of course – a crowd of those.
There had been screaming, but all were saved,
thank God. An old lady raised her arms, stumbled
but I managed to help her. A girl in a blue shawl
looked on, tears in her eyes for what she had lost.
Returned home as if nothing happened;
the small birds still chasing the hawk.

FATHER EAGLE AND THE CARNIVAL

Small white wooden church in Tunapuna –
I remember the Masses there, the hellfire sermons.
Father Eagle we called him, huge-beaked man,
grey cassock always patched to make a point.
Craggy-faced, his arms aloft to summon angels,
belabour souls on the verge of being lost –
our little village was a lewd bad place.
How he thundered, smashed shut the doors of heaven,
beat down the congregation with his awful voice.
One time, though, I saw him full abashed.
Necklace of pearls at her slender throat,
reddest of red dresses devilishly swinging,
a woman swept up the aisle to receive Communion.
I swear I saw his big hand all a-tremble
as he delivered up the Host to Carnival.

MIDNIGHT MASS

Dreams of lost Decembers wake me and I shake
with grief. A cold wind from the mountain,
the monks' chant at midnight and I stayed long
after to kiss a girl. Rain was coming down,
the last stars of morning had gone when we
parted. I could not sleep for thinking of her.

STONE

One Carmody Road, St. Augustine Trinidad –
home to my sweet mother, my dear father.
I, among my sisters, remember only love,
fairness, strong advice, laughter, good example.
Airy bedrooms full of sun and books,
orchard "up the land", fruit eaten straight from trees,
great dining room where bustling preparations
anticipated feasts and parties. We were confident
in ourselves, parents proud of us. Their bedroom
balcony, open to the wind, looked up to the high abbey
of Mount St. Benedict, above the Northern Star,
steady as our lives, where we gathered,
tousled out of sleep on Sunday mornings,
talked about our lives and planned our grace-filled days.

Fifty years have gone. I visit our old home to see
a gravel pit. Apartments will be built, I'm told,
everything levelled bare – no remnant left.
One great samaan tree still stands; it overhung
the servants quarters where we often played.
Under its spreading shade, mother grew red anthuriums.
Stones lie in piles, clutter from the excavation.
Amidst that disarray of rock I search for memory.
One stone – crescent-shaped, heavy, black and silver-veined –
I keep, weave stories round, pass on.

CAMBRIDGE

Played tennis hard – winter didn't stop me,
hit with gloves on the frozen courts –
got my summer blue. My tutor advised
Stretch the muscles of the mind. Read Kant,
and over sherry we discussed the Tudors.
I cycled through winter winds to early morning lectures,
John Saltmarsh on the wool trade in the 13th century,
striding around the lecture stage without a note,
explaining great beauty in an ordinary world.
I hungered for the days to come, the hours
filled with gifts and testimonies the years redeem.
One weekend Pandit Nehru visited –
how nervously he touched the red rose at his breast,
told us, sadly, how millions died for freedom.
Sunday, Dylan Thomas staggered from a pub.
We sniggered as he fell about the podium,
then read "Fern Hill". I still recall the silence.
In the gold-lit shadows of the College chapel,
I hear still a young girl singing softly,
a young man playing the flute.

CUTTING CANE

Once I cut cane, Caribbean's most bitter occupation.
"See how it's done" – the corporate plan.
To command is to know what is commanded,
as if history's blood could practise to be shed.
The driver showed me how; it looked easy.
Not long from a Cambridge junior common room,
hardly started, my pale skin suffered in the sun,
fit enough for Wimbledon, but definitely not this.
In half an hour, pouring sweat and sick,
panicked, embarrassed, I signalled my despair.

The driver sternly hushed the laughter of the gang.
"Look, boss-man, this is chupidness for true.
I going tell Manager you could cut cane very good.
Come rest." He laughed and waved the others on.

SMALL JOURNEY OF THE SOUL

Walked out of the forest to find a far horizon,
the heavens afire in the morning sun;
a humpbacked whale of shining black
heaves out of the flat, far-bright savannah.
Started a long walk along a mossy stream;
the grass shining after days of rain.
Disappeared in the land, I had brought no companion,
on all sides no human habitation,
not even a plane overhead.
Now a strange impulse: if I strip to nakedness
and bury everything behind a rock,
I will find myself, this one and only time,
utterly freed of all connection with what
man has made against oblivion, the single
sign of what man is or does contained
in myself alone. Until now, ashamed
of this absurd conceit, I've never told
this tale of pure abandonment of what
we take for granted, even in the solitary
hours of our lives. I saw a fox quick darting
between bushes; hawks balanced in the air
exactly poised. I threw jade stones gleaming
in the little stream. I shouted loud and threw
arms in the air. It's sixty years, so why tell it now,
this small journey of the soul?

THE DHOTI

Late one night, back road in Berbice, flat tire
in days when flat meant flat. No spare. Walked for
help, in truth a little worried – wind and rain,
remote – thin moon made it more dramatic.
Came upon this little house on stilts, paraffin
lamp flickering at the window. Soaked to the skin
they let me in. Old man greeted me, his back
badly bent, upswept white moustache, courtesy
in his blue-grey eyes. His wife was there and others
came to see – sons and daughters, other children too.
How could this place hold so many? Could they get
a message sent for me? No phone of course,
but two miles away a place "have communication".
Sent one boy bicycling in the rain-swept night
to pass the message which I wrote out for him.
Meanwhile, the wife brought me a huge bowl
of fish broth, peppery hot. The old man said,
You got to dry your skin, can't stay like that,
From an ancient gold-handled chest of drawers
he took this gleaming white dhoti
for me to wear until they dried my clothes.
Stripped, he showed me how to dress myself. I made
some limber moves; he smiled. My grand re-entrance
went down very well. Old lady put her hand
up to her mouth, boys clapped and laughed, but best of all,
girl pretty as a flower fled giggling from the room.

PROVIDENCE FISH MARKET

Weekend sport, nice buzz from El Dorado,
DJ's sharp music, slow dancing, building to jump-up.
Cry go up, *Providence for the fresh fish catch*!
Boats just coming in morning light, fish jumping

in the briny, heaved-out baskets; serious buyers going
boat to boat. We had the cash not to bother bargaining.
Good mood all about, big catch that morning.
They were cutting up big fish – smell of salt
and sweat and guts and gasoline. We bought
snapper ice-packed in a box. Claim go up
he could cook red snapper nice, fry it up
in cutlets with tarragon butter sauce.
Don't let that time, don't let that life be over.

MIDNIGHT HERON

River party, fun, tall tales and drink.
After midnight puttering outboard takes us home,
young Amerindian boatman piloting for safety.
Blue mist rising in the moonlit trees, river glittering
full of stars. Suddenly, a mighty bird emerges,
gleaming yellow-eyed, mightier than any heron
we'd ever seen before. We point and shout
with wonder. It flies, huge wings extended along
the side of us – shines white as with an inner light.
Great heron flies ahead and circles back,
keeps close company as we point and shout –
beauty we cannot begin to find a model for.
Boatman, cowering, speeds and slows the boat,
trembling, stricken to his knees, lashing
with a boat-hook when the bird comes close.
Lands us at our river-home, offers not a word,
leaves the boat unanchored, stumbles to his room.
Great bird swoops around us one last time,
white wings beating slowly in the night.
Silence seized us as it disappeared,
dark darker – when it went more night.

LOVE-BROKEN

Love-broken, my dear friend, miserable
as a sick dog in our midst, growled of betrayal
one instant; another, keening of beauty
he had lost, vowed he would never love again.
Books were better, doing good deeds – an
old story told a million times. We laughed
and embraced him in his vow, when this girl
with olive eyes entranced him.

LOSER

When I played tennis in my youth
I had a friend who was good but never won.
He trained an hour more than anyone,
he followed the manuals perfectly,
his technique was superb, well-coordinated,
strong, quick – you could not fault
his preparation, his application and ambition,
but in the big matches he failed.
There must be a lesson, I thought.
Perhaps too much thought of victory
tripped his body up, all-out to win distracting
the zest and joy of playing, targeting the prize
and not performance. When he got older
it was different; he didn't worry about winning
so much, his skills become more beautiful to see.
But then his body was diminished,
and still he did not win the games.

PERFECT FORM

Too much to drink at the Club one afternoon,
carousing with the boys late into the night;
when they all left I stayed, quietly drinking
some more alone. Went down at last to sit
by the squash courts, switched on the lights –
no one about – stretched out on a bench, thought about life:
good things, bad things, getting along quite well.
After a while, walked on the court, took off my shoes,
ran around like so many times, but no racket, no ball,
an imaginary game, gliding about making shots
corner to corner, bent low, leaped high, my form perfect –
match against the furies winning points.
Then something caught my eye high up behind me;
a girl was sitting where the spectators go, her hair
caught in a red ribbon. I didn't know her, thought her pretty,
went on playing corner to corner. Thought she might clap –
I would have bowed – but she got up, left
in the middle of a rally. Soon I stopped playing,
my mind much clearer. We met once or twice after that –
never really got to know each other.

KANHAI AT BOURDA, 1956

Before I saw him, first I heard him,
heard the silence, looked around bewildered –
pavilion bar where friends and I were drinking –
not much happening on the field of play:
BG batting v Barbados in that year's inter-colony.
Barbados bowling, one wicket down, slow scoring,
pitch dead. Bar was where it was best to be.
Shout went up, another wicket gone.
Now nothing was the same, scene transformed

from practice pitch to where the Gods perform;
silenced audience moving quickly to the front.
He springs down the pavilion steps in a stride or two,
tossing the bat from hand to hand, raising and swinging
to loosen up his shoulders; he looked so young for fame
to mark him – from Berbice his wondrous talent
was reported, breaking the stranglehold of class and race –
lithe, handsome peoples' man blazing in the sun.
He gave the waiting bowler the honour of a glance
as he took his perfect stance. Drama gripped the crowd's
collective heart. I sat beside one Club veteran
gripping the balustrade in front us hard.
You see how not a sound? They bowing down to he;
I only see that once when great Headley came to bat.

With passion that night I wrote my father,
Today I saw the greatest batsman I will ever see.
The years have flown; I've never seen a better,
that first golden drive flashing past the cover fielders.

AN ANCIENT EYE

We had come from inspecting first-crop cane,
walking across a field in Mon Repos
towards the public road, a friend and I,
where we had left the parked Land Rover,
talking of yields and ratooning cycles,
the farmer's eternal need to cut his harvest costs.
Sun was going down in a golden sky,
becoming a deeper gold, quick quick,
and then the cloudy sky ripened into red,
deep red for not more than a single minute,
but in that minute a bull across the field
stood out black silhouette on red.
It stopped us in our tracks. I remember
seeing that same ox, he said, ten thousand

years ago, not different, against that same
blood-red sky. I could see my friend was serious
and caught his eye and nodded.

RIVER CONVERSATION

Big rain brought a heavy river down
past churning Mazaruni rapids, a killing
turbulence glistening with flame. In the dark
Bartica rum shop, loud words: two Amerindian
youths stood up, looked fiercely into each
other's souls; sudden crash of knives in fists
on table. Room stopped and sang with silence.
Who knows how long they looked, then took their hands
away as one, knives now with no killing work
to do. Whole room breathed; talk began again.
Our old boat captain shook his head. "They rash.
Death don't bother them." Outside,
wind blew the river into silver edges.

RIVERMAN

Captain, he die this morning, early.
Only last week he wave me breezy.
Man, he smiling, strong, indestructible.
Sad, sad – Da Silva   no better river man than he,
knew every Essequibo rock and fathom,
thick white hair, features carve deep deep;
lifetime laughter crease his weathered face,
handsome in his age, eyes always dancing,
life-pitcher full of wine drink deep.
Lean, fit from sea-work most his life.
He love the sea when waves grow white with rage,
retired to the great river long his home,
settled with one woman. He was good to she.

I said I loved to hear him talk his adventures,
all the racing rapids of the Mazaruni,
abundant tales, taller than bamboo.
No, he laughed, every word is true.
There are monsters in the deep called death;
forests hide moon-witches all about, my brother.
Yes, water-moomahs take men to their bridal beds.
Cap challenge fate. Gods are mischief-makers –
they like to test us, sometimes let us win.
Where Essequibo springs from earth, they come
down from heaven wrapped in shawls of stars,
sit among us, tell us how the world began –
vanish from us when the clouds first blush.
Will miss his goodwill and his fellowship –
ranks high among all men I ever knew.
Life good, he said. Best gift I ever had
the look of him I swam to save from drowning.

COMMUTE

Travelling in one of the Bell family boats,
hired to go up from Roed-en-Rust to Bartica
on the great river, running back in the afternoon –
a simple commute for those who do it –
farmers, salesmen, civil servants, priests.
Sat near a man wearing a red bandana,
machete at the ready, no doubt for cutting plantains,
and a beautiful Indian girl with a sad face.
Passed the wild banks, saw macaws and herons,
sundrops gleaming in the wind-thrown spray.
Thought of this between Spadina and Bathurst Central Line,
blank unEssequibean tunnel flashing by.
But in the carriage a man goes up and down dancing a jig,
a woman's laughing with a big basket of colourful clothes,
and on the wall a marvellous poem by Derek Walcott.

THE FOX

I can't get out of my head the black eyes
of a skinned fox. Thirty years have passed.
Walking by the jasper-floored river,
water clear, I saw foxes run so lithe,
shining quickness, red diamonds in the sun.
That night, at the village shop, buying beer,
saw behind the shopman, on his wall, dead
black eyes – a fox he'd caught and skinned. It was
for sale, he said – the dull skin, the dead black eyes.

GRIEVANCE

Gone to the village office to settle some complaint,
I saw three young men in pouring salt-wind rain,
behind the broken-down Presbyterian Church,
best clothes soaking on their skins, heads bowed,
hands clasped, huddled round a fresh rose-scattered grave.
Two hugged the other, held him upright, close.
Didn't bother to make my grievance known.

OLD MAN LIT BY A PARAFFIN LAMP

I'd expect to remember long-gone beauty,
the sweetest moments with my love,
marvellous events going down in history –
memory's organized to keep these bright. So why
does the old man in a battered hat qualify?
Sixty years ago I passed him in his cart,
bony donkey barely able to pull his load,
the old man hunched, coconuts piled behind him,
lit by one of those old-time paraffin lamps.
He looked up as we passed, face carved in shadows.

Seemed to me his eyes saw his death.
Sixty years later I am still seeing that.

DONKEY RIDE

On the public road near Skeldon, I begged a lift
on a donkey cart. I didn't need it. I was walking idly,
going to tennis with the manager. I scrambled
on the cart and we clattered on our dusty way,
bags of tangerine and squash around me.
Cartman talked of his hard times, arm muscles
tense cords, tired eyes. Twenty years older than
he should look. He barely made a living
selling vegetables, fruit, cows' milk, duck eggs,
charcoal when he could. Big family, so it was
a regular struggle. His wife worked hard, too,
making do, and a son would soon be cutting cane.
I said that wasn't the right idea at all. He should
get all his children taught – though I well knew
the business I was in could not survive for long
without cane-cutting carrying on. I told him,
Make any sacrifice. Go home right now and
tell your wife your son will go back to school.
Go tell him. He seemed to hear what
I was saying. When I got off he chopped
a coconut and I drank deep and thanked him.
Later, many times I made sure to see him.
He sent the boy to school. He is doing well.
Now and then we should take a ride to nowhere.

RESPECT

The old foundry served the sugar mills
in my time when I was a director there;

the young manager never forgot I appointed him –
his big chance in life – again and again he reminded me.
When his grandmother died, he arranged the ceremonies –
she had brought him up, done everything for him,
taught him respect. He invited me to attend,
tears in his eyes. All day she'd sewn clothes,
given him bread and school until she could no longer.
He ordered the best casket; foundry men in black
carried her reverently in slow military step.
He asked me to walk with him to the grave.
It mattered more than most ceremonies I've attended.

PEARL OF WISDOM

On public holidays I loved the swift goat races
on the track laid out with Government money,
wind off the sea flapping the joyful flags.
Crowds came to hail, carouse and bet;
vendors, stirring pots of fish and savoury meats,
shout their wares and ladle helpings out –
the knowledgeable eager with race advice and tips.
Bright-harnessed animals, their agile runners
all alert, jockey at the starting line.
Small, neat-footed Pearl of Wisdom
is my favourite. I place my bet on him.
Started well, but the big ones ran him down.
That's one he used to win, old-timers said,
now age hobbles his last fifty yards or so.
Champions are worth one thousand US dollars
at their peak, but when at last they fade,
what happens then? Do not ask, my friend.
Rictus of a smile prepared, I await the standing joke:
Why you think goat curry so popular down here?

SANTA ROSA

I'd given the children books, golden-apple drink;
bantered with the nuns; bathed in sweet
root-stained water; walked through forest trails
on small adventures, creek gleaming in late golden light;
marbleu dipped and flashed blue masterpiece of flight.
Stopped where bamboos made green shade,
talked about the good days full of beauty.
One of us played guitar and some sang.
I was quiet, knowing I would not forget
the guitar's strum and a girl's voice gentle:
Who owns a leaf floating in the wind?
Candle in the daylight, candle in the dark;
I was young. Something shattered in my heart.

THEY HIDE DOWN IN THE LILY ROOT

Birdsong beginning and a half-moon in the sky,
early dawn in this silver world of water,
kingfishers flying just above the surface.
His figure slight, white wisps of hair, a kindly look,
old Narine takes me out to catch fish –
gleaming lukanani river-rainbows here.
He paddles the boat through reeds and lily-pads.
I know nothing of the art of fishing,
just want to say I've caught these treasures,
brought them back to cook for breakfast.
I cast as he directs in all the likely places,
green haunts and deep tacouba water.
I cast and cast again without success.
It isn't luck; I haven't got the art.
The sun comes up and burns the morning mist.
After a good hour I laugh at my attempts
and hand the sterile rod to old Narine
who caught ten thousand fish before my birth.

For sure he casts and strikes at once
and three times more without a miss.
I sigh and smile and give his hand a shake.
At least I'll bring them breakfast, thanks to you.
He nods. *They hide down in the lily root.*
Next time, trust God, you will catch them good.
He has calm unaccusing eyes, no scorn.
Wind ripples the water of this lovely glade,
spurwings jump from lilies, leaf to leaf.
Forty years have fled; I never tried again.

APPOINTMENTS

Half an hour between appointments,
I went in the Cathedral to pray, light a candle,
put some coins in St. Anthony's box.
A solitary man caught my eye, carrying flowers,
going from altar to altar, hunched, old,
a ragged shawl hid his face. He bowed as he placed
the flowers carefully, raised his hands
coming to the Virgin Mary. I went up near to him.
He wasn't old at all; his lustrous eyes
looked like the pictures of Christ you see.
It was very strange going to my next appointment.

HOW MY SON WAS BORN

(*My wife remembers*)

Seven weeks too early, two weeks more to put
on the weight for safety that he needed;
suddenly he is there, insisting to be born.
Terrible pain. No no, too soon, not now;
trauma will be too much for him.
"Prepare quick, we must take him out."

Desperate tension, young nurse hugging me,
steel tray falls – a brute and cruel sound.
I feel a barrel rolling, tumbling out.
He came in bursts of helpless pain,
my emptying womb, my rising fear.
Forceps in hand, the doctor caught him,
so small, crumpled, no hair, no nails.
What's in this world that will defend him?
Agony feeling he'll die, he's not alive.
He does not cry. No breath, he has no breath.
Nor can I breathe. Try, try, they tap him.
He will not cry. I see his face forever.
My son he will not try. They take him,
guard him from my sight. He will not cry.
I tell him with all my fervent heart,
Try, my son, try try. He cries, he begins to cry.

REWARD

He had asked to see me in my big office,
the old man, white beard neatly trimmed.
From its green velvet pouch, he put
the gold sovereign reverently in my hand.
It felt quite heavy in my palm. In formal
ceremony it had been given him by
a governor for loyalty in long service
to the Crown. He wanted me to have it –
a reward for getting his only grandson
work in the office, where he had to wear
a tie. I would have liked to take the golden
gift – unusual souvenir – and for its
beauty too, but thought better of it. Smiled,
a generous "no", under the eye of eternity which
belongs to all. When he left the old man bowed
to me and I with some awkwardness bowed back.

CLOSING THE OLD DISTILLERY

I decided to close the old Port Mourant distillery;
no longer profitable; wooden stills had had their day.
Went to tell the staff there, mostly old men.
How you could do this? Rum here still the best.
A secret in the wood does give the rum a taste.
It was true. Looking back, those ancient stills were good;
they made that famous rum people still remember.
But nothing to be done; the bottom line was red.
Leaving the meeting at the old distillery
we didn't look at each other. Perhaps we all knew
the foolishness men do they often know is foolishness.
I remember walking past a pasture with a few cows
peaceful in the shadow of a spreading samaan tree.
Three of the cows were shitting at the same time.
I remember that exactly: cows shitting
that day we closed the old distillery.

SPIDERS

Solemnly invited to a seance, a few of us,
all prominent citizens, attended. Preacher
from Trinidad, all-white robe; red cord tied
the waist; gaunt, long-locksed, looked the part
of Jesus. After lentil soup and spicy loaves of bread,
he spoke quietly for an hour about evil; spiders of evil
were crawling in the world; obsessed by spiders –
it was his only metaphor – spiders of hate and crime
and jealousy and greed. I wondered what the point
was at the end. Supposed to be a big conversion.
A friend said, *Ian, let's go get a rum*.

RATOON

Hadn't been in Berbice for years, before this visit.
Saw the stained glass windows in the Church
of the Ascension, got some old books I'd been told about,
took a drink with Father Montrose, asked a favour:
Ride me around places I used to know so well, sugar estates
where I worked fifty years ago. Passed some fields
near newly metalled roads, tough tangled bushes
in hard earth, scrub and weeds. Fields looked familiar,
yet how could this be so? Amidst the rough growth
waving in the wind, some old ratoon stalks
growing sweetly green. He must have seen my face,
my friend, the priest. *What's wrong?* he said, looking
in my eyes. Nothing I could do but smile in sudden shock.
I shared with him; he hugged my shoulders.
I knew those fields for sure. Proof of work well done,
the good of everyone increased:
tall, well-tended cane, silvery arrows in the wind.

RADIANT WINDOWS

A car drive took us to New Amsterdam,
to the beautiful windows of the Church
of the Ascension, we'd heard needed restoring –
the golden robes of saints, bright wings of angels.
Share the bread of life, the priest with the black,
spade beard, shining eyes, said when we took Communion.
Afterwards, seated at his presbytery table,
he gave us glasses of red wine, a simple meal –
cooked it himself with herbs from his garden.
Why did that seem to add to everything?
He clasped our hands, said we were kindness itself.
Coming home in the passenger seat I noticed everything:
a rainbow far out over the ocean,

rain sweeping in, the clouds low and dark,
a stretch of miles, the evening a red fire,
herons in the field, fading as shadows fall.
Night came fast, thin-nailed curve of moon.
All the way back, patches of fireflies.
Earth stars, my small son said, earth stars.
We never stopped talking of the radiant windows;
it was one of the very good days of life.

UNWRITTEN DIARY

Between the pages of a diary left unwritten,
decades old, I find such keepsakes as stamps
I must have thought were valuable, Bourda Test card,
TIGER scrawled in capitals, photograph of a farewell:
I count the faces – five died out of ten. Who will be next?
Note to myself I must have forgotten:
Check the children's vaccination (exclamation mark);
a page of cash transactions no longer making sense;
list of books for ordering, urgently, it says:
Frost's *Collected Poems*, Wodehouse's *Gardens of the World*
for Mary. Yes, I remember how she hugged me;
sister's postcard from Hodges Bay Antigua,
telling me the laughing gulls have come again,
how my father used to say, *It's Ian's birthday then*;
advertisement for an antique Irish pendant
a spark with jewels – but I never bought it;
invitation to an evening of dub poetry – I recall it –
there were drums, Ras Michael's eyes were bright;
wine list with the Madeira twice underlined,
from Miles – his word was law on horses, jazz and drink;
notes on code of the Samurai, the Stoic's creed
linked to lines I wrote and kept the scrap;
New Yorker cover – a splendour of peacocks;
most of all empty pages. What happened to my life?
Yes, notes from Mary with simple lines of love.

THE SILK GLOVE

Past eighty, it's time to make a reckoning:
getting rid of old stuff, clearing out a life.
In an old suitcase treasures and emblems
not worth keeping. Life is not a museum.
Found a silk glove, yellowing, still fits;
haven't thought of it more than half a lifetime.
Strange to think a doctor ordered it;
fingers on one hand were festering, a mess.
Not fungal, she said; *you have sadness in your life;*
nothing to be done, no ointments, salves.
Gradually it will heal. All will be well,
as gradually your life is healed, *by time and love.*
I've seen such things before. I wore the silk glove
nearly one whole year; it became a part of me,
an elegance. People found it strange;
I thought up explanations. Gradually, indeed,
my hand was healed by work and love, the glove
discarded. So why did I keep it, so long
not even thought of? Now what to do with it?

2: LIVES

WHY PETER FORSYTH SPOKE FROM THE SKY

In the Camp Street prison he found a way
to scale the roof-top where he balanced,
angry, half-naked, to the world:
Evry day dey come fo a confession. Don know
a ting dey talkin bout. Wouldn let me sleep,
even close me eye. Force dis soul drink me piss for tea.
Balls get beat til I faint away. Try get a frien to see dat ban.
Get a match, light mattress fire. Dey hose it out
then put water down me throat.
Ise INNOCENT INNOCENT INNOCENT
God betray me. INNOCENT, Ise INNOCENT!
Hundreds gathered for the show. Armed guards
came up to get him down. He tried to jump;
they caught him just in time. How events rush and go.
He was a headline. I don't recall what happened after that.

LAW AND ORDER

Chief Justice of the bedraggled streets,
withered body of dainty bones,
he rode his bicycle around the town
equipped with bells and whistles,
with noticeboards depicting famous crimes
and criminals, and a little coffin showing skulls.
Now and then he would dismount
and give a graphic picture show.
Shackled prisoners stumble in a row;
he puts on black hat and tattered gown
and with stately dignity announces
the guilty verdict. Nothing else would do.
Death by strangulation rope he called it.
Set up his cardboard gallows
to show the fate of executed men.

With grimacing and lolling tongue,
staring eyes to put fear in children,
he flung his hanged head to and fro.
Public nuisance you might have thought, but no,
some always gathered to see the show.
They said he was a judge gone crazy.
I doubt it, but you never know.

CONVERSATION ON EASTER MONDAY

Rain-washed sky, good wind blowing along the coast,
joyful festival of kites aloft, thousands, thousands
of bright kites flying, swift-winged birds swerving with them,
the spirits of everyone soaring skywards, dash and dot
of brilliant colour, a thousand lines lifting up to heaven,
resurrection singing in the Easter wind, a blazoning
of pennants high and wide streaming, flashing
in the sun, pointillist carpeting for miles and miles.

Father and his son come walking by; he hands the boy
the humming twine. *What happen if I loose? It gone.*
The box kite half-lifts him off his feet. *Straight to heaven
it will go*. Even so, stumbling, he holds it tight.
Feels the singing of its soul.

SKIPPER OF STONES

Came across this frail boy skipping stones,
must have been about twelve years old,
hands of swift grace, whip-cast at the end.
What an art! Seven, eight times they skipped.
How beautifully the stones skim and skip
as if his fingers tell the stone the way.
I asked to try a few; it didn't work.

Stones skipped once, twice, perhaps, and sank
like dull iron – even the best stones he gave me.
Show me, I said, but he couldn't teach the art,
just threw marvellously on the bright water;
didn't know what practice is. On days
of mirror calm he skipped a stone twelve times.
Turned his eyes to me, knew he could do more
if he found the perfect stone and perfect water.

POTS

He tried spinning pots for a living, not well-
made pots, lopsided in different ways, splotches,
dribbles of bright colour down one side not the other,
patterning not at all well done. We gave him a chance.
He delivered the pots slowly; trial and error
clearly shaped them, some really badly botched,
always strong though, balanced OK. One day
we looked at each other; something in the pots
we loved. Flowers looked good, rightly placed
in those strong, haphazard pots. He got better
and better making them, got more and more
business, corporate commissions, took on assistants.
He thanked us for giving him a start, proudly gave us
big discounts. How could we tell him flowers
lived best for us in those beautiful first pots.

AN OLD WOMAN SMOKING A PIPE

Looking forward to the rum punch barbecue on Sunday,
the car parked a short walk from the house,
I hear noise and laughter. It will be good to relax
after a hard week. Barman will have my favourite drink
already poured; jokes and conversation. Welcome the good life.

I pass a woman squatting on a stone. Old, black, withered,
one eye a lump of flesh, she is not seeking alms,
just smoking a black-bowl pipe, removing it only
to spit and cough and spit. Red-rose dress
ragged and smelling, she settles on her haunches,
as if forever. I catch her terrifying eye and wonder
what's the purpose in her great sun's orbit,
the heavens' curve. Whole worlds unreasonably deflected,
I turn away and slightly change my course.

PLAYGROUND

For three days the big tree in the park
was out of bounds; children couldn't go there
to play on swings. A vagrant in stinking clothes
had made his home under a brilliant red sheet.
Outside, he'd built a fire, boiled water for eggs,
roasted fish on a stick, seemed quite happy
and well-behaved. Of course they came for him,
made things neat again under the big tree.

THE JOB

Bearded, old clothes, bandaged leg, black sandals,
every day I passed him at the gate of Sacred Heart;
rattan chair, jute sacking, enamel bowl for coins
clanged in. Laughing boys he'd swing at with a stick.
Some said he was a fraud, did good business.
He looked haggard and sick to me. He was there
every day, like a job. Begging shouldn't be a job.

THE BOWL OF SOUP

My monthly visit to the orphanage coincides
with his arrival, deposited today, a five-year old.
The administrator speaks about his case: Years of abuse
his mother suffered, butchered by his father in his view.
"Blood over everything, including him". No old aunties
to the rescue. What is to be done, what is to be done?
Little stick-limbed creature, he is eating soup
in a corner; he is looking deep in the bowl.

AT THE PARLOUR

I should know, she said, I should know
the clean smell of him. Fifty years I washed
his clothes, used the special soap he liked.
Once I used a different brand; he knew –
he didn't blame, but his kind eyes looked at me
and I knew, never again. He liked to come across me
ironing his clothes; he would watch a while,
give me a lover's pinch. When he was younger,
played games in the sun, I took the sweat
right out of his clothes, made sure he was always
well turned out. I should know the smell anywhere.
My son was a comfort to me, always a comfort.
I should know he was a good man. I loved him.
I did everything for him. I always washed his clothes.
No, I'm not going to distress, but I should know...

WITH HER SON IN PARADISE

Morning's first silver coming in the sky,
early walkers found her, woman in rags,
one swollen leg bandaged, seeping blood,

sprawled by St. George's entrance at the back,
her long long hair spreading silver grey.
Summoned, bent as a broken beanpole,
the Cathedral deacon nodded; he knew her,
knew her only son drowned playing, laughing,
sporting in a trench one Sunday morning.
She went mad, never right again. Sang in the choir
sweet-sweet, he said. God gave her that voice,
blessed her. He wouldn't forget she. Now
in Paradise, she and she son. Can't forget she son.

NO

Near me in the cancer room, needles bandaged
to his wrists, tubes snaking under the blue gown,
frail old man wheeled in began to scream,
low and hoarse, *No no no no no no no no*,
on and on. Black eyes in face papery and white,
stern and distant, but out the open mouth,
hollow, dribbling, came *No no no no no no no.*
No more of this! Put an end to me! No no, no no,
this agony cannot be. That I have come to this.

Young woman comes at last. She comforts him
most tenderly. *Papa, Papa, be at rest. I am here.*
I love you, be at rest, Papa, Papa be at peace.
She strokes his thin hair, white as winding sheet,
but it starts again. *No no no no no no no.*
It hardly can be borne. She turns to tell the room,
He's ninety, he should be at rest. We love him.
Oh my God, no no no no no no, please no no no no.

OLD BOY PASSES

A call at midnight: *The old man pass. You*
could come tek he? They had finished with him,
put him on one side, their business tidied up;
it was for us to deal with his hereafter.
Wrapped in cotton white as ice, white binding
cords parcelling the body, white gowned attendant
unwrapping him, whiteness of death beneath
the Indian colour; poor bare remnant on display.
Of what's not there there's utter silence – what
life the old boy led. His centre was himself
alone. He sought the pleasures of the day;
the years would take care of themselves. A hundred
jobs he had throughout the land; with high
intelligence he did them well, but never
saved a cent, nor owned a house, nor had a bank
account – what people called collateral.
His desires needed no collateral,
yet those in life he never cared for saw
that he was blessed with care. The strength of
family prevailed; their piety protected him.
The benefits of respect and home were his.
Now their distress is natural, the children's
bitterness real and heavy. He should not
have ended up like this. But there is another
view to take. *So what?* I hear the old boy say,
I wasn't there. I didn't know why you
taking things so hard – my last times. What I
received you gave me – all the peace I know.
Like all of us he passed this way.

SISYPHUS

Passed a building-site, corner of Robb and Camp,
stopped in traffic, watched workmen glistening in the sun.
One pushed a wheelbarrow filled with stones
one spot to another on that site. A while later, returning,
he was still at work, pushing the wheelbarrow
from one spot to the other, filling it with stones,
emptying it the other side, one spot to another
of equal unimportance. I stopped mesmerised.
He was talking to no one. Was it a punishment?
Watched for quite a while in the hot sun;
the two piles of stone didn't change much.
I wanted to enquire what was going on,
but you can't ask about everything that happens in life.
Last time I looked the stones were still in two piles,
the wheelbarrow upturned near one of them.

GRIBBA

Old and bent by his work, he never missed a day,
they said. Thirty years stacking sugar bags
high as his head takes strength. I was the soft
white boy giving out prizes for tasks
I could never do. I reward him now by remembering.
I see his eyes undimmed, fearing no one,
feel his iron-strong handshake,
do not forget this measurement of worth.

THE STAND PIPE

Taking a walk on the seawall for the freshness,
dawn a golden goblet shattering in the clouds,
opening my lungs to the sea wind, took a detour

through Ogle Village. I've known so well
the little shops and houses. At one stand pipe
a young woman bathes her child; he squirms and shouts
in the coldness of the water; she slaps him gently,
kisses him, roughly towels him and lifts him to the sun.
I was glad I passed that way in Ogle Village;
there was something good about it, there was love.
I entered home, heart and body full of joy.
The gardener was standing at the gushing stand pipe,
our dog being washed and cleaned with Ivory soap.
I was unsettled by the conjunction.
A big bunch of cut flowers lay on the steps.
I hesitated, took them inside, thinking of many things.
What was a good thing, no longer seemed so good.

THE PERMANENCE OF INDIVIDUAL JOY

When the rains came storming out of grey heavens,
sweeping silver curtains lashing the land hard,
rushing in the choked alleyways, making torrents
of the streets, beating down gardens of flowers,
covering the green earth thick with gutter-muck,
swirling in bottom-houses around belongings,
cascading in the marketplaces, destroying stalls
piled with goods, threatening the livelihood of people;
bringing down trees, telephone poles, lights,
stalling cars everywhere. Then everyone complained
endlessly about the damage done: produce destroyed,
priceless merchandise ruined, wet reams of cloth,
stained brocade, warehouses yards-deep in the deluge,
imported spices, ham, brandy floating back out to a sea.
In outlying districts cattle drowned, food plots inundated,
roads scoured into gravel pits. Uninsured millions
lost and soiled. Oh the voracious bankrupting flood!

THEY BLAMED THE CITY COUNCIL

Hollow men on plump behinds, the Mayor
a man of importance, the useless yawning
bureaucrats dreaming of visas, writing their reports –
This month nothing happened; money is requested –
and the Government, of course, in whose hands
our lives are not spared. Silted-up trenches, fallen culverts,
blocked canals, no power to drive drainage-pumps,
broken-down kokers rusting in the sea-wind –
neglect and confusion abroad, each feeding avidly on each.
I too was angry, joined my muted curses to the multitude's
mass accusing, inventing swearwords to suit the new absurdities,
vowed this must have an end, but how, but how?

MEMORY CAUGHT ON A THORN

With a jolt I remembered an old man –
I hadn't thought of him for years and years –
memory's bright cloth caught on a thorn.
Suddenly I see him selling cones,
riding up and down on his bike.
I would go looking especially for the coconut.
He gave good helpings, always shared a laugh.
Loved his cricket – Rohan's cover drive,
Lance bowling his stiletto ball, as he called it.
One day a drunk's truck knocked him flying,
killed him on the spot, amidst his cones.
It was long ago, thirty years at least. Yet I remember.
The evening our hostess served a special sweet –
chocolate fudge with cream of coconut –
I saw him stopping for me, shaping ice cream
on the cone, sharing news from Bourda,
bike bell clanging as he went his way.

THE WIND WILL BLOW A LITTLE SWEETER

(For Edward and Audrey Glover)

Diplomats come and go like stones
dropped into water lightly;
they scarcely make the smallest mark;
the water surface smooths again,
the wind that brings the bitter rain
does not cease to blow.

But you were not so lightly thrown;
you broke the surface of our world
as a farmer pierces soil to grow green plants
for precious food, or a miner dips his pan
in Mazaruni river depths and brings up gleams
of golden sand, or a teacher opens a child's mind
to poetry's song, and what he does bears fruit forever.

You cared for us and made a difference.
My friends, you were not superficial;
in Guyana you went in deep
and you will be remembered long;
the wind will blow a little sweeter.

ACTS OF KINDNESS

Family visiting, cousins from the old days,
hadn't been back for forty years, refugees
from the bad days of nothing in the shops, fear
of always being below, no future for the children.
They came with gifts, brought back memories.
Then it was bare food my wife didn't have;
now it was a tablecloth wonderfully embroidered
and, for me, bottles of Niagara wine. They were lovely.
We gave them a good time, laughter and memories.

When they left, my wife lamented, *Not enough*.
Next morning I found her in the garden
preparing a big basket of lettuce, fruits, herbs,
bunches of flowers to send where they were staying
in Industry, where they had lived so long ago,
where my wife endured her sad good memories.
I feel better, my wife said. *Kindness filled their lives.*

GIFT WRAPPING

The old Spanish lady
on her feet behind the counter
all day on minimum wage
giftwrapped my orchid;
she took such care
choosing the ribbon of gold,
choosing the tissue of red,
the most important thing
in the world she was doing;
it always will be

JOHN CUT-MAN

For sixty years John Cut-Man has groomed our grass
for a fee. Well-groomed himself, white moustache
neatly cut, he looks more the scholar type,
but never went to school. He's slowed so much
it's sad, but still he comes to us for work.
Even if the grass is low, give him the job to do,
he makes the lawn immaculate. He likes
the praise he gets more than the money, it seems
to me, but that perhaps is sentiment.

THE SHINING BOOTS

A man we trust, who watchmanned our home
for thirty years, faithful beyond compensation,
this morning came to tell us, tears brimming in his eyes –
would not have thought it, the big tough man –
He dead last night, my old father dead.
You see me here, I cry, I never cry before.
All he life he try he best for everyone;
never go to school, anything like that.
Stevedore for thirty years. When strength done,
he try with any little job he could get to do.
He never beat he wife or family, never beat –
talk rough sometimes, true, but never beat.
He protect, he encourage, he really care;
every little thing he really try for me.
When I get this job he lecture me, buy clothes,
shining boots, bright-buckled leather belt,
always check me how I doing, any help I need.
Never even one time anybody ever thank he.
I myself does know I never thank he.
(Softly), *How that could be right*, he said.

IMMIGRANT

Kamran, Persian warrior, comes to fix our pipes,
face grey parchment, hobbling in his gait,
lungs half destroyed, shrapnel in his hip;
he has such kindness in his eyes, forgiveness.
Fixes anything plumbing or electrical.
Summon him any hour day or night –
You are family, you have cared for me.
Takes his time and drinks our cups of tea.
When his jobs are finished they are perfection.

For the Ayatollah he fought Saddam Hossein.

Faith first inspired him, then he was enforced,
wounded half a dozen times, near to death;
gassed, he felt he'd never breathe again.
How he got from there to here, his odyssey,
hardship, mystery, miracle multiplied.
When I deserted they would have killed me sure.
Now in this well-ordered, ordinary land,
he unfolds his tale: village of his youth
so beautiful, remembers farmland in Iran,
rising by his father's side, unforgettable dawns.
Will he go back when all is calm again?
He sighs and smiles and goes about his work.
It never will be for a hundred years;
this is my home now, I will never leave.
Peace, he says, *peace, where there is peace.*

THE RED SERVIETTE

Old man sits at the corner table,
red serviette in his lap,
sipping white wine in a crystal glass,
silky-white hair well-groomed.
Alone, he looks into distances,
sighing sigh after sigh.
I wonder about his story.

JUDGE HIM

He never led good causes, though he followed them.
He did nothing evil, but did not intervene.
He fiercely loved his own; others did not matter.
Animals in misery he shot. One time he asked forgiveness.

PRESENCES

KAIETEUR STONE

The downfall of huge water raises rainbowed
mists high and glorious over the horizontal brim;
small golden frogs hop on the mottled mossy rocks;
I bend low and see their small wet eyes.
One blue stone, exactly oval, lies near their leaping.
Thirty years on my ordinary desk.

VENUS'S GLITTERING CANDLES

I thought I saw candles glittering on the water.
It was Venus casting her gold net with sweetness
in the air past midnight on the Essequibo river.
I saw huge fish surfacing in pools of light;
it might have been a wild hog swimming.
Over my head the forest swaying, creaking
in a big wind, and mind whirling further and further
out to the end of firmament and time, the ancient fabric
of how all things started. I grew dizzy, my mind collapsing
into small concerns like love and the beauty all around,
and the light, the inextinguishable light at the beginning.
Then lamplight, sound of voices, dredges running
down river slow and heavy, interruptions to my mind's
crazed direction; but there again a-dance are Venus's
glittering candles: testimony of nothingness defeated.

BUFFALO POND, RUPUNUNI

Spurwings skim the bright surface here,
Buffalo Pond, most beautiful of places.
Wind blows rain in sweeps of silver,
green lily pads crowd the stretch of water,
white flowers reddened at the heart

in thousands lightly scent the air.
There is no future that is as good as this.

Rain abruptly stops. Blazing azure arc
creates a deeper shade of blue below;
herons, boat-billed, light, black-crowned,
strut sharp-eyed in the shallow reaches;
aeons they have been here patrolling.
Black hawks balance in surrounding trees,
swoop and swerve in fearsome hunting flight;
otters break the surface of shining water
shimmering, playful, sleek.

I wait for dark to hear the late birds sing,
a kindling in the night crackling, star-net
thrown high above the darkening lily-field.

GOLDEN HARVEST

The fields are golden in the sun,
the kendel poles have done their work;
parrots swoop over the fields
in great arcs of flight;
red-winged dragonflies hover
over the silver pools;
herons gulp small mud-frogs.
Cousins from afar are coming to assist –
they are young buffaloes trampling,
scoldings take a small holiday.
Yes, the air is ripe with joy.
The village fathers warn the rumshops,
Leave money in the women's hands.
Girls are eyeing gold bangles,
thinking soon there may be weddings.

HUNTING FOR THE WILD PIGS

Out early to hunt the wild black pigs,
morning's first light barely stains the sky,
mist drifting in the low spots of the forest,
drapes of silver, everything dripping wet and green.
Overnight, heavy rain battering in the dark,
moon in and out of heaped and sailing clouds,
over the great river an unforgettable beauty.
What else can one say of such a night?
Now morning finds us wreathed in mists
of vapour rising round the mighty trunks of trees,
small gold frogs hop in streams of rainwater.
Not much of an adventure, slogging and slipping,
tracks hard to cut, we walked in mud for hours.
Some sun begins to leak through dripping green,
and body steam clings to wretched clothes.
Debris of falling timbers clog and bar the way.
Not a single sign of the wild black pigs
whose fierce, gleaming reputation we craved to see.
Enough. Too weary to take our own long track back,
we cut a new path to the river bank much nearer home,
the swim through gleaming water a sort of happy ending.

A GATHERING OF HAWKS

Grey day, clouds fleeing the wind, small white waves
ruffling the wide water, the great river
preparing for tumult, I watch an extraordinary
gathering of hawks. Four swoop past, then more
arrive, flying above the trees – there must
have been a score – the single-minded power
of their flight gleaming in the silvery light,
then off, dropping to some ordained and secret place.
What rage or danger summoned them, proud, imperial

birds of the tall air? Some instinct old as pyramids?
I would have given gleam of river gold
to see that rare gathering grace one place,
a great tree's branches become their throne,
fierce-eyed, bright-taloned, spreading
their strong wings as one in the wild wind
when the storm came over the great river.

FOREST SONG

Where old trees grow tall, long ago a small
church stood, the ancient riverman assures me;
it had a golden window, he remembers.
I went exploring, cut a path, rotting
smell of purple plums, monkeys roaring in
the treetops. A mile aback I found wooden
shards and lost amidst thick vines and roots one strange
substantial thing – a foot-long, lichen-speckled bell,
angels etched around its inner rim. I knocked
it and sound still came, a ringing from long ago.
Why was it not rescued when all had failed?
I knocked it, and it sang again as it once rang
in the blue air. In the sunless forest I left it there.

THE ORCHID MANTIS

Wind brings scents from the forest
as we pass bruised berries, blossoms
tangled in vines on the green branches,
field of waves tufted with white flowers.
This time I've come to find the creature
a friend told about, somewhere in the dark forest,
feeds on singing crickets, biting them in two:
the orchid mantis fragile as a petal.

BLUE TILES

Walking near the river, stones blue like the sky
underfoot, rough-hewn, half-hidden in the earth,
I look for other signs near the gleaming river.
Nothing, only the blue tiles. A circle it looked like,
red stone at the centre twenty yards in circumference,
a heavenly floor.

COLD

Grey dawn, colours rubbed from the sky;
one cloudless patch where stars glittered like ice.
Walked along a stony path by the river,
the water as icy as the stars. Stepped
on white sand beneath a gnarled tree,
black-branched, dying, hardly a green leaf,
its roots exposed. Silence except for the small
lap of water; cold wind through to the bone.
Jagged moon low in the sky amid cloud,
colder than any moon I'd ever seen. Shivered.
There was beauty in the world but it was hidden;
there were golden suns but it was not their time;
the old tree was a crucifix in the wind;
that was how the black branches grew,
hard nails hammered into the feet of Christ.
That came to me for no reason, except the iron cold.

HALF-WAY TO THE END OF TIME

The small fish gleam, bright life wiggling in the clear water,
caught there when the high water fell, rough rock basin
beneath the evening sky, reflecting piling clouds.
Beyond the sea, emperors bathe their bloodied hands.

When did this begin, what hope is there?
I watch them for a while; they will die.
Carefully I carry them to the lower waves.
Night falls on the vastness where they swim.

STRANGE SKY NEVER SEEN AGAIN IN MY LIFE

Strange sky never seen again in my life,
high white cloud completely covering the sky,
no rain, no wind, sun seeping through like milk,
the river glassy, not a black ripple on it,
colourless mirror reflecting white all day –
white, not a shining white, transparent white.
Once or twice pelted stones. Stillness returned.
Watched for hours, determined to be silent.
Not reading, trying not to think, subsided into stillness
like the water, quieter and quieter. Does death come on
like this – a quietness, no sound, no colour in the mind –
clear mirror of the river, the bread-white sky,
end-images, only whiteness, quietness?

WHITE HUT

White hut on a hill, three boys come leaping down
to the shining river, a man follows slower,
laden with fishing nets, a woman waving.
Easy to notice their faces full of joy.
Back in the big town I haven't smiled in a month.

FOREST SUNSET

We face the wrong way for sunsets on the river.
Dawn, yes, early mornings radiant beyond compare –

immortal paintings – if only I was Turner.
Unseen, the sun drops behind us in the black forest.
To miss no offering from the God of rivers, in his balahoo
lithe Dominique takes us to the great river's heart. We'll see
the sun go down, golden cup pouring into the ancient forest,
sky descending into the river. Dominique rests his oars;
we are quiet. Forest dark slips across the shimmering water;
nightfall quicker than dawn; burst of fireflies as we drift home.

SILVERQUICK

This bird was strange to me, a wayfarer,
black-crowned, grey and white-winged,
gleaming as if it shone, delicate curved bill
piercing rose-ripe mangoes in the tree,
such knowledge and grace in what it did.
I looked the bird up in the handbook:
there it is named ugly banana quit;
there it is beautiful on the green branch,
flying now swift-winged to a flower,
poised in a dance-step to suck honey
from the heart of all the flowers of the world.
Swift, sweet stranger in this sunlit garden,
thought flashes as I look. Call it silverquick.

JOURNEY OF AN ANT

I sat reading in the shadow-dappled garden,
a black ant on the arm of the white chair,
a single ant, quite big, very unusual.
I flick it hard off the chair into the grass.
Wouldn't a man be killed by the flick,
the fall, if everything was in proportion? Not the ant.
Perhaps stunned a little it begins its jittery walk

between the grass-dense undergrowth. Getting up,
I follow it. No ants came to its rescue or in
companionship. It hesitates, if that is the right word
for an ant. Maybe it is thinking, finding its bearings.
It sets off quite fast in the thick grass until it comes
to a gutter which halts it – not for long –
it finds a piece of grillwork over the running water,
crosses there safely, full of purpose. I follow it
a long way – bed of earth, roadway, more grass,
under a parked car, concrete patch, along the wall
of our home, not stopping. Sun or shadow makes
no difference to the ant; it just progresses, zig-zagging a bit,
basically going in one direction. But when
it labours over the top of a stone and it does not go around it,
pauses to examine a shred of blossom, I wonder why.
Seems now to have no destination, no intent.
It moves on agitatedly. I've other things to do.
I think of flicking it again, but do not.
Leave it to its own devices, like God, I suppose.

THE RIVER HAS NOT CHANGED ITS BEAUTY

Morning mist drifts on the river,
April wind rumples my white hair.
Beneath the ceaseless singing of the trees
bateau lands on the rippled sand.
Stiffly a big man alights and stands.
I hobble down to greet this stranger –
paunchy, red-faced, clean-skulled, old –
until he gets closer and I see his eyes.
Fifty years ago we were young together,
full gallop we rode the world-horse,
close as brothers in life's adventures.
The river has not changed its beauty;
soon the sun will burn away the mist.

THE GREAT TREE

Heaviness in the air; huge clouds build all day.
After midnight, the storm struck brutally.
Tempest of sound, wind lashing the dark forest,
almighty crack of thunder joined a lightning flash;
blinding white filled the room. We all jumped up.
Morning saw the tallest tree split open,
towering mighty under heaven, star-witnessed
before our father's fathers lived. Along its length
the long wound raw and black. I knew we were
in the presence of a great death.
For miles and miles the river people came,
hushed sad-eyed slow they came and went.
Called a sawmiller: the tree was dangerous.
More hard wind might bring it down.
Three old men asked, before the tree was cut,
for a ceremony of reverence, a simple blessing,
not taking long. The ancients passed around
fire in a gourd and lifted it to the sky,
some simple words and at the end they bowed.
When it was cut in pieces, it was hard to look.

THE SILVER CUPS OF RAIN

Rain poured in the hot afternoon
leaving water-pockets in the grass
silver cups shining in the sun
birds flit down to sip
and flirt wings gleaming
sun-shone feathers,
their delight in fallen rain.

HIBISCUS

Cold in the night wind, alone in the crowd of stars,
counted one hundred hibiscus in the garden,
every one beautiful. One day's light they last,
adorn the world and are gone. Eighty years
the same – at least it seems so at the end.

KILLING THE BEES

In the kitchen one morning I stepped
on a honey bee; gold-black it stings me sharp.
Swatted many more swarming, wind blowing them
through the window, ricocheting in the sunlight.
Traced them to the Orchid House; smoke soon
kills the hive; dead golden bees everywhere.
Honeycomb tasted crisp and sweet, as I thought
of the beauty of bees out of control that bright morning.

FOREST CREEK BY SAVORY

Gleam of water in green shade,
gold glints descending
through a precision of shaking leaves,
wind-rustle the eye can hear.
There, a white flash of bird wing
balanced on a branch curving with its weight.
I look carefully: a diamond-drop
at the bird's beak – must just have dived;
red ballyhoo drifting at an angle,
on the prow four golden leaves.
Where has the woodsman gone,
leaving his black paddle?
I cannot get this perfect composition

in words, however well I write.
I wonder if he's tried poetry
he would make masterpieces.

UNTITLED

Blue enamel cup
filled with sprigs of green,
marigolds, red buds of roses;
two blackbirds with golden eyes
near the enamel cup,
their wings glisten in the rain;
a shiny black beetle
crawls a silver path.
In this famous exhibition
everyone is drawn to this picture.

ESSEQUIBO HAWK

Hawk shines across the river,
lands in sunlight on a golden rock,
preens in beauty by the gleaming water,
soars aloft, darts into the forest trees.
Such offhand and sudden grace
makes me smile, think about the Maker.
There he swoops again on the golden rock,
a bright green lizard dying in his beak

THE TUGBOAT

Thinnest slice of pomegranate in the sky,
river of cloudless night reflecting
the radiant stars. I am exultant and at peace.

A tugboat hauling fresh-cut wallaba poles
chugs into sight trailing oil and smoke.

WINTER CLOUDS

Cold galleons sweep across the black sea of the sky;
shriek of strange birds in the wind along the waves;
nets of beaten gold brim with red fish; iron-armed
men pull the oars of the world towards a green port.

SPECULATIONS

CONFESSION

Dined well. In his private library,
I confess my inmost sins
to my good friend, the priest,
not so much to restore a shattered faith
as ease the burden of an uneasy heart.
He is anointed and absolves me:
Life is a path of thorns
no one walks down unwounded.
He refills my glass with rum and ice,
refills his own. We sit and he tells
tales of his seductions, moral cowardice
and sacred lies, despair the rankest sin of all.
When he's done I sign the cross,
rise and clasp him to my breast.

ON THE VERANDAH

Told my oldest friend today, avid monitor
of his blood-pressure, heart-rate, diabetes, lungs:
Better at our age we monitor our souls.
He smilingly agreed and took another tablet.

My old Jesuit now dead, I have to confess myself,
not proud at all of how I've lived, too many
wrong things done, treated poor people as if
they did not matter, lost my temper with
the innocent, justified self-interest
with special pleading, showed no bravery
when bravery was needed. No use to go on.
The record is undistinguished. But I
was never cruel by intent and, though no evidence
can be offered, at the end when it all must stop,
and the great thing is decided, perhaps
mercy will find me, and if not mercy, peace.

SUNDAY MASS

Why waste an hour on old ritual,
hard pews thrown in and a boring sermon,
stuttering reader butchering the epistle,
a weary priest offering dogma set in stone –
a fossil faith for museum more than church,
where hardly any youths are ever in attendance?
I recite, by rote, responses grown inert
and wonder at the habit which brings me here.
And yet and yet, there's something directs me
which does not come from inclination or reason,
which I often wrestle to defeat and find
redemption in intellect and pure sense.
Perhaps it is simply the loyalty I have for
what was taught me as a beloved child, or
is it Pascal's wager I decide to make, and
this is how I approach the betting booth?
These reasons have to do when I explain
to friends who long ago cut church-religion loose.
But I don't know. The Mass proceeds, the host
is lifted, the ancient faith declares that all
are saved from sin and nothingness, love
soaring in a marvellous ascension. In my
mind and in my throat I feel the heartbeat
of it and pray with passion that it is so.

EXTINCTION

In the dream I crossed Australia,
everywhere I walked charred under the sun's gold glare,
stones heaped in what were river estuaries,
no sign of anything alive except leafless red-barked eucalyptus
in an empty landscape of rock and dirt, fires in the distance,
the skeletons of cities. I could not even shut my eyes

to make dark come. Endless dream of brass expanse,
iron outcrops, plains of Martian rock – no escaping the dream
within a dream, because in the dream everyone
was dreaming it. No matter how hard I tried,
I could not think of water.

CONSULTATION

The unborn, who never get to live,
haunt me, almost fully formed,
perfect limbs, fingers curled in sleep,
ear whorls you can see are ready
for the sweet songs of the world,
delicate eyelids closed on eyes.
For mercy's sake, one instant give,
the universe is so full of light.
A woman weeps in the corridor
holding an envelope from the Imagery;
they must have tried their very best.
My thumping heart, my thumping heart.

WARUM

On one plantation, it was recorded, a slave's clothes
were wrung out every hour, sweat collected
in an iron pail measuring devotion to the daily task.
Experiment in how to punish: too little sweat, so many lashes?
Not so bad compared with one where recalcitrance
was judged deserving of staking in a cane field naked,
honey smeared on genitals. Well, in Colombia,
not too long ago, a closet found in one commandant's home
revealed a heap of "dried up peaches", found to be
the severed ears of rebels who could not be traced.
Now a village in the Middle East reports thirty decapitated

corpses in a row, heads carefully re-attached
to different bodies to warn and "tease" the families.
At Auschwitz, Levi asked the German guard
Warum? To which the answer spat:
Hier ist kein warum – here there is no why!
And then and now and always that was that.

HOW IT HAPPENS

First appears a thin green whip perhaps,
doesn't really hurt, no not at first.
When used more and more, well then...
Still plenty time to act get things right again.
But soon a stroke quite solid surprises.
This has got to stop, but it does not.
The blows begin to raise dark ugly bruises,
not anymore is this the slightest fun.
Cease this nonsense! Fight back must begin.
Blows are now delivered which break the skin;
blood smears real now. How could this be so?
Now the clubs are out in full display,
limbs and skulls are discriminately cracked,
knives thrust into guts as an example,
greater weapons in reserve all planned.
People, friends hang on iron poles by bedtime.
Should have noticed when it all began

WHAT WE WANT OF LOVE

So much we desire of love, so much:
that it be perfect, that it be absolute,
that it take us across astonishing gulfs
of danger and harm and hurt and fear,
that it heals all wounds inflicted by the world;

when we are young, that it be passionate,
set fire to the skies of day and night,
be honey on the bread of life,
a gleam of beauty always present,
that it should bear rich fruit.
But when the last comes, as it must,
all we want of love is narrowed down:
whom we love need not be glamorous or strong,
brave or exciting or providing everything;
what mattered once does not matter now.
Do not leave me leave me to the black night coming
be with me with me one day one hour
one more day one hour more be with me
one more hour one last hour forever.

WHAT TO EXPECT OF AN ORDINARY DAY

Frogs, chips of gold, feast of the hunters,
barrels of salted codfish, snarl of the gadget world,
sway of the sea, song of Johnny Woodpecker,
in his madness a white hawk's immortal flight,
the wanderer's sorrow, rain in the hills,
scattering of children in the far world,
overflowing septic tank, wine bill to be paid,
dancers in the distance, inexplicable histories
of those you meet, whisper of music,
salves made of honey, reminders of death,
horse with one eye in the neighbour's yard,
no more no less than what comes next.

ROUTINES

How important they are in this life which has an end:
keep the salt in the salt cellars flowing easily,

fill the morning vases with fresh and dewy flowers,
chilled water in the red clay pitchers, shoes polished
to a Sunday shine, day's laundry fresh and folded,
replace the cake of soap before it's half a nub,
carefully sweep under the bright carpets,
take down the curious ornaments to clean each one –
chores that could regularly be skipped –
such things not really noticed if not done.
My wife goes out, says *See you later*, is gone.
I'm reading at my tidy desk. She stops, comes back,
gives my grizzled cheek a kiss.
There's something in being told I love you,
especially when you're not expecting it.

AT THE OASIS COFFEE SHOP

Crowded, lively, warm and welcoming,
we were drinking coffee and discussing death.
I said I'd like to have notice so I could make plans,
tie up loose ends, arrange to do things one last time,
see the great moon spreading across Essequibo,
sit in the white chair in Mary's garden at six,
waiting to say farewell to the hummingbirds,
talk with old friends like you about old days,
tell my wife and sons how much I have loved them,
embrace the grandchildren, write poems for them
to remember me. No, my friend said, I'd want to die
in peaceful sleep, forever thinking I will wake up
in another morning, not knowing when it will ever end.
I choose what is responsible. Think of those you love.
What has death to do with responsibility, he asked,
what has death to do with others, what has death
got to do with love? I looked around. Let's take a poll I said.

STRAVINSKY'S FINGERS

I can understand when death beckons, at the last
I will find it hard to go, will not want to leave
the green trees swaying in the wind, the sea's scent,
arbors hummingbird-haunted, wing-flash blue and gold,
sun breaking through clouds at the day's end,
never-ending newness of things – just the wonder
of what comes next – grandson, ball at his feet
shouting with joy; no more to ask my friends
what else, what else; to do without the companionship
of love, the infinity of small signals and exchanges.
Stravinsky, in whose mind songs of the wild earth
soared all his life, in his last days, it is recorded,
"made his fingers into little hooks of flesh"
as if to cling to those he loved in life.

LAST WORDS

He wished there was a little hope.
Do you hear the thrush singing over the field?
I think it may be a sign of milder weather.
There was none, only thorns in his throat.
Such a rush of blood came to his lungs
he felt he would stifle in his blood and die.
What torment to be young and dying.
My own eyes fill with tears at the desperation,
the girl he loved healthy as the day is long.
I wish I was in your arms full of faith
or a Thunderbolt would strike me.
At the last from Rome he wrote her mother,
My love again to Fanny – tell Toots
I wish I could pick her a basket of grapes
and tell Sam the fellows catch here
with a line a little fish much like an anchovy
pull them up fast – I see him scribble,

his one comfort. He often told her,
My sweet love, send me your words
good night to put beneath my pillow.

MY FRIEND, THE GOOD NIGHT

Blur of wood-ash, fires burning countrywide,
the wide sky is a peculiar blue, distant
dim shadow of endless time, wind rising loud
in the trees: good day for a funeral by the sea.
The piled and fragrant wood lit, red flames driven
taller by the wind, ashes cooled by the sea-wind
collected. What he wanted done is this:
take the linen bag under a great moon
out at sea, throw me to the sky.
My friend, the good night will take care of me.

EVENING STAR

All day thought of love and death
when no one is around to divert attention.
Now night is upon me, no sailing moon
but necklaces of light and their central pearl
the evening star casts its marvellous
lonely light over the shadowed world.
Who else is watching? No one as aware
as I am of the central facts of life.
Hours, hours I walk the night alone,
crazily thinking of the great star growing
greater in my soul. My birth was its birth;
it never shone before. When I die it will
go out forever. No beauty anywhere will
survive my death. Sun beneath the night
shapes the world anew; life will fill with
friends and ordinary conversations.

QUESTIONINGS

SOAR

At playground swings we played a game
my small beloved son, just the two of us.
I swung him high and high and higher,
each swing a stronger push to take him up
to where he stopped and came rushing down again
and up again faster, higher, to steeper levels.
Earth, I said, moon, sun, planets, stars –
almost by then as high as it would go,
and he was shouting – half-terror, half-excitement –
holding tight the ropes preventing tumbling out.
But there was more to go – galaxy would be next.
By then the risk was there that he might spill
and I myself was filled with cautious fear.
No no no no, Daddy, not galaxy no!
I would let him down by slow degrees
and he would laugh and shout, *Again again!*
and we replayed the game a thousand times,
hugged him tight each time he came to earth,
pleading, *Again again; this time will be galaxy!*
Ah, my beloved son, what marvellous ascensions.
He grew strong and stronger still until galaxy palled.
Final swing was universe when childhood's end had come.

THE FACE OF GOD

Will we see God one day? he asked,
my beloved son when he was a boy.
I'd educate him solemnly and smartly,
I thought, tell him how God
was in all the beauty of the world,
in sunset clouds, the moon that rises,
crashing ocean waves, the creatures of the world.
I gestured – *He's in all of us.*

Look at those orchard plums ripened by God!
I impressed myself with the point I'd made.
He didn't seem very interested,
soon went away to play with his friends.
Now I am old I see he meant *his* meaning –
no nice distractions – *I want to know myself.*

UNTIL THE HEAVENS CLEARED WHISTLE-BRIGHT

Gentle evening blue and gold,
and my small grandson's eyes alight,
excitement trembling in his limbs,
puts on his tall black boots, revelling in
the high water, wading through
the lustrous mire, calling out in amazed delight:
Come and see me in the great flood!
Adventure exultant, dream his whole desire,
such delight made my own life sing.
Later, the shadow of the rain-god gone,
night cleared luminous and crystal black;
huge stars – Orion the fearless Hunter –
a great moon climbing to her silver throne
gleamed on the expanse of water,
sleek and slippery eel-glistenings, dark lake
afire with slowly dripping gold – Heaven's lights
come down to rope the flood in pearls.

MEETING MY GRANDSON AT SCHOOL

When children see those who come for them,
who knows how far the reach of heaven goes?
Smiles light their faces and those who meet them
light with love and pride. Such reciprocities
bring tears to my eyes as I see again and again

pure love in my land. Jacob, a little late, sees me,
gives a little leap, waves shyly with his serious-solemn smile,
runs into my open, universal arms.

GRANDCHILDREN PLAYING

Ah they had a good day,
a river outing with their parents –
I knew that shining water once;
later chased the falling sun
beautiful as hummingbirds,
in the green-dressed garden;
curious they see how cherry jam is made;
Zoey danced for us that night,
spun until she fell down laughing;
Jacob asked his serious questions –
what happens to today tomorrow;
time for favourite songs and stories
before they go to sleep;
tired out they come for hugs;
last thing in their eyes I see is joy.

SHADOWS

(With apologies to Jacob aged 4)

Walking with my grandson in the garden
so many things catch his attention –
falling leaves, spiders, the possibility of snakes.
He kicks a mushroom. I say it is poisonous –
thoughtless because I do not really know.
I have to give it much more thought than that.
Everything he asks, I try my best to answer;
it's good to see things completely new again,
lodge fresh experience in the mind.

Then: *Granddad, can you cut a shadow?*
No, you can cut what makes the shadow.
Will the shadow bleed if you are cut?
Well, no. Still, there will be blood,
the shadow will not ever be the same.
He thinks about that. So do I.
Looks up at me expectantly.
Black passing clouds obscure the sun.
Look, look, there's a hummingbird I say
cravenly – a chance to explain the start of storms.

THINGS THEMSELVES

Can I feel what snow is like? my grandson wants to know.
I put cubes of ice in big bags of cloth, batter them,
grind them into dusty diamonds, glittering, beautiful,
but it is not snow. I take him to the factory making ice
in Water Street – I know the manager. In an inner chamber,
on pipes of iron in a dark and wintry silent room, a frost
accumulates; scrape, collect it, dishes of white sift,
light as fluff so he can plunge his hands in. He takes
my hand as we go home, wants to know how
rope is made. Thank god I know a man in Non Pareil
makes rope out of green blades of coconut.
Jacob, snow today; tomorrow rope.

THE GAME

Aged four when we began the game – villain
was the green crocodile – from him the village
had to be protected. Jacob had to make defences,
intricate walls and battlements from his Lego sets,
platforms from which robots fired laser beams.
I would describe the latest evil plan against the fearful villagers;

he had to be endlessly inventive to confront
the sinister new strategies I devised to test him.
Beguiled, astonished, he relished every challenge, built
traps and fresh defences to frustrate every trick,
repelling terrors the crocodile was planning –
new creations, forts, moats, even booby traps,
once an "epic headquarters" defended by a zoo.
What a game! It never seemed to stale,
imagination expanding to find new ways to fight
death-invasions the green crocodile attempted.
So comes this day; we play the game once more.
He has found a way to defeat the latest plot
to crush the villagers and drive them to destruction –
intricate defensive works manned by super heroes.
He thinks each creation through, tells me step by step
his latest plan to make the village safe.
I praise such work: the green crocodile will not win,
you have beaten him again; he's no match for you.
He goes on explaining; I marvel at his wit and calculations,
his counter-plans, none of them repeated.
Suddenly he pauses in his thought, his serious eyes
catch mine. *Granddad*, he says, *I want to know –*
the green crocodile – what is he really?
I think I'll never really beat him, will I?
He's learned the lesson I never meant to teach.
I praise his new creation better than all the rest.

JACOB'S QUESTION

Where am I in me? my grandson asks.
At six he's serious, he has worked it out,
the question, not the answer, clear.
I say the me is all of you that wants
to be attended to. It tells me when
to laugh or cry, tells me when to love or hate.

Where is I? Let's make a start.
I think it is the centre of the heart.

STARLIGHT

Before, now and then are all the same,
my grandson says. I ask him how.
When I think now, it is before;
then is now, so that's before.
Of course, he's right: the night is clear,
filled with stars which are and were.

A NORMAL BOY

Good time talking, my friend's mind sharp –
plantation, sugar, indenture and of course West Indian cricket.
Called Jacob over from his block-creations play –
rescue ships, aerodromes, fortresses and trucks.
Reluctant three-year old came to say hello.
What do you do? he challenged seriously;
dark eyes intent, he looked from visitor to me.
Well, Jacob, I'll tell you I was once a farmer,
minded cows in Berbice a long long time ago.
How would you like that, Jacob, tell me –
be a farmer and mind cows on a farm?
He considered it, at once made up his mind,
looked at me, then turned to meet his fate.
I don't want to be like that at all,
he said, *I want to be a normal boy*.
I love you, Jacob, the young professor said,
raised his arms in joy, hugged him close,
and smiling turned to me,
I'll wait with awe to see what normal is.

CLIFF HOUSE

Where I walked seventy years ago
I walk again but very slow,
boyhood's jump across the rocks
becomes a careful clamber.
As of old the sea leaps against
the storm-carved shore,
green sea-grapes in the wind
sting my aged face again.
Coral necklace gleams near prickly pear,
sea gulls caw-clatter in the sky.
Five-year Jacob tugs my hand.
Granddad, come, I want
to show you something new.

THE EDGE OF THINGS

Children love edges; should they see a cliff
they climb to see what depths are; watch them
in their beds, they roll towards the margins
ready to fall to find out. They incline to where
mysteries are, they crave the discovery of ends,
not fearing to fall into the unknown.
Older they grow cautious. See them thinking twice.
They slow down near precipices, observe
boundaries, limit themselves to the middle ground,
to solid footing, the outcome calculated.
Strange, now I am old the urge begins anew –
adventure in high places of the mind,
risking, little knowing. Soon I will
fall over the edge of everything.

MATURITIES

THE NEXT STEP

Once I danced on green courts, now youth's perfect
balance has deserted me, middle age's more
deliberate poise has gone, beginning to stagger
when I walk. Still can right myself in time.
Make sure I hold handrails; can't skip up and down
stairs without balancing grips. Extra careful
on uneven surfaces; small edges cause bad stumbles;
can't afford to be instinctive any more. If you fall
and break a hip, recovery cannot be guaranteed.
Stern advice from loved ones: Don't carry things in both hands,
keep one hand free to break a fall. I've slowed
right down, don't take chances; time to think about
the next step. At an art exhibition long ago
I bought a sturdy walking stick, "People of the Forest"
work, marvel of carved purpleheart, snarling
jaguar head its handle, beads of gold for its wild eyes.

MY BODY WHICH I STILL LOVE

I never used to examine my body when it was good,
admire it, yes, regularly – that was different.
Now, saggy at the throat, bags beneath the eyes so sad,
not a day passes I don't check with sad distaste
some new blood mark, pain spot, muscle ache.
What is this new sign of age and disrepair?
What brittle joint gives under time's unrelenting pressure?
When will the next tooth crack, gum begin to bleed?
What cataract will blur the beauty of the world?
What is going on inside, what new conspiracies?
Swellings which newly hurt – might this not be cancer?
Chest pain means the heart is giving out for sure;
rose-coloured rash – must be that new headline affliction.
Can one delay this dilapidation? If I walk or run,

will half of youth's easy spring return?
I know, of course, it won't, but it may buy time,
fend off old age, which ends how old age always ends.

CRABS

The day I was diagnosed with cancer,
I said the right brave things, of course,
but didn't give myself much chance.
I remembered the crabs below Cliff House,
ugly grey creatures climbing on the rocks,
the waves would roar in covering them.
Surely they would be gone after that cleansing;
the strong water would recede and there they were,
still clinging on, as if they'd put down hooks in stone.
I thought hurricane seas would rise up, crash
in a welter of fierce water, scouring the rocks
bare and clean. No, grim invaders still undislodged.

GLOSTER VALE

At my desk overlooking the garden,
well-made over years of love and work,
sweet wind this morning rustles the green leaves
in the great trees, sea-tang in the air,
marigolds, hibiscus in April profusion.
Hawk alights not six feet away;
see his gold unblinking eye, his lifting wings –
keep stone-quiet, keep him for a while –
but he launches heavenwards, flash of wing
above my head. Tears in my eyes.
Time's distance unmans me; we are young again.
I heard my old friend died a day ago,
reading, thinking, in his favourite place.

Looked up to see the green mists of a Gloster Vale,
Unaware, we think, of any problem.
As I have done, he long looked out on beauty.

THE DANCING

Quiet dinner party, friends for years,
some taking wine, some not. Crab-meat starters
in willow-patterned plate, elegant crystal glasses
glinting in the candlelight; stories – many told before –
still comfortably good – light gossip, not vicious,
and indulgent laughter. Headlines of the day touched on,
a death or two, births also, boasting the life-force
of grandchildren. Coffee served, brandy for the gentlemen.
Feel like dancing, she said. *A Marley song,* and her partner
took her hand, and then two more, then all of us
were dancing, all of us trying moves.
It never happened before, not since either
but that one time: the dancing, the dancing!

FORGOTTEN IN THE DANCE

Blessings of a quiet birthday at our pleasant home;
friends salute me with love and warm good wishes,
send bottles of good wine, one now joyfully shared
in the Orchid House; tinge of russet becoming night,
spices blowing in the wind. I say, *Come, love,*
let us dance a little. We fall into well-remembered steps,
close embraced, settling comfortably into each other's arms
as of old when we were courting.
Whisper to each other thousand-year-old clichés.
I've had my share of favours and good name.
How little it seems to matter now,
forgotten in the dance memories down the years.

WAITING FOR THE NIGHT

Day began with white egrets on the lawn,
slices of ham and sweet paw-paw,
Mary arranging marigolds in the vases.
I went out to a shirt factory to see the work –
a clean fragrance to the place I did not expect.
Carrot soup, warm bread rolls for lunch;
discussed with friends the history of cricket
and various books about travels in Guyana,
telling stories wild as Waterton's,
a caravan in the Pakaraimas full of gold,
and an old poem called 'The Indian Maid'.
In the afternoon paid taxes at City Hall,
astonished at the courtesy of service.
Visited an old friend – known each other sixty years –
on his breezy balcony laughed over old times
and spoke of current difficulties – so little love –
and swirled ice-laced El Dorado in our glasses.
Unspoken was our sadness how time goes.
Later, walked in Mary's garden in light,
counted the hibiscus, walked to the Orchid House,
praised her quietly in my inmost heart.
Sat in the theatre of a blazing sunset
waiting for the hummingbirds to come
just at six and the bell-frogs starting in the night.

THE STARCHING IRON

Fatherless for so long, nine children
and a mother fending for bare bones of life,
food just enough and sometimes not,
cramped shelter and recycled clothes,
and something must be left for school.

In market place from morning light,
the mother weary all the time,
eldest daughter nine years old
shares interminable chore of starching irons,
a little wetting, sprinkled starch,
pressing neat the shirts and cricket whites
and singlets patched and patched
and patched to use again.

We go out now to grand occasions,
my wife lovely in her party dress.
I pause in front the standing mirror,
see how perfectly my blue shirt falls
smooth and shining, no crease nor crimp.
I turn and hold tight her hand in mine,
tell her how beautiful she is.

LATE MARIGOLDS

Cold November wind flutters the last marigolds,
butterfly wings in the dark. Ah my love,
tears gather in my eyes thinking of when youth
was sweet in our limbs. Your dark eyes turn to me
giving permission. Forty years gone, unforgotten.
Old now, I remind you; grasping my hand you smile,
hearts beating, as I remember.

TOASTING THE MOON

Once in my fine clothes, returning from a party feeling good,
I drank wine alone in our quiet moonlit garden
full of sleeping flowers, green trees black against the glow,
fragrant, singing, silvered dark. Lifted my wine to the moon
sailing in cloud, my heart bursting with the joy of love,

that moment of life, the beauty of the night,
the shadow of my hand. My wife called, *Where are you?*
I'm toasting the moon, come down come down.
We danced under the moon and jostling stars.

THE COVERLET

I wake beside her in the night, air turned to cold,
the soft woven, old, red-flowered coverlet –
family bequeathed forty years gone by –
slipped down her body lightly clad, her arms
clasped round herself, her legs drawn up.
She looks lost, lonely in the cold of night.
Adjust the cover carefully as I can.
She stirs and murmurs; tense limbs relax.
Thank you, my husband, I am safe again.
Sighs, falls asleep. Enough, it is enough.

DRY

Incomparably beautiful are the dancers
in the rain, these young lithe girls.
Clothes threadbare, they are laughing,
their eyes are bright as they dance;
they swing each other in swirls and loops
signalling joy to each other, laughing
all the time the rain is pouring.
Looking on, huddled and dry and old,
I remember something like that dancing.
Love and courage were my companions then;
I was young dancing in the rain.
I feel like clapping, but I do not.

BLACK FOREST

In depth of blackest night, blow inside the skull awakes me.
Timeless instant; all there is to know in this shuttered room's
dim curtained light. Heavy heavy hours fixed in place
by drugs and needles, bottled air, heart measured on a chart.
Please let me find a better end, facing the river's beauty,
far sky stretching to the end of time, flames of sunset lingering
into night, near my beloved, waiting for the dark,
moon honey-gold and tilted, its rising beauty we've
so often shared, coming up over the black and endless forest.

CONVALESCENCE

A week lost, sick with the fever,
fiercely beating down my defences,
breaking my bones as they said it would,
a strange taste of ash and pepper in the mouth
impossible to spit out. Disgusted with my body,
teeth hurt, sure my hair had whitened;
nights endless, a sweaty pit of nightmares;
miserable, weak, not worth reading, thinking.
Family and friends come to talk, soon leave bored,
wasting time on someone not dying, but morose.
My wife brought me salmon cakes, golden apple juice;
her kind words and comfort hardly acknowledged.
Late one afternoon, struggled out of bed, shaky,
to sit in the balcony by my restless self,
overlooking the wind-dance of green trees.
Beside me, against the wall, a Savory forest painting,
red canoe in shadowed water-gleaming creek.
First pipes of evening start to sound and sing –
the woodpecker chattering his love song,
hidden mate suddenly replying; at exactly ten past six
the hummingbirds, as they always do,

sip nectar in the hundred hibiscus,
moon-lantern hanging low in flaming skies.
Knew I was getting better.

MYSTERY

A fountain plays in the green pool
by which I sit; the sound soothes me;
a hummingbird skims back and forth
sometimes kissing the water.
I am reading about Nicholas Winton
who rescued 669 children destined for the camps.
I think of the children who were not saved,
shuffling bones, eyes unfathomably hollow
as they approach the ovens, not understanding.
Again the hummingbird kisses the water and is gone.

THE MASSACRE OF THE MYANMAR MUSLIMS

Not a good day for me; high wind stripped
the red flamboyants last night, their flame of beauty lost.
Morning saw me quarrelling with the garbage men
who scattered rubbish by the gate. Come home
from buying groceries, I noticed weevils
in the packets of red beans. Car exhaust
making a racketing noise; so much money
and time to fix that. Tired, had to attend
an unnecessary meeting; I am intelligent
enough to value time highly. A Jehovah's
Witness accosted me; I lost my temper,
was loud and rude. Raged inwardly at these
continual disasters. Realizing I was being a fool,
I suppose something was saved tonight
when I decided to write all this down.

ON JABBERWOCK BEACH

Big storm far out in the roaring sea
Met. forecast not quite a hurricane,
waves piling in, crashing on the shore,
sea rising beyond the tidal debris mark,
drifts of seaweed, storm-strewn salt and raw,
sting and wet my face. I'm enjoying this walk.
Crashing of lightning, in the distance sunbursts.
Spit on the sand between waves and rainbows;
phlegm-speck gone, vanished, swallowed up.
The dead are dead forever. I'm alive.

NOTHING MEMORABLE TO REPORT

No burst of joy I can think of today,
no whirlwind or even, to be honest, stir
of excitement in the calm circumambient air.
There was no exceptional beauty in the sky
save a glorious flamingo-red sunset
sinking into the dark sea gradually;
and a good meeting with the Prison Board
to get relief and rehab for those remanded.
No special gathering of comrades-in-arms
from the old days when we all excelled;
a very ordinary day pottering about the garden
picking a few herbs my wife requested.
Sat in the wind-filled veranda for tea,
talked and laughed about the day's events,
talk which included a few mild arguments.
Their parents dropped off the grandchildren
who came with their victories and disasters;
we listened, encouraged and hugged them a lot.
I told their favourite stories, which never bore them.
Once upon a time heroes walked upon the earth.

TOASTING SCHOMBURGH

He collected old books all his contemplative life,
loved dry sherry and sweet Madeira wine;
his library was our preferred meeting place,
beautifully kept, catalogued by category and author.
Talked mostly of history and politics and sport,
of all things really – life is rich and strange.
He had shelves of books of poetry in his stock.
As names came up we loved to cite and quote,
got up with satisfaction to take one or another down:
Cavafy, Walcott, Yeats and Donne our favourites,
and of course Carter, who was his friend from youth.
Recalled how Martin would scribble sudden lines
in this same room years ago on torn-off flaps
of packs of cigarettes and crumple them and tear
and throw the unsatisfactory leavings on the floor.
He shook his head at that and filled our glasses
so we could toast the memory of his friend –
as we raised toasts to many books and authors.
Of all his treasured acquisitions, bought and kept as holy
over sixty years of love, most prized of all was
Schomburgh's Travels, illustrated first edition; he handled
it like gold. I remember well as I left his hospitable room
he said, *Let us meet soon again and drink among the books.*
When he died his widow grieved for him intensely,
but not for books, her rivals. She dispersed them quick.
Salvaged for myself Rohlehr's great calypso book
and Noel Deerr's *History of Sugar*, volumes one and two.

STEAMSHIP SAILINGS, 1928

When you walk early, the rubbish bins are full.
This morning I noticed a dead cat's shining eyes,
a bunch of rotting figs, cardboard cartons,

oily rags, pieces of splintered wood, scent bottle,
cut branches with green leaves still on.
Big flies were beginning to get at the dead cat,
but in there a thick almanac, missing covers.
Lover of books, how could I not be sorely tempted.
Looking around in case of company, I got it out:
British Guiana 1928. I couldn't believe it;
rummaged to get that treasure safely in my hands –
phases of the moon, list of councillors, steamship sailings...

NIGHT FEVER

One last time the darkness is coming.
I am going out to see the starlight,
the trees in the wind, the softness
of the night air, fireflies, white drops of fire.
One last time I hear the night frogs chiming,
see the curve of the moon in the black branches,
the drumming of time in my pale heart.
One last time to draw sweet breath,
the wings of birds unseen singing in the night;
never again the brightness, the immense depth of sky
the climbing sunlit clouds of morning,
the flame of blue above all living things.

THE GOLDEN HORSES OF THE SUN

Lush pawpaw trees all mottled-tatter –
hot and stony season is upon us;
solitary white clouds are flying high –
nothing to stop the golden horses of the sun.
Crickets whirr in the brown grass, birds keep
out of sight, bushfires redden the noonday air,
water trickles from the far conservancy,

lilies wither in the cracked-mud trenches,
hose pipes are banned – cans of water
cannot save the flowers. We walk around
in huge Cuban hats, nothing sweeter
than green coconuts in the almond's shade,
cut for jelly and cool water.
I love how she gives a rueful smile:
At least no drought will kill our great green trees.

SMELL OF BASIL

I wander about in great contentment, watch her dig
the kitchen garden, great-boled tree undressing in the wind,
gold blossoms on the browning grass. Not far across
the ancient wall, high tide sends up leaping waves,
sea-froth scenting the garden air, mixing with the smell
of sunlight, black earth dug with mould in beds.
She crumbles soil and sets the plants in place –
lettuce, pakchoi, peppers red and sweet. Half-barrels
sit in the big tree's shade filled with herbs she tends
with special care – parsley, thyme, rosemary, mint and dill –
she shows with pride their flourishing – sage and tarragon,
marjoram and bay. *Smell this*. She picks me leaves of basil
scrunched between her fingers at my nose.
Years, years ago, still sharp and green.

POETRY

Shimmering cloth, green and gold,
in two hours she knits a scarf,
every now and then she shows me
her work unfolding perfectly,
every movement poised and deft.
Line after line repeats her art,

astonishing how quick her fingers dart.
I sit beside her reading poems,
find lines I love to read to her.
Don't, she says, *don't. I'll drop stitches.*
Be calm, be calm, you agitate my mind.
And so I mark the lines, for when she's done:
Carver's Fragment, Walcott's egrets,
Jeffers' passion for his dying wife in Hungerfield,
whose sprawling lines obsess me.
Sipping El Dorado and black Jamaican coffee,
fifteen year old liquor warms the heart.
She warms it, too. The glittering scarf unfolds;
she holds it up complete. *For you when winter*
comes, she says. Now read me your poetry, love.

RAW GOLD

I went to Stabroek Market with my wife,
she to a master craftsman at his unassuming stall,
who for forty years shaped beauty out of crude materials,
raw gold into burnished bracelets. She has brought
him honey-coloured ore to see what wonders
he can make of it. I leave them to seek out treasures
of my own in that mazy labyrinth of wares:
crucifixes made of mother of pearl, holy books in tatters,
brass Hindu gods, Buddhas, stripped rabbit loins,
ribs of bloody bone, nets of onions hanging from the roof,
stuffed salamanders, silver bedspreads, saris,
pictures made of sky-blue marbleu wings, cachets
of lavender, sapodillas, limes, stuffed piranas,
plain salad bowls carved from purple heart,
chilled cane juice on a counter with fruit and cakes,
wrapped roti takeaway – brave efforts to make ends meet.
My wife is waiting, delighted, tells me the old man
will make a double bracelet with enough left over

for a grandson's ring. Ah wonders, gaieties, messages
from God. Tonight we have showers of meteors.

THE GRANDCHILDREN VISIT ON CHRISTMAS EVE

I sleep on flowers on the bed,
the curtains ring with windswept bells,
home is all anew created –
lanterns, wreaths and gold-red candles,
lights welcoming everywhere,
embracing with love our fellow man.
Music fills the festive rooms,
decorations deck the garden
amidst the flowers every corner,
the great tree's branches lit and starred
to join this year's amazing moon.
The kitchen's work is never done,
in and out to taste the fare,
fragrance spiced throughout the home,
red sorrel and the ginger beer,
mince pies and the Christmas cake
laced with rum, the garlic pork,
hams, pepperpot and pickled onion,
home-baked loaves fresh and hot:
a feast for family and friends.
Wrapped the gifts with loving care
which in a flash will be undone –
doesn't matter, all brings joy,
life and love are everywhere,
no better place or time I swear.
Excited shouts sound at the door
the grandchildren are here,
intent on knowing what's in store;
they tumble and they dance about.
Yes yes yes, we have been good.

Well then, one more night to wait
come meanwhile and give a hug.
Oh what joy lights up their faces,
Jacob four and Zoey two;
how we love them through and through.
They skip and dance, complete delight.
The starry river of the night,
the music and the celebrating rooms,
no gifts are greater than their joy,
no light shines brighter than their eyes.
Rejoice and cherish them forever.

AN OLD FRIEND PAYS A VISIT

He rang late, could he come over.
Tell the truth, I was looking forward
to an evening by myself, an anticipated book
by the falling water, evening colouring
a thousandth time. But how could I say no?
Got us glasses of rum. After a couple of hours
he went home. It didn't seem much – a lot of laughter,
talked cricket, latest nonsense of politicians,
sad how earth was burning to a cinder, memories,
spoke well of friends, some who died long ago came alive,
how the years go like morning dew.
Don't think we said anything immortal.
As he left we embraced warmly.
After, I thought about him, long.

PERFECT FOOD

Going out on errands in a hurry,
monthly meeting with the bank manager,
posting poems to Stanley Greaves

in cold America, his heart still here –
what was he painting now, that master spirit?
When you're coming back, my wife said,
pick up sweet corn and a ripe breadfruit.
I also got a packet of small mushrooms –
my own idea – and a tin of red salmon.
I knew very well what was going to happen;
my wife was making a huge pot of soup.
I'll even put the salmon in, she said.
At the same time she baked wheaten bread,
cut garlic butter into the hot loaves.
Perfectly remember that meal for itself,
also the shower of gold orchids blooming.

THE MOMENT

Just this morning, I stood by the kitchen window
drinking a glass of water, Mary cooking the perfect omelette,
the wind swaying the orchids, bringing a shower of gold
and leaves down; the dog curled asleep in the shade
until I called him and he woke; clouds sailing
in the blue blue sky I seemed never to have seen before;
kiskadees on the telephone wires – thought idly
of what messages of love were passing.
In the shade, the dog was sinking back to rest;
a young man and woman laughing on the road
hitting each other, playfully, skipping along.
Finished drinking the water, put it down.
There was the moment when life mattered most.

GONE TO GET RIBBONS

Ah my beloved, my rare beauty,
my heartfire, how I have loved you.

Without you I am lost.
Do not die, I pray, I am selfish, do not die.
Heaven protect me from that worst thing –
to be the witness of your death.
I cannot sensibly exist if you do not exist,
darkness would come upon me worse than death.
No more to see your eyes alight with life,
no more to feel the calm comfort of your arms
which once with such sweet passion embraced me,
no more to hear the way you sing when you
think no one is listening – I smiling in
the other room – no more of that:
I cannot bear to think of such desolations.
You went out this morning to buy fruits,
get ribbons for our granddaughter's hair.
Back soon! In a hurry you kissed me, touch-quick.
Wait, wait wait – putting out my hand.
Gone with a look-back, knife sliced my gut.
I got up distracted, rattled pearls in my lucky-box.

CASTLES

All day I have felt this sorrow I can't explain.
Late at night I sit alone on the verandah,
everyone else gone to bed, tired out. I watch
the Essequibo river-gleam spread out under
a rising moon, a silver spangle of stars.
The children had so much fun in the water,
building castles in the sand as if this was the sea.
I breathe deep and some flower from the forest
scents the air. This place, this great river has touched
my life. On the beach I see the river-tide come up
and the children's castles go one by one.

RIVER OF STARS

I ache with loss tonight: the long death of my friend,
his last days bad, weary for him. A rafter
has fallen in the house of poetry; our lives
are less secure. I've been drinking with others,
lamenting the loss, his terrible struggle
shouted out loud in his agony, the look
in his eye fierce and steady: Poetry
doesn't matter; this is real. I am going out
now alone in the night. In this same windblown
garden, he spoke ecstatically of the river of stars.

CLINGING TO THE UNIVERSE

Three deaths announced: two old rivals
and a boyhood friend. Yet the beauty
of the morning is the same as I remember
all those years ago, a time of combat and of love.
Nothing has changed. Here is a young girl
passing by, looks aside as the boys whistle.
The great green tree I've known for fifty years
still rustles in a strong wind, and look –
the heaven's still full of stars at eight o'clock.
I've picked pears from the avocado tree
a thousand times; the fruit tastes just as good today.
I will take a glass of wine and send condolences.

TEARS

It's no good sobbing for the dead. They're gone,
they'll never be back. Do not expect that a visit
in your dreams will be the same thing as sweet life,
memories of love and laughter real again.

They won't return, they've left on their endless journey.
So no tears fall from the stone heart, better
so much better that grief be defeated.
Yet sometimes when the moon rises and the last
birds wing for home, I suddenly remember
and sob for those I loved and are gone.

THE FIERCE PASSION OF LIFE

When an old friend died, sadness pierced my heart.
We'd had good times together, and he'd seen
me through big troubles. Earlier in the day
there were storm-bursts. Now the evening sky's
ablaze. Grandchildren dancing in the garden –
still strong enough lift them high. Life seems
so good; a hunger in my soul for more of life.
My friend's wife – in her grief – what shall I say?
I have an overwhelming sense of love
and abounding joy. Know it's given to us
only for a while – the embroidered sky at night
alone worth being born. Pulse of blood beats takes
my breath away. I will tell her he made
a good visit to life – a stupid thought,
no comfort. How could anything be for
the final boundless loss of all he was?
Oh, the selfishness of being alive
when others die! The grandchildren dance around
me in their play. I throw my fist high towards
the unseeing sky. Heart asunder, raging
towards death, his world slipping away,
I think of John Keats' urgency of love
to his beloved: "I cannot live my life
on water-grass and smiles."

PROCESSIONS

A cold wind blows for me today.
On the Conservancy long ago
I remember kingfishers graced by Christ
chased us on the Courantyne.
I remember flights of herons
kept our Essequibo company.
In Antigua seas one holiday,
from Hodges Bay to Prickly Pear,
silver fish leaped beside the boat
all the way, shillings in the sun.
Now the slow and endless passage
from Cathedral of the Sacred Heart
to sad neglected Repentir,
route though shabby built-up areas.
A green field, children flying kites.
The terrible silence in the car.

STRAWBERRIES, CANADA

I slip on dog mess underfoot, carrying strawberries
in a bag. This land is cold, shining snow
piled in high drifts frozen under silver skies.
Strawberries spill red on white, scatter everywhere
beautiful as flowers. Sunset – hummingbirds
fly and flash among green branches;
bougainvillea flame red against white garden walls,
in the golden sun, white as snow.

BABA'S GIFT

(*With acknowledgements to Philip O'Meara*)

I broke them on Christmas day, biting hard
on a nutty cake, three front teeth smashed

in spat-out splinters. The gums were carved
to get the roots out, prepping made for simulacra.
In this condition I walked out, salt grain scattered
on the ground, tramplike in a saggy pants to meet
my Katie in the coffee shop with her young companion,
rugged, gritty, handsome (but how's his heart?)
bundled up and weather-fattened – no one is lean
in winter wind. We stood and stamped; she kissed
my cheek. Would she like to see my teeth?
Of course, Baba, that very thing! I gaped and showed
the stumpless gums – fine sight for anyone you love.
The young man measured up to it: That's the eye tooth
you have lost. Hey look, I smashed mine too, shattered
on a hockey rink! Ah sweet Kate, my lovely
daughter's kid, I served you well; he deserves you.

HOME, CANADA

If the truth be known, my friend, it is not
as good as I expected. Yes, there is
wealth here, much wealth, and no doubt I can get
my share. There is peace and order; laws rule,
and a sort of honour. I know these things;
I will get used to new customs. For sure
I will settle into advantages I never dreamed
of in all my years. The food in one supermarket
down the road could feed every village along
my beloved coast. I can hardly believe
how good the hospitals are. Above all, the children,
the children's children, they for certain will
have greater opportunities. They will do well,
they will bless the day. I cannot explain,
but you asked. I'll tell you what is in my heart.
Often unshed tears sting behind my eyes.

THE DAILY LIST

Give myself a stern lecture, the days drifting by,
nothing getting done – unanswered letters, tax return,
old uncle owed a visit, Red Cross fund raiser,
letter to the editor necessary – country slipping
towards tyranny, things must be done quickly.
By the time night comes, a friend visits out of the blue;
I laugh a lot with him. I read "The Windhover"
a hundredth time; have an interesting conversation
about spiders with a river man; send an email to my
artist friend – he tells me how "ideas arrive in my mind".
The luminous hummingbirds fly in the garden, as always.
I do a couple of things on the list: trim the hibiscus hedge,
keeping the flowers intact, shop for the wine.
Tomorrow I'll do better.

IT IS WHAT YOU HAVE

It is what you have – the emerald green lizard
in the morning light, darting amid white stones;
hammer of hot noon; white almond blossom
falling in the wind, fragrance in the air;
the pure joy of being; the chance of knowing love –
and now this day coming to an end.
It is what you have, what you will not have.
Take note of the tall clouds climbing the heavens,
the torrent of light cascading in the sky,
birds tinged with gold, soaring, swerving,
wind carrying them in curves and dives;
the world's edges filling with night.
I am waiting for the blaze of red,
the death of the day I have loved.
Take note of the great moon rising,
its cape of silver thrown across the earth.
Do not forget to take note of this.

THE LAST DAY OF ALL

Early, the sun gleamed at the window,
a different way it seemed to me;
a bird's song was piercingly vivid.
In my 85th year it came on me: my last
day on earth had arrived. I got up,
abruptly terrified, alert. All day I was
closely observant; there seemed to be
so much to love – the orchids on the old trees,
the sky aflame heralding the end of time;
also the sound watering the plants makes,
freshening the grass; a lizard in the sun
on stonework; the omelette garnished with herbs
in the pan; laughter somewhere – things like that.
Everything. That was two weeks ago.

ABOUT THE AUTHOR

Ian McDonald was born in Trinidad April 18th 1933 and educated at Queens Royal College. Honours Degree in History at Clare College, Cambridge University (1951-55). In July 1955 he joined Bookers in British Guiana, as it was then, and spent 52 years in the sugar industry. He rose to be Director of Marketing & Administration in Bookers Sugar Estates and after nationalization in 1976 continued in that post with GuySuCo until 1999. Between 2000 – 2007 he was Chief Executive Officer of the Sugar Association of the Caribbean. He was an Editorial Consultant with the West Indian Commission 1991-92. In January 2009 he was appointed Chairman of Guyana Publications Inc., publishers of Stabroek News. He has been a director of the Hand-in-Hand Group of Companies since 1988.

As a lawn tennis player he played at Wimbledon, captained Cambridge, then Guyana and also captained the West Indian Davis Cup team in the 1960s. He was Guyana's Sportsman of the Year in 1957.

A novelist and poet, he has published short stories, six poetry collections (*Mercy Ward*, *Essequibo*, *Jaffo the Calypsonian*, *Between Silence and Silence*, *The Comfort of All Things* and *River Dancer*), a collection of essays and speeches, *A Cloud of Witnesses* and a collection of essays, *A Love of Poetry*. His novel *The Humming-Bird Tree* was first published in 1969; in 1992 it was made into a BBC film. In 2004, Macmillan published a new edition. He won the Guyana Prize for Literature – for poetry – in 1992, 2004, and 2012. He edited the magazine *Kyk-Over-Al* from 1984 to 2000. He has edited the following: *AJS at 70: The Collected Poems of A.J. Seymour* jointly with Jacqueline de Weever; *The Heinemann Book of Caribbean Poetry in English,* jointly with Dr. Stewart Brown; with Lloyd Searwar, Joel Benjamin and Laxshmi Kallicharan he compiled and edited *They Came in Ships*, an anthology of Indo-Guyanese writing; *The Bowling Was Superfine*, an anthology of West Indian cricket writing, edited jointly with Stewart Brown. In 2008 Macmillan published his *Selected Poems*, edited and with an introduction by Professor Edward Baugh, in honour of his 75th birthday. *Selected Poems* was shortlisted for the Royal Society of

Literature Ondaatje Literary Prize in 2009. His one-act play, *The Tramping Man*, first produced in Guyana in 1969, was published by UWI's School of Continuing Studies in *A Time and a Season: 8 Caribbean Plays*. His weekly column, "Ian on Sunday" has appeared in *Stabroek News* for thirty years.

He has written extensively on cricket and in 2005 delivered the Inaugural Lecture entitled "Cricket: A Hunger in the West Indian Soul" at the London Metropolitan University in the Sir Frank Worrell lecture series. He was a member, with P.J. Patterson (Chairman) and Sir Alister McIntyre, of panel set up by the West Indies Cricket Board in 2007 to report and make recommendations on the governance of West Indies Cricket. He assisted in the compilation and production of *Cricket At Bourda*, celebrating the Georgetown Cricket Club, in time for the World Cup, March 2007.

He was elected a Fellow of the Royal Society of Literature in 1970. He is a recipient of the Golden Arrow of Achievement Guyana national award (1986). In 1997 the University of the West Indies conferred on him the Honorary Doctorate of Letters for services to sugar, sport and literature. In 2013 he received the Theatre Guild of Guyana Lifetime Achievement Award. He is consulting Editor for the Guyana Classics series being published by the Caribbean Press. He contributed, with his sister Robin McDonald, to the publication of their mother's Memoir, *Beloved, Memoir by Thelma Seheult*, published by Paria Publishing in Trinidad, 2016. With his sister he is compiling a companion volume *Inheritance, The Story of a West Indian Family*, to include their father's memoirs. *An Abounding Joy*, a collection of essays on cricket and sport, edited by Professor Clem Seecharan, is to be published by Hansib in 2018. He and his wife, Mary Angela, have two sons, Jamie and Darren, and he has a son Keith from a previous marriage.

February 6, 2018.